WHEN MIGRANTS FAIL TO STAY

New Directions in Social and Cultural History

Series Editors: Sasha Handley (University of Manchester, UK), Rohan McWilliam (Anglia Ruskin University, UK), and Lucy Noakes (University of Essex, UK)

Editorial Board:
Robert Aldrich, University of Sydney, Australia
James W. Cook, University of Michigan, USA
John H. Arnold, University of Cambridge, UK
Alison Rowlands, University of Essex, UK
Penny Summerfield, University of Manchester, UK
Mrinalini Sinha, University of Michigan, USA

The *New Directions in Social and Cultural History* series brings together the leading research in social and cultural history, one of the most exciting and current areas for history teaching and research, contributing innovative new perspectives to a range of historical events and issues. Books in the series engage with developments in the field since the post-cultural turn, showing how new theoretical approaches have impacted on research within both history and other related disciplines. Each volume will cover both theoretical and methodological developments on the particular topic, as well as combine this with an analysis of primary source materials.

Published:
New Directions in Social and Cultural History, ed. Sasha Handley, Rohan McWilliam, and Lucy Noakes (2018)
Art, Propaganda and Aerial Warfare in Britain during the Second World War, Rebecca Searle (2020)
Captive Fathers, Captive Children: Legacies of the War in the Far East, Terry Smyth (2022)
Family History, Historical Consciousness and Citizenship: A New Social History, Tanya Evans (2022)
Welfare State Generation: Women, Agency and Class in Britain since 1945, Eve Worth (2022)
British Humour and the Second World War: "Keep Smiling Through", ed. Juliette Pattinson and Linsey Robb (2023)
When Migrants Fail to Stay: New Histories on Departures and Migration, ed. Ruth Balint, Joy Damousi, and Sheila Fitzpatrick (2023)

Forthcoming:
Capital Labour in Victorian England: Manufacturing Consensus, Donna Loftus

WHEN MIGRANTS FAIL TO STAY

New Histories on Departures and Migration

Edited by
Ruth Balint, Joy Damousi, and Sheila Fitzpatrick

BLOOMSBURY ACADEMIC
LONDON • NEW YORK • OXFORD • NEW DELHI • SYDNEY

BLOOMSBURY ACADEMIC
Bloomsbury Publishing Plc
50 Bedford Square, London, WC1B 3DP, UK
1385 Broadway, New York, NY 10018, USA
29 Earlsfort Terrace, Dublin 2, Ireland

BLOOMSBURY, BLOOMSBURY ACADEMIC and the Diana logo are trademarks
of Bloomsbury Publishing Plc

First published in Great Britain 2023
This paperback published 2025

Copyright © Ruth Balint, Joy Damousi, and Sheila Fitzpatrick, 2023

Ruth Balint, Joy Damousi, and Sheila Fitzpatrick have asserted their right under the
Copyright, Designs and Patents Act, 1988, to be identified as Editors of this work.

For legal purposes the Acknowledgments on p. 219 constitute an extension
of this copyright page.

Series design by Liron Gilenberg, www.ironicitalics.com
Cover image © The Drescheris Family aboard USS General L. M. Hersey traveling to a
"New Land" of Peace and Opportunity. Courtesy of Oscar Drescher.

All rights reserved. No part of this publication may be reproduced or transmitted
in any form or by any means, electronic or mechanical, including photocopying,
recording, or any information storage or retrieval system, without prior
permission in writing from the publishers.

Bloomsbury Publishing Plc does not have any control over, or responsibility for,
any third-party websites referred to or in this book. All internet addresses given in
this book were correct at the time of going to press. The author and publisher
regret any inconvenience caused if addresses have changed or sites have ceased
to exist, but can accept no responsibility for any such changes.

A catalogue record for this book is available from the British Library.

A catalog record for this book is available from the Library of Congress.

Library of Congress Cataloging-in-Publication Data

Names: Damousi, Joy, editor. | Balint, Ruth, editor. | Fitzpatrick, Sheila, editor.
Title: When migrants fail to stay : new histories on departures and migration /
edited by Joy Damousi, Ruth Balint, and Sheila Fitzpatrick.
Description: London ; New York : Bloomsbury Academic, 2023. | Series: New directions in
social and cultural history | Includes bibliographical references and index. | Summary:
"Explores how migration has shaped and restructured the order of society after the Second
World War"– Provided by publisher.
Identifiers: LCCN 2023022771 (print) | LCCN 2023022772 (ebook) |
ISBN 9781350351110 (hardback) | ISBN 9781350351127 (ebook) |
ISBN 9781350351134 (epub)
Subjects: LCSH: Australia–Emigration and immigration–History–20th century. |
Return migration–Australia–History–20th century. | World War, 1939-1945–Refugees.
Classification: LCC JV9125 .W54 2023 (print) | LCC JV9125 (ebook) |
DDC 304.8/940904–dc23/eng/20230609
LC record available at https://lccn.loc.gov/2023022771
LC ebook record available at https://lccn.loc.gov/2023022772

ISBN: HB: 978-1-3503-5111-0
PB: 978-1-3503-5114-1
ePDF: 978-1-3503-5112-7
eBook: 978-1-3503-5113-4

Series: New Directions in Social and Cultural History

Typeset by RefineCatch Limited, Bungay, Suffolk

To find out more about our authors and books visit www.bloomsbury.com
and sign up for our newsletters.

CONTENTS

List of Illustrations — vii

INTRODUCTION: DEPARTURES—WHY MIGRANTS FAIL TO STAY — 1
    Ruth Balint, Joy Damousi, and Sheila Fitzpatrick

Chapter 1
THE AUSTRALIAN GOVERNMENT RESPONSE TO MIGRANT
DEPARTURES, 1947–1973 — 19
    Justine Greenwood

Chapter 2
HOPSCOTCH AUSTRALIA: DISPLACED PERSONS TAKING
THE LONG WAY AROUND TO THE REST OF THE WORLD — 35
    Ruth Balint

Chapter 3
FAR RIGHT SECURITY RISKS? DEPORTATIONS AND EXTRADITION
REQUESTS OF DISPLACED PERSONS, 1947–1952 — 51
    Jayne Persian

Chapter 4
REPATRIATION OF POSTWAR MIGRANTS FROM AUSTRALIA
TO THE SOVIET UNION: THE AUSTRALIAN VIEW — 67
    Ebony Nilsson

Chapter 5
REPATRIATION FROM AUSTRALIA OF POSTWAR RUSSIAN
MIGRANTS: THE SOVIET PERSPECTIVE — 85
    Sheila Fitzpatrick

Chapter 6
UNDERSTANDING BRITISH RETURN MIGRATION: THE AUSTRALIAN
DEPARTMENT OF IMMIGRATION, BRITISH YOUTH CULTURES, AND
THE FAILED PROMOTIONAL TOUR OF AUSTRALIA IN 1960 — 103
    Rachel Stevens

Chapter 7
"UND ICH DREH' MICH NOCHMAL UM" (HILDEGAARD KNEFF):
GEORGE DREYFUS, GERMANY, AND THE REVOLVING DOOR
OF RETURN   125
    Kay Dreyfus, with Jonathan Dreyfus

Chapter 8
GREEK DEPARTURES: SHIPS, STOWAWAYS, AND THE
POLITICS OF RETURNS   145
    Joy Damousi

Chapter 9
"STARTING FRESH, AGAIN AND AGAIN": FAMILY EXPERIENCES OF
MULTIPLE MIGRATIONS TO AND FROM AUSTRALIA   161
    Alexandra Dellios

Chapter 10
STAYING OR DEPARTING: DISPLACED YOUTH IN AUSTRALIA   187
    Karen Agutter

Chapter 11
DEPARTURE BY DIPLOMACY: A HISTORY OF REFUGEE RESETTLEMENT
OFFERS BETWEEN AUSTRALIA AND THE UNITED STATES   201
    Claire Higgins

Chapter 12
MOVING ON: WHEN MIGRANTS DEPART, AND WHY IT MATTERS   221
    Tara Zahra

Index   233

ILLUSTRATIONS

Figures

6.1	Settler arrivals from the UK and Ireland, 1947–8 to 1969–70.	104
6.2	Former settlers departing by age and gender, 1961.	107
6.3	Itinerary of tour of Australia, with maximum temperatures in capital cities.	116
6.4	David and John are sprayed with a special chemical that prevents sunburn at Surfers Paradise on Queensland's Gold Coast.	119
6.5	Mr. Doug Hyles, of Uriarra, thirty miles from Canberra, shows the wool of one of the 12,000 sheep on his 7,000-acre property.	119
9.1	Dellios family, 1965, Nigrita, Greece.	164
9.2	Anastasios, Dimitra, and Kyriakos Dellios and other people from their village (Therma, near Nigrita)—sometime in the mid-1960s.	165
9.3	Leaving Party, in the Dellios' home, Therma, July 1969.	166
9.4	Map showing Greek territorial gains and losses, 1832–1947.	167
9.5	Athanasios and Olympia Joseph, after they fled Smyrna in 1922.	168
9.6	Marianthy and Kyriakos Miltsos with baby Dimitra (my grandmother), 1934–5, eleven years before their deaths during the Civil War.	170
9.7	Dimitra and Anastasios' wedding photo, 1957.	172
9.8	On board the ship *Patris*, 1969. The children putting on a play—dressed as pirates. Kyriakos is center-right, in the dark shirt.	173
9.9	Community event, South Melbourne, 1971–2.	175
9.10	Kyriakos posing outside their home in South Melbourne, 1974.	176
9.11	Therma, taken in 2005.	180
9.12	Anastasios working in a tobacco factory in Thessaloniki, 1974.	181
9.13	Kyriakos, family, and friends (his godparents) seeing a "friend from the village" perform at a pub in Brunswick, 1976.	184
9.14	Back in Greece, 1984, visiting the village, Therma.	185
9.15	Back in Greece, 1984, Athens trip.	186

Tables

6.1	Emigration of Commonwealth citizens from United Kingdom by sea (in 000s)	105

6.2	Permanent departures of former settlers by nationality and occupation, 1961	106
6.3	Factors influencing return migration (in percentages)	108
10.1	Data sourced from ships nominal rolls held by the National Archives of Australia	191

INTRODUCTION: DEPARTURES—WHY MIGRANTS FAIL TO STAY

Ruth Balint, Joy Damousi, and Sheila Fitzpatrick

Australia is a country built on immigration. Many of those who came to Australia stayed and made their homes there, but some did not. It is the latter group, often neglected by scholars and commentators, that is the subject of our book.

Australia's first immigrants were involuntary—the convicts, expelled from Britain, and the British servicemen and administrators sent to look after them. The servicemen and administrators returned home after their tour of duty was up, but most of the convicts stayed, presumably because of lack of funds or stomach for the long-distance journey home as well as opportunities discovered in the new settlement. Later Australian immigration was voluntary, although passages were often assisted by colonial and later Commonwealth governments. Permanent return rates were low throughout the nineteenth century (though part of the wave that washed in for the gold rushes in mid-century washed out again), especially before the introduction of steamships on the Australia route in the 1870s. But until the mid-twentieth century it remained common for Australians to refer to Britain as "home." Australians, like other Commonwealth members, could still enter Britain freely on their Australian/British passport, and as affluence increased in the 1950s, a trip (often lasting a year or more) to England became almost a rite of passage into adulthood for the young.

In the mass migration from Europe of the postwar period, Australia was a major migrant destination despite its small population. Australia's big immigration boom after World War II was the result of the state actively seeking to encourage recruitment of permanent migrants outside the traditional source of the British Isles, who were not coming in the desired numbers to stimulate population growth. The new immigrants were "displaced persons," Eastern Europeans displaced by the war and held in camps in Germany, Austria and Italy before resettlement by international organizations, and Southern Europeans, primarily Greek and Italian. Australia's population grew by around 3 million in the two decades after 1945 and at least 2.5 million of these were European migrants.[1] By the end of the twentieth

---

1. Eric Richards, *Destination Australia: Migration to Australia Since 1901* (Sydney: UNSW Press, 2008), 204.

century, Australia had become a much-celebrated multicultural society. But success is only part of the immigration story, in Australia and elsewhere. Accepting that arrival is not necessarily the end of the migration process opens up a number of promising new perspectives for the historian, as the chapters in this book demonstrate.

If migrants decide not to stay, there are two main options: going home, or moving on. The East Europeans who came to Australia after the war generally did not seek to go back to original homelands that now had Communist governments. But Australia had rarely been their first choice of place of resettlement, and some of them undoubtedly wanted to move on to third countries (particularly North America) where there was a national diaspora. For those without valid identity papers, this was impossible before naturalization (bringing with it an Australian passport), since departing Australia required a passport. The Greeks, Italians and Maltese, who generally retained the old passports of their homelands as well as often acquiring new (Australian) ones via naturalization, were in a different situation. Some returned, and a subsection of these returnees were disappointed for one reason or other and retraced their steps to Australia. But even in the twentieth century, with faster steamships supplemented by air travel, the great distance of Australia from Europe was a deterrent for frequent moves back and forth. To be sure, there were many in Asia who would willingly have migrated to Australia, but that, as well as migration from Africa and the Caribbean, was hindered for much of the twentieth century by the so-called "White Australia Policy".

The big returnees in the three postwar decades were the British, many of them brought out as "£10 Poms" (assisted migrants). Over one million British migrants came to Australia during the peak period of mass migration after the war, at least 86 percent of them on assisted passages. But there was a high return rate of around 25 percent. This aroused official concern in Australia—all the more because the British government, grappling with labor shortage and inflation, was increasingly reluctant to subsidize the passage of its citizens to Australia—and led to an investigation in the late 1960s and again in the early 1970s of the reasons for return. Such a concern was quite foreign to the United States—Australia's successful competitor as an attractor of migrants—because North America was the mecca for immigration of all sorts throughout the nineteenth and twentieth centuries. When immigration became a political issue in America, it was because there were too many would-be immigrants, not because there were too few. Britain, similarly, was too preoccupied with ways of keeping out undesirable (colored) immigrants, to be bothered about those who departed under their own steam. Only the Canadians, faced with the perennial problem of immigrants using Canada as a staging post for the United States, could have much fellow-feeling for the Australians.

These peculiarities of the Australian migration experience make it an exceptionally interesting case study, in a field where the United States as a destination and the transatlantic passage (much shorter than the Australian one) are often the unstated basis of generalization. Yet Australia, after the US, is the second-most immigrant country in the world, with its own concentrated forms of dispersion, concentration, and mobility.² Migration studies have burgeoned in Australia in the past decades, but the emphasis has been on arrival and assimilation, not on subsequent departure. In the Australian scholarship, and in Australian popular understanding, migration has often been treated a momentous one-off event that brings with it an irrevocable change of identity. From the 1980s, "multiculturalism" started to undermine this, and now both scholars and the public have become interested in what it was the migrants (now often parents and grandparents) left and what they remembered of it.

In this volume, we proceed from the assumption that arrival is only the beginning of the story. Regardless of formal and informal assimilation procedures, newly-arrived migrants generally live in ethnic communities which for years remain their primary reference point. They retain connections with their homelands through family ties, correspondence, and memory, and they may also maintain connections with an international ethnic diaspora, particularly in cases where the original homeland is inaccessible. They generally think about the possibilities of return, and, while this is often a fantasy born of homesickness, a proportion actually do voluntarily return, while another group of migrants moves on to a new destination. A smaller but interesting group departs because the government judges them undesirable after arrival and deports them.

Australian Scholarship on Migration

Pre-World War II Migration

Immigration studies of nineteenth-century Australia are focused on Britain as the departure place of the great majority of arrivals, and the status of the arrivals (convicts or settlers) and their choices and experiences in the various colonies that would become states of the Commonwealth of Australia only in 1901. Founded as a penal colony in 1788, New South Wales relied on convict labor until the 1820s, when free migration was introduced for British emigrants. As the new states emerged, the reliance on convict labor waned and free immigration was encouraged.³ Onward migration falls in the same category, except for the exceptional case of the gold rushes of the 1850s and 1860s.⁴ Return migration was of interest to several historians who considered British return prior to World War II. This work challenged the concept of immigration as a one-shot permanent

---

2. Eric Richards, *The Genesis of International Mass Migration: The British Case, 1750–1900* (Manchester: Manchester University Press, 2018), 2.

3. Eric Richards, "How did poor people emigrate from the British Isles to Australia in the nineteenth century?" *Journal of British Studies* 32, no. 3 (July 1993): 250–79.

4. Mae M. Ngai, "Chinese Gold Miners and the 'Chinese Question' in Nineteenth Century California and Victoria," *Journal of American History* 101, no. 4 (March 2015): 1082–105.

change of state, on the basis of British (English, Scots and Irish) data. They point to the fact that many long-distance migrants (UK to Australia) have, before or after their migration to Australia, been remarkably mobile, both within national boundaries and beyond them. This suggests that at least some migrants—women as well as men, interestingly—seem to belong to a particularly enterprising risk-taking and perhaps competent and organized subset of the general population, far from the victim stereotype that has been popular in studies of Scots (Highland clearances) and Irish (oppression by the English, Famine) out-migration.[5]

The only ethnic groups that get noticed over this period, apart from the English, Scots and Irish, are the Chinese and to a lesser extent non-white laborers brought in from various parts of the Pacific.[6] They are an object of particular interest because of the antagonism that developed against them, culminating in a policy of exclusion adopted by the Commonwealth in 1901. The Immigration Restriction Act of 1901, or the White Australia Policy as it became known, was specifically designed to keep Australia "white" and British and especially aimed to exclude the entry of non-Europeans.[7] Further restrictions during the interwar years stressed the desire to retain Australian "whiteness." Because of this policy, exclusion, racial prejudice, and concepts of "whiteness" have been an object of particular attention by scholars.[8] Some of the same issues were raised in Australia's response to the pre-World War II possibility of the immigration of Jews in danger in Nazi Germany, although in this case some Jews were taken, albeit reluctantly, in the late 1930s despite ongoing discrimination against Jewish immigrants.[9]

---

5. See Richards, *Destination Australia*; Eric Richards, "Return Migration and Migrant Strategies in Colonial Australia," in David Fitzpatrick (ed.), *Home or Away? Immigrants in Colonial Australia* (Canberra: ANU Press, 1992); Eric Richards, "Running home from Australia: intercontinental mobility and migrant expectations in the 19th century," in Marjorie Harper (ed.), *Emigrant Homecomings: The Return Movement of Emigrants, 1600–2000* (Manchester: Manchester University Press, 2005); Margrette Kleinig and Eric Richards (eds.), *On the Wing: Mobility before and after Emigration to Australia* (Adelaide: Flinders University, 2012); David Fitzpatrick (ed.), *Home or Away? Immigrants in Colonial Australia* (Canberra: ANU Press, 1992); David Fitzpatrick, *Oceans of Consolation: Personal Accounts of Irish Migration to Australia* (Ithaca, NY: Cornell University Press, 1994); Ken Inglis, "Going Home: Australians in England, 1870–1900," in David Fitzpatrick (ed.), *Home or Away?*

6. Kay Saunders, *Workers in Bondage: The Origins and Bases of Unfree Labour in Queensland 1824–1916* (Brisbane: University of Queensland Press, 1982/2012).

7. Gwenda Tavan, *The Long, Slow Death of White Australia* (Carlton North, Victoria: Scribe, 2005); Sean Brawley, *The White Peril: Foreign Relations and Asian Immigration to Australia and North America* (Sydney: UNSW Press, 1995).

8. Michele Langfield, "'White Aliens': The control of European Immigration to Australia 1920–1930," *Journal of Intercultural Studies* 12, no. 2 (1991): 1–14.

9. Andrew Markus, "Jewish Migration to Australia 1938–1949," *Journal of Australian Studies* 7, no. 13 (1983): 18–31.

Postwar Migration

After the opening up of Australia to large-scale non-British migration in the wake of World War II, demographers, sociologists, and geographers took the lead in migration studies for several decades—a period that coincided with the emergence of the social sciences in Australia and the establishment of connections with international scholars and institutions. In the immediate postwar period, when migrants arrived in Australia in unprecedented numbers, it was sociologists who were immediately drawn to studying the impact of migration and the challenges of resettlement.[10] Pioneering scholars who began to develop a sociological interest in these experiences included Jean Martin and Jerzy Zubrzycki. Demographers and economists began identifying the significant impact on the Australian population of these new waves of migrants. Charles Price, R. T. Appleyard, and W. D. Borrie especially focused on the demographic shifts in their studies of this new historical phenomenon.[11]

But they were not only interested in the ebb and flow of population shifts. Of particular interest was the question of why migrants came, their experiences in Australia, and why they left. Assimilation became a theme of enduring interest, especially for Borrie and Richardson in their considerations of how best to assimilate migrants and the factors that contribute to a successful or otherwise assimilation program.[12] This focus engaged historians too. The program of assimilation that was developed by successive postwar governments has been the

---

10. Ruth Balint and Zora Simic, "Histories of Migrants and Refugees in Australia," *Australian Historical Studies* 49, no. 3 (2018): 378–409.

11. Jean Martin, *Refugee Settlers: A Study of Displaced Persons in Australia* (Canberra: ANU Press, 1965); Jean Martin, *Community and Identity: Refugee Groups in Adelaide* (Canberra: ANU Press, 1972); Jean Martin, *The Migrant Presence: Australian Responses 1947–1977* (Sydney: Allen & Unwin, 1978); Jerzy Zubrzycki, *Immigrants in Australia: A Demographic Survey based upon the 1954 Census* (Melbourne: MUP/ANU Press, 1960); Jerzy Zubrzycki, *Settlers of the La Trobe Valley: A Sociological Study of Immigrants in the Brown Coal Industry in Australia* (Canberra: ANU Press, 1964); Charles Price, "Australian Immigration: 1947–73," *International Migration Review* 9, no. 3 (1975): 304–18; Charles Price, *The Method and Statistics of Southern Europeans in Australia* (Canberra: ANU Press, 1963); Charles Price, *Australian Immigration: A Review of the Demographic Effects of Postwar Immigration on the Australian Population* (Canberra: Australian Government, 1975); W. D. Borrie, *The Peopling of Australia* (Sydney: University of Sydney, 1959); R. T. Appleyard, "The Return Movement of United Kingdom Migrants from Australia," *Population Studies* 15, no. 3 (March 1962): 214–25.

12. W. D. Borrie, *The Cultural Integration of Immigrants* (Paris: UNESCO, 1959); Alan Richardson, *British Immigrants and Australia: A Psycho-social Inquiry* (Canberra: ANU Press, 1974).

subject of several studies and approaches to the topic.¹³ In tandem, a consideration of migrants as a cheap source of labor used to build the Australian economy after the war drew attention to the working conditions of migrant communities as well as their political mobilization.¹⁴

While the study of British migrants continued, a plethora of studies began to examine non-British communities.¹⁵ These have included studies of Greek, Italian, Jewish, Muslim, Maltese, Chinese, Vietnamese, and Indian communities.¹⁶ Recent scholarship on displaced persons in particular has focused attention on Slavic

---

13. Anna Haebich, *Spinning the Dream: Assimilation in Australia 1950–1970* (Fremantle: Fremantle Press, 2008); Gwenda Tavan, "'Good Neighbours': Community Organisations, Migrant Assimilation and Australian Society and Culture, 1950–1961," *Australian Historical Studies* 27, no. 109 (1997): 77–89; Andrew Markus and Margaret Taft, "Postwar immigration and assimilation: a reconceptualization," *Australian Historical Studies* 46, no. 2 (2015): 234–51; Joy Damousi, "'We are human beings, and have a past': The 'Adjustment' of Migrants and the Australian Assimilation Policies of the 1950s," *Australian Journal of Politics and History* 59, no. 4 (2013): 501–16.

14. Jock Collins, *Migrant Hands in a Distant Land: Australia's Post-war Immigration* (Sydney: Pluto Press, 1988); M. G. Quinlan, "Australian Trade Unions and Post War Immigration: Attitudes and Responses," *Journal of Industrial Relations* 21, no. 3 (September 1979): 265–80; Centre for Urban Research and Action, *"But I wouldn't want my wife to work here"... A Study of Migrant Women in Melbourne Industry: Research Report for International Women's Year* (Fitzroy, Victoria: Centre for Urban Research and Action, 1976); Andrew Markus, "Labour and Immigration 1946-9: The Displaced Persons Programme," *Labour History* 47 (1984); Andrew Markus, "Labor and Immigration: Policy Formation 1943–5," *Labour History* 46 (1984).

15. James Jupp, *The English in Australia* (Melbourne: Cambridge University Press, 2004); Michele Langfield, "'To Restore British Migration': Australian Population Debates in the 1930s," *Australian Journal of Politics and History* 41, no. 3 (1995): 408–19; Benjamin Wilkie, *The Scots in Australia 1788–1938* (Woodbridge: Boydell Press, 2017); Alistair Thomson and James A. Hammerton, *Ten Pound Poms: Australia's Invisible Migrants* (Manchester: Manchester University Press, 2005); James Hammerton and Catharine Coleborne, "Ten-Pound Poms revisited: battlers' tales and British migration to Australia 1947–1971," *Journal of Australian Studies* 25 (2001): 86–96.

16. Suzanne D. Rutland, "'Waiting Room Shanghai': Australian Reactions to the Plight of the Jews in Shanghai after the Second World War," *Leo Baeck Yearbook* 32, no. 1 (1987); Suzanne D. Rutland, "Subtle Exclusions: Postwar Jewish Emigration to Australia and the Impact of the IRO Scheme," *Journal of Holocaust Education* 10, no. 1 (Summer 2001): 50–66; Suzanne D. Rutland and Sol Encel, "No room at the inn: American responses to Australian immigration policies, 1946–54," *Patterns of Prejudice* 43, no. 5 (2009): 497–518; Antonia Finnane, *Far from Where? Jewish Journeys from Shanghai to Australia* (Melbourne: Melbourne University Press, 1999); Michael Blakeney, *Australia and the Jewish Refugees 1933–1948* (Sydney: Croom Helm, 1985); Sheila Fitzpatrick, "Migration of Jewish 'Displaced Persons' from Europe to Australia after the Second World War: Revisiting the Question of Discrimination and Numbers," *Australian Journal of Politics and History* 67, no. 2 (2021): 226–45; Charles Price, *Southern*

migration, which Australia experienced after World War II under the International Refugee Organization resettlement program.[17] Another sub-theme in the scholarship on postwar immigration has been exclusion-related in the opposite sense—*failure* to exclude Nazi war criminals and collaborators among East European and German migrants of the late 1940s and 1950s, a corollary of the Cold War emphasis on the paramount importance of excluding Communists and Soviet sympathizers.[18]

Europeans in Australia (Melbourne: Oxford University Press, 1963); C. Lever-Tracey, "Return migration to Malta: neither failed immigrants nor successful guestworkers," *Australia and New Zealand Journal of Sociology* 25, no. 3 (1989): 428–50; Constance Lever-Tracy and Robert Holton, "Social Exchange, Reciprocity and Amoral Familism: Aspects of Italian Chain Migration to Australia," *Journal of Ethnic and Migration Studies* 27, no. 1 (2001): 81–99; Francesco Ricatti, *Embodying Migrants: Italians in Postwar Australia* (Bern: Peter Lang, 2011); Joy Damousi, *Memory and Migration in the Shadow of War: Australia's Greek Immigrants after World War II and the Greek Civil War* (Cambridge: Cambridge University Press, 2015); Anastasios Tamis, *Greeks in Australia* (Cambridge: Cambridge University Press, 2005); John Fitzpatrick, *Big White Lie: Chinese Australians in White Australia* (Sydney: UNSW, 2007); Mei-fen Kuo, *Making Chinese Australia: Urban Elites, Newspapers and the Formation of Chinese-Australian Identity, 1892–1912* (Melbourne: Monash University Publishing, 2013); Nancy Vivani, *The Long Journey: Vietnamese Migration and Settlement in Australia* (Melbourne: Melbourne University Press, 1984); Kama Maclean, *British India, White Australia* (Sydney: UNSW Press, 2020); Nahid A. Kabir, *Muslims in Australia: Immigration, Race Relations, and Cultural History* (London: Routledge, 2004).

17. E.F. Kunz, *Displaced Persons: Calwell's New Australians* (Canberra: ANU Press, 1988); A. Dellius, "Displaced Persons, Family Separation and the Work Contract in Postwar Australia," *Journal of Australian Studies* 40, no. 4 (2016): 418–32; Nonja Peters, *Milk and Honey—but no Gold* (Perth: UWA Press, 2001); Jayne Persian, "Displaced Persons and the Politics of International Categorisation(s)," *Australian Journal of Politics and History* 58, no. 4 (2012); Jayne Persian, *Beautiful Balts: From Displaced Persons to New Australians* (Sydney: NewSouth Publishing, 2017); Sheila Fitzpatrick, "'Determined to Get on': Some DPs on the Way to a Future," *History Australia* 12, no. 2 (2015): 102–23; Sheila Fitzpatrick, "Soviet Repatriation Efforts among 'Displaced Persons' Resettled in Australia, 1950–1953," *Australian Journal of Politics and History* 63, no. 1 (2017): 45–61; Sheila Fitzpatrick, "Russians in the Jungle: Tubabao as a Way Station for Refugees from China to Australia," *History Australia* 16, no. 4 (2019): 695–713; Sheila Fitzpatrick, *White Russians, Red Peril: A Cold War History of Migration to Australia* (Carlton, Victoria: Black Inc., 2021); Ruth Balint, "Industry and Sunshine: Australia as Home in the Displaced Persons' Camps of Postwar Europe," *History Australia* 11, no. 1 (2014): 106–31; Ruth Balint, *Destination Elsewhere: Displaced Persons and their Quest to Leave Postwar Europe* (Ithaca, NY: Cornell University Press, 2021). Ebony Nilsson, "The 'Enemy Within': Left-Wing Soviet Displaced Persons in Australia," Ph.D. dissertation, University of Sydney, 2021.

18. Ruth Balint "The Ties that Bind: Australia, Hungary and the Case of Károly Zentai," *Patterns of Prejudice*, 44, no. 3, (2010): 281–303; Mark Aarons, *Sanctuary: Nazi Fugitives in Australia*, (Melbourne: William Heinemann Australia, 1989); Mark Aarons, *War Criminals Welcome: Australia, a Sanctuary for War Criminals Since 1945*, (Melbourne: Black Inc, 2001).

Alongside specific studies there were also broader histories which emerged to take a longitudinal approach to migration histories. In particular, James Jupp's work sought to chart the history of migration from the nineteenth century onwards and captured the range and scope of migrant communities who have arrived throughout Australia's history. Discussions have also focused on the historiographical trends and directions of the field over time.[19]

With regard to immigration policy, the central focus of the scholarship was on assimilation. But by the beginning of the 1970s, concerns were being raised about what was perceived as high rates of return by British migrants. This made visible the long-held Australian assumption that once Australia had accepted people as migrants, and often assisted their passages, they were meant to stay. "Multiculturalism" was the new orthodoxy—not peculiar to Australia of course, but locally particularly significant because of the extreme narrow Anglo-Celtic parochialism of the country only a few decades before. From within different ethnic communities, "contribution" histories emerged such as European Jewish migrants and their contribution to arts and intellectual life.

From the 1990s a new political development changed the focus of the scholarship again. In the name of "border protection," successive Australia governments adopted an aggressively unfriendly posture towards refugees and asylum seekers fleeing displacement and homelessness in Asia and the Middle East arriving on its shores without permission. Exclusion was once again the order of the day, but this time not ostensibly on the basis of race (although those excluded were non-white) but as people breaking the law and trying to "jump the queue" to immigrate. The refugee question has dominated the migration scholarship for the past twenty years, with scholars generally taking a strongly critical attitude towards Australian policy and the victim motif kept in central place in migration studies. Notable here is a recent contribution by Ruth Balint and Julie Kalman that points out that the "people smugglers" excoriated in official border protection statements at the beginning of the twenty-first century were in fact often the functional equivalents of those who, in Europe half a century earlier, had helped Jews escape and were often warmly remembered by them for a lifetime.[20]

---

19. James Jupp, *Arrivals and Departures* (Melbourne: Cheshire-Lansdowne, 1966); James Jupp, *From White Australia to Woomera: The Story of Australian Immigration* (Melbourne: Cambridge University Press, 2002); James Jupp (ed.), *The Australian People: An Encyclopedia of the Nation, Its People and Their Origins* (Cambridge: Cambridge University Press, 2001). See also Jacqueline Templeton and John Lack, *Bold Experiment: A Documentary History of Australian Immigration since 1945* (Melbourne: Oxford University Press, 1995); Ruth Balint and Zora Simic, "Histories of Migrants and Refugees in Australia"; Catriona Elder, "Immigration History," in Martyn Lyons and Penny Russell (eds.), *Australia's History: Themes and Debates* (Sydney: UNSW Press, 2005).

20. Ruth Balint and Julie Kalman (eds.), *Smuggled: An Illegal History of Journeys to Australia* (Sydney: NewSouth, 2021), 43–53.

Much of the focus of discussion over the past few decades has been on refugee policy and legal and illegal settlements of refugees.[21] Studies of refugees, humanitarianism and human rights throughout the twentieth century have added a further aspect to the study of Australian migration, where migration is seen through the lens of the shifting parameters of humanitarianism as well as transnationalism.[22]

In recent times, histories of migrant activism and the ethnic rights movement has shifted the focus to radical ethnic movements especially from the 1970s onwards, which has been framed within transnationalism and the movement of ideas and practices between Australia and other countries.[23] The emergence of activist migrant groups has taken the migration story to another framework—that of the migrant as activist—which also includes memoirs and autobiographies.[24] A

---

21. Klaus Neumann, *Refuge Australia: Australia's Humanitarian Record* (Sydney: UNSW Press, 2004); Klaus Neumann, *Across the Seas: Australia's Response to Refugees—A History* (Melbourne: Black Inc., 2015); Jordana Silverstein and Rachel Stevens (eds.), *Refugee Journeys: Histories of Resettlement, Representation and Resistance* (Canberra: ANU Press, 2021); Clare Higgins, *Asylum by Boat: Origins of Australia's Refugee Policy* (Sydney: UNSW Press, 2017); Peter Mares, *Borderline: Australia's Response to Refugees and Asylum Seekers in the Wake of the Tampa* (Sydney: UNSW Press, 2002). See Balint and Kalman, *Smuggled*, esp. editors' Introduction, "People Smuggling and Australian Migration History," 1–11, Julie Kalman, "Escaping the Holocaust by breaking the law: courage and disobedience," 12–28, and Ruth Balint, "A Jewish refugee racket," 29–42.

22. Joy Damousi, "World Refugee Year 1959–1960: Humanitarian rights in postwar Australia," *Australian Historical Studies* 51, no. 2 (2020): 212–27; Joy Damousi, "The campaign for Japanese-Australian children to enter Australia, 1957–1968: A history of postwar humanitarianism," *Australian Journal of Politics and History* 64, no. 2 (2018): 211–26; Joy Damousi, *The Humanitarians: Child War Refugees and Australian Humanitarianism in a Transnational World, 1919–1975* (Cambridge: Cambridge University Press, 2022).

23. Simone Battiston, "Migrant Radicalism and Activism in Australia: The Transnational experience of Pierina Piris," *Journal of Australian Studies* 43, no. 2 (2019): 160–73; Evan Smith, "Shifting Undesirability: Italian Migration and Australian Authorities from the 1920s to the 1950s," *Immigrants and Minorities* 40, no. 1–2 (2022); Con K. Allimonos, "Greek Communist Activity in Melbourne: A Brief History," 86 (2004): 137–55l; Alexandra Dellios, "Marginal or mainstream? Migrant centres as grassroots and official heritage," *International Journal of Heritage Studies* 21, no. 10 (2015): 1068–83.

24. George Zangalis, *Migrant Workers & Ethnic Communities: Their Struggles for Social Justice and Cultural Rights: The Role of Greek-Australians, Migrant Workers and Ethnic Communities* (Altona, Victoria: Common Ground, 2009); Simone Battiston, *Immigrants Turned Activists : Italians in 1970s Melbourne* (Leicester, UK: Troubador Publishing Ltd., 2012); Toula Nicolacopoulos and George Vassilacopoulos, "Migrants' Struggles to Transform the Political Landscape of Post-War Australia," *Agora* 49, no. 2 (2014): 24–32.

part of this development has been studies of migrant organizations as well as their creative and cultural expressions.[25]

Recent Trends in International Scholarship on Migration, Return and Diaspora

Return was a significant phenomenon in transatlantic migration well before the 1870s, when steamships replaced sailing vessels carrying passengers from the British Isles and Europe to New York and other North American ports. Suddenly, a journey across the Atlantic that had typically lasted more than a month, if not two, could now take as little as eight days. Fares, too, were drastically reduced, as shipping lines competed fiercely for customers. The spread of a railway network across Europe, linked to ports of departure, also shortened the distance between European villages and the West. This enabled emigrants to rethink their passages as something short-term, rather than permanent. As Mark Wyman found, "the old patterns of seasonal migration, and of short-term migration to earn some money for home expenses were juxtaposed on Atlantic emigration to the New World."[26]

Between 1846 and 1940, around 55 to 58 million Europeans moved to North and South America, peaking in the first decade of the twentieth century. As Tara Zahra points out, this movement was not unique: between 48 and 52 million people, mainly from India and Southern China, moved to Southeast Asia and to islands in the Indian Ocean and the South Pacific during the same period, and similar numbers left Northeastern Asia and Russia for Manchuria, Siberia, Central Asia, and Japan.[27] Yet at least 30 percent of transatlantic emigrants returned home, and some estimates put these returning migrant numbers even higher. Economists have found that between 1850 and 1913, a staggering 40 to 60 percent of Southern and Eastern European migrants left the United States and returned home.[28] It has also been estimated that 40 percent of emigrants from England and Wales departing between 1870 and 1914 subsequently returned permanently, although

---

25. Michele Langfield, *Expresso Bar to EMC: A Thirty-Year History of Ecumenical Migration Centre* (Clayton: Monash University, 1996); Catherine Dewhirst and Richard Scully (eds.), *The Transnational Voices of Australia's Migrant and Minority Press* (London: Palgrave Macmillan, 2020).

26. Mark Wyman, "Emigrants Returning: Evolution of a Tradition," in Marjorie Harper (ed.), *Emigrant Homecomings*, 20.

27. Tara Zahra, *The Great Departure: Mass Migration from Eastern Europe and the Making of the Free World* (New York: W. W. Norton & Co., 2016), 4.

28. Ran Abramitzky, Leah Boustan, and Katherine Eriksson, "To the New World and Back Again: Return Migrants in the Age of Mass Migration", *ILR Review* 72, no. 2 (2019): 303.

statistics vary widely.²⁹ Interestingly, Europe is now seeing a revival of this trend. Recently, the *Economist* reported a great reverse migration, as those who had sought work abroad, mainly in the United States or Britain, returned home. This included around 1.3 Romanians, perhaps 500,000 Bulgarians, and similar numbers of Poles, Estonians, and Lithuanians. The magazine cites the pandemic, a shifting economy, and changing work patterns, with a growing emphasis on remote working, as the primary reasons.³⁰

As Tara Zahra argues, return to Eastern Europe in the early twentieth century was often also a product of political engineering, in the interests of creating nationally homogeneous populations after the collapse of the Habsburg Empire. Nationalists in Poland and Austria, she writes, "plotted to discourage the emigration of Hungarians and Poles, while encouraging the emigration of other national minorities."³¹ Similarly, in Czechoslovakia, government officials actively encouraged the "emigration of national and linguistic minorities and the return of nationally 'reliable' and 'productive' citizens from abroad."³² These earlier efforts in the interests of purifying national populations had their later manifestations in the deportations of unwanted refugees after World War II, when politicians engaged in what Peter Gatrell has called "a merry-go-round of demographic engineering."³³ Around 7 million ethnic Germans were expelled from Czechoslovakia, Hungary, Poland, and Yugoslavia between 1945 and 1950. When they arrived in Germany they were excluded from the welfare assistance given to refugees, or "displaced persons" as they were called by the Allies, from Eastern Europe. Elsewhere, around a quarter of a million Turks were expelled by Bulgaria, but Turkey refused to admit them; Romania also expelled its Armenian population to Turkey, where they faced persecution as Armenians and as former "Communists." Meanwhile, Soviet POWs and former *Ostarbeiter*, forcibly repatriated from Central Europe in 1945–6, became a political *cause célèbre* in the West when their resistance to repatriation became clear.³⁴

The "displaced persons" who had been forcibly uprooted by the Germans during World War II were also repatriated, sometimes forcibly, back to their countries of origin by the Allies in 1945. But as the Iron Curtain descended across Eastern Europe, many refused to repatriate, and remained under Allied care in DP camps

---

29. Harper, "Introduction," *Emigrant Homecomings*, 2.

30. "How the Pandemic Reversed Old Migration Patterns in Europe," *Economist*, January 28, 2021.

31. Zahra, *The Great Departure*, 16–17.

32. Zahra, *The Great Departure*, 112.

33. Peter Gatrell, *The Making of the Modern Refugee* (Oxford: Oxford University Press, 2013), 92.

34. Nikolai Tolstoy, *Victims of Yalta: The Secret Betrayal of the Allies 1944–1947* (London: Hodder and Stoughton, 1977); Mark R. Elliott, *Pawns of Yalta: Soviet Refugees and America's Role in their Repatriation* (Urbana: University of Illinois Press, 1982).

until resettlement countries were found for them.³⁵ The scholarly focus on the aftermath of World War II is partly because of the unique scale of forced displacement in this period. To the European theater of mass displacement must be added the incredible upheavals created by the end of empires in Africa, India, and Southeast Asia, in which millions were forcibly uprooted, becoming refugees in the process. Policies of forced removal across the globe in this period were underpinned by populist concepts of state sovereignty rooted in racial and ethnic prejudices and propelled by technologies of warfare.³⁶ The massive numbers of those uprooted and displaced in this period was only superseded in the twenty-first century by the war in Syria and other Middle Eastern conflicts, producing refugee numbers never before witnessed in modern history. The Russian invasion of the Ukraine has recently invited comparisons with the postwar era refugee crisis, as huge numbers of Ukrainians uprooted by the crisis seek refuge across Europe.

Studies of migrant return have burgeoned since the 1993 publication of Mark Wyman's seminal *Round-trip America*.³⁷ Since 2000, this field has evolved to

---

35. Mark Wyman, *DPs: Europe's Displaced Persons, 1943–1951* (Ithaca, NY: Cornell University Press, 1989); Ben Shephard, *The Long Road Home: The Aftermath of the Second World War* (London: Vintage, 2010); Gerard Daniel Cohen, *In War's Wake: Europe's Displaced Persons in the Postwar Order* (Oxford: Oxford University Press, 2012); David Nasaw, *The Last Million: Europe's Displaced Persons from World War to Cold War* (New York: Penguin, 2020); Ruth Balint, *Destination Elsewhere*.

36. R. Bessel and C. B. Haake (eds.), *Removing Peoples: Forced Removal in the Modern World* (Oxford: Oxford University Press, 2009); Kelly M. Greenhill, *Weapons of Mass Migration: Forced Displacement, Coercion and Foreign Policy* (Ithaca, NY: Cornell University Press, 2010). An area of focus among scholars has also concerned the repatriation of former colonists to their home countries as a result of the dissolution of empires after World War II. See Sharif Gemie and Scott Soo, *Coming Home?* Vol. 2: *Conflict and Postcolonial Return Migration in the Context of France and North Africa, 1962–2009* (Newcastle upon Tyne: Cambridge Scholars Publishing, 2013), on Pieds-noir coming back from Algeria to France. Pamela Ballinger, *The World Refugees Made: Decolonization and the Foundation of Postwar Italy* (Ithaca, NY: Cornell University Press, 2020); Elizabeth Buettner, *Europe after Empire: Decolonization, Society and Culture* (Cambridge: Cambridge University Press, 2016); Lori Watt, *When Empire Comes Home: Repatriation and Reintegration in Postwar Japan* (Cambridge, MA: Harvard University Asia Center, 2009); Jordanna Bailkin, *The Afterlife of Empire* (Berkeley: University of California Press, 2012).

37. Mark Wyman, *Round-trip America: The Immigrants' Return to Europe, 1880–1930* (Ithaca, NY: Cornell University Press, 2023). Precursors included Wilbur Shepperson, *Emigration and Disenchantment: Portraits of Englishmen Repatriated from the United States* (Norman: University of Oklahoma Press, 1965), Theodore Saloutos, *Expatriates and Repatriates: A Neglected Chapter in United States History* (Rock Island, IL: Augustana College Library, 1972), and George Gmelch, "Return Migration," *Annual Review of Anthropology* 9 (1980): 135–59. See also Harper, *Emigrant Homecomings*; Russell King and Katie Kuschminder, *Handbook of Return Migration* (Cheltenham: Edward Elgar, 2022); Zahra, *The Great Departure*.

include a wide range of literature investigating different geographies, historical periods, and archives that yield new questions and new discoveries. Yet, as the editors of a welcome new *Handbook on Return Migration* argue, it remains difficult to find dedicated chapters in mainstream migration histories on the phenomenon, despite its prevalence in practice.[38] Despite this relative neglect as a discrete topic within the broader field of global migration studies, there have been a number of recent books solely concerned with migrant return, and a significant reconceptualizing of the topic in recent years.[39] Scholars have addressed different theaters of return beyond a transatlantic focus, including India, Israel, and the Caribbean.[40] More recently, Africa has attracted a lot of attention regarding the return of skilled migrants, much of which stems from a development perspective.[41] This has coincided with a strong political interest among developing nations in promoting the return of their skilled citizens through national policy. As Åkesson and Baaz show, African returnees are often expected to bring home economic capital, knowledge, and skills, but the reality is often vastly removed from these expectations, and they often struggle to establish the local connections necessary for a successful return. This contrasts with the more optimistic findings by historians and economists of European return, both after World War I and at the end of the Cold War: since the 1990s, the Central and East European region has seen a strong rise in return migration. In these instances, East European returnees often had a dramatic political impact on their homelands. "Exposure to democratic processes and elections has helped several returning emigrants move up the political ladder in their homelands," notes Wyman.[42]

Alongside the impact of return on countries, there is a renewed interest in the motives for return and the question of how returned migrants, or in some cases, their offspring, manage their reintegration.[43] There has also been a rethinking of

---

38. King and Kuschminder, *Handbook of Return Migration*, 1.

39. Jean-Pierre Cassarino, "Theorising return migration: the conceptual approach to return migrants revisited," *International Journal on Multicultural Societies* 6, no. 2 (2004): 253–79.

40. Nir Cohen, "Israel's return migration industry," *Journal of Ethnic and Migration Studies* 47, no. 17 (2021): 400–17; Ori Yehudai, *Jewish Emigration from Palestine and Israel after World War II* (Cambridge: Cambridge University Press, 2020); George Gmelch, *Double Passage: The Lives of Caribbean Migrants Abroad and Back Home* (Ann Arbor: University of Michigan Press, 1992).

41. Lisa Åkesson and Maria Erikkson Baaz (eds.), *Africa's Return Migrants: The New Developers?* (London: Zed Books, 2015).

42. Mark Wyman, "Emigrants Returning," in Harper, *Emigrant Homecomings*.

43. See, in particular, Mark Wyman, "Emigrants Returning," in Harper, *Emigrant Homecomings*; Abramitzky, Boustan, and Eriksson, "To the New World and Back Again"; Scott Soo, Norman Laporte, and Sharif Gemie, *Coming Home?* Vol. 1: *Conflict and Return Migration in the Aftermath of Europe's Twentieth-Century Civil Wars* (Newcastle upon Tyne:

return migration as a gendered process. Aija Lulle and Russell King have pioneered research in this respect, arguing for an "entwined" approach that recognizes the influence of both aging, gender, and migration together.[44] As Russell King and Katie Kuschminder note, of growing importance in the field of return migration is the need for a more intersectional approach that recognizes "experiences of different types of return migrants across gender, age, generation, race, class, education and other intersectionalities."[45]

What has become evident in recent decades is that for many migrants, the return to their country of origin is not necessarily the end of their journeys, and the phenomenon of periodic returns may be more common than permanent ones. This leads to a consideration of diaspora, for within diasporic communities, multiple return is often commonplace. Diaspora has become an important concept since the journal of that name was established in Toronto as a "journal of transatlantic studies" at the beginning of the 1990s. The dictionary meaning of diaspora is a "scattering or decentralization, as of national or religious groups living outside their homelands but maintaining their cultural identity,"[46] but as Robin Cohen shows, the term has undergone a number of phases since its original formulation to describe the dispersal of the Jewish people after the sixth century.[47] The classical use of the term described a traumatic and cataclysmic event, he writes, "creating a historical sense of injustice at the hands of a cruel oppressor."[48] It referred principally and originally to the Jews, but gradually also was used to describe the African, Armenian, Irish, and the Palestinian dispersions. During the 1980s, the term was further extended, becoming a metaphor for hundreds of different groups of people, with different experiences, histories, and relationships to homeland and host land.[49] This enabled a definition that encompassed "not only

---

Cambridge Scholars Publishing, 2013) (focused primarily on returnees to Spain after the Spanish Civil War); Mariusz Dzieglewski, *Coming Home to An (Un)Familiar Country: The Strategies of Returning Migrants* (Cham: Palgrave Macmillan, 2020); A. White, "Double return migration: failed returns to Poland leading to settlement abroad and new transnational strategies," *International Migration* 52, no. 6 (2014): 72–84; David Fitzpatrick, *The Americanization of Ireland: Migration and Settlement 1841–1925* (Cambridge: Cambridge University Press, 2020).

44. Aija Lulle and Russell King, *Aging, Gender and Labour Migration* (New York: Palgrave Macmillan, 2016), 28. See also their chapter "Gendering Return Migration" in King and Kuschminder, *Handbook of Return Migration*, 53–69.

45. King and Kuschminder, *Handbook of Return Migration*, 11.

46. *New Webster's Dictionary of the English Language* (New York: n.p., 1975).

47. Stuart Hall, James Clifford, and Paul Gilroy have all written pioneering work in this field.

48. Robin Cohen, *Global Diasporas: An Introduction*, revised edition (Abingdon: Routledge, 2008), 1.

49. Cohen, *Global Diasporas*, 2. Cohen refers in particular to William Safran's influential intervention in the field.

victim diasporas, but also trade diasporas, imperial diasporas, labour diasporas, and so forth."[50] A decade later, postmodernist scholars sought to expand the concept still further, arguing that as identities had become de-territorialized, it was necessary to deconstruct two of the major building blocks that had previously defined the parameters of the diasporic idea, namely homelands and communities based on ethnicity or religion. At the turn of the twenty-first century, however, there has been a partial return to its original definition, what Cohen calls a "phase of consolidation," in which the postmodern critique is partly accepted, without emptying the notion of all of its analytical power.

Despite the constant tussle among theorists about how to define diaspora, there is a certain tacit acknowledgment of some key features. This includes the feature of dispersal from an original homeland, usually to two or more foreign regions, and, alternatively or additionally, the expansion from a homeland in search of work, trade, or other ambitions. This more recent development has allowed scholars to include Chinese, Indian, Turkish, and other labor types of diasporas, but it could also include certain aspects of the Jewish experience as well. As Hasia Diner notes, in her recent discussion of this history, while the Jewish diaspora was a product of expulsions, forced conversions, and massacres, to see this history only as one of unbroken suffering is misleading. Indeed, she notes, Jewish migrations were also sometimes movements in search of better economic opportunity in new places.[51] Yuri Slezkine went further, linking the Jews with Gypsies, Chinese, Indian traders, and Irish tinkers not by virtue of victimhood, but because all of these groups were what he called "Mercurians" or "service-nomads." They had survived not by owning or tilling the soil but by their mobility, their literacy, and their mercantilism:

> Their principal resource base was human, not natural, and their expertise was in "foreign affairs". They were the descendants—or predecessors—of Hermes (Mercury), the god of all those who did not herd animals, till the soil, or live by the sword; the patron of rule-breakers, border crossers and go-betweens ... what all of Hermes' followers had in common was their mercuriality or impermanence. In the case of nations, it meant that they were all transients and wanderers—from fully nomadic Gypsy groups, to mostly commercial communities divided into fixed brokers and traveling agents, to permanently settled populations who thought of themselves as exiles.[52]

50. This summary of the scholarly dichotomy is taken from Paul Basu, "Roots tourism as return movement: semantics and the Scottish diaspora," in Harper, *Emigrant Homecomings*, 138–40.

51. Hasia R. Diner, *Oxford Handbook of the Jewish Diaspora* (Oxford: Oxford University Press, 2021), 11–12, https://academic.oup.com/edited-volume/37080/chapter/323168059. For an early statement on diaspora focused on its original Jewish context, see Simon Dubnow, "Diaspora," *Encyclopedia of the Social Sciences* (New York: Macmillan, 1931). A more recent approach is in Daniel Boyarin and Jonathan Boyarin, "Diaspora: Generation and the Ground of Jewish Identity," *Critical Inquiry* 19, no. 4 (1993): 693–725.

52. Yuri Slezine, *The Jewish Century* (Princeton, NJ, and Oxford: Princeton University Press, 2004), 7–8.

Other features that define diasporas include a collective identity and myth of a homeland, a commitment to its safety, prosperity, and history, and the frequent development of a return movement. Return is rarely nowadays as permanent as it once was, but rather, as mentioned above, periodic or intermittent. In the Jewish case, for example, and since the creation of Israel, Safran has observed a dezionizing of the Jewish diaspora in recent decades, and has since shifted away from his original definition that made the homeland and the wrench away from it of vital importance, to softer notions of a "found home" in the diaspora.[53] Indeed, as the concept of diaspora has come to embody the importance of cementing ethnic and cultural connections outside of a homeland, rather than a return to it, its analytical relationship to migration and mobility has weakened.

Serial (onward, multiple, third-country) migration has received less attention, partly because it confounds older notions of migration and partly because it is so difficult to track.[54] Under the influence of transnational studies, the figure of the mobile migrant has often morphed into a cosmopolitan global citizen who calls no single country home.[55] Australia-based Eric Richards was a pioneer in this field, drawing upon his knowledge of the British migrant to Australia:[56] "Humanity seems always to have been a mobile species. And now we seem more mobile than ever, forever dislocating and relocating within and between countries."[57] His own track through the twentieth and twenty-first centuries mimicked this pattern, with grandparents who lived on the land, but whose children and grandchildren soon dispersed, leaving the land for the city. Within two generations, the radius of his family had widened across the globe, and Richards himself had emigrated to Australia.

Like Richards, the editors of this volume have personal connections to the field of migration and human mobility. Both sets of Ruth Balint's grandparents were part of the two waves of Jewish refugees from Europe that bracketed World War II, and going further back, *their* parents and grandparents had been part of the Jewish movement out of the stetls of Eastern Europe and into the assimilated middle-class world of Europe's cities. Joy Damousi's parents were part of the postwar exodus from Greece. Arriving in Australia in the late 1950s, their journey became a familiar one for many Greeks seeking employment, opportunities, and prosperity after the devastation of the world war and the Greek Civil War that followed it.

---

53. Cohen, *Global Diasporas*, 12.

54. Susan Ossman, *Moving Matters: Paths of Serial Migration* (Stanford, CA: Stanford University Press, 2013).

55. Aihwa Ong, *Flexible Citizenship: The Cultural Logics of Transnationality* (Durham, NC: Duke University Press, 1999); White, "Double return migration," 72–84; Catherine Gomes, *Transient Mobility and Middle Class Identity: Media and Migration in Australia and Singapore* (London: Palgrave Macmillan, 2017).

56. See particularly *On the Wing* and his article in David Fitzpatrick (ed.), *Home or Away?*

57. Richards, *The Genesis of International Mass Migration*, 2.

Sheila Fitzpatrick's Anglo-Celtic ancestors arrived in Australia in the mid-nineteenth century, but she herself has been both a migrant (to the UK and then the US) and a subsequent returner to Australia after almost fifty years away. Her first foray into migration studies was *Mischka's War*, a book on the experiences of her husband, Michael Danos, as a displaced person from Riga.[58]

Our volume takes as its starting point the pioneering work of Richards on migrant mobility in an Australian context, and his insights about mobility as an historical phenomenon of global consequence. Our contributors have come to their research from many different directions, with a range of areas of expertise which we hope will further expand the scope and depth of discussion on departures. We have grouped the essays thematically to illustrate the range of aspects captured by the departures theme. There are four themes. We begin with policy issues as these frame and direct many of the activities of those who take the initiative, or consider the possibility, to depart. This is followed by migrants who definitely leave and then those who go back and forth. The final theme explores those who are unable to make their own decisions about going or staying.

In her chapter, Rachel Stevens explores the British case that so disturbed the Australian authorities in the late 1960s and '70s, by looking through the lens of adolescent British winners of an essay prize whose impressions of Australia left them with little enthusiasm for permanent return. Sheila Fitzpatrick and Ebony Nilsson each look at the voluntary repatriation of a few Russian (Soviet) DPs, through two disparate perspectives on their actions. Fitzpatrick examines that of the Soviet authorities, who did their utmost to persuade DPs resettled in Australia and elsewhere to return, while Nilsson traces the reaction of Australian intelligence, whose officers observed the process with suspicion and monitored both the Soviet recruiters and their targets.

As Nilsson's chapter shows, return to the Soviet Union was a process that was very difficult to reverse if the repatriant changed his or her mind. But that was not so for other types of return, and our volume provides some intriguing examples. Alexandra Dellios examines a family history of back-and-forth migration/movement between Australia and Greece over decades that makes it difficult to sustain any simple notion of "home." Kay Dreyfus gives a fascinating study of the composer George Dreyfus, German-Jewish born, who came to Australia as a refugee with his parents just before World War II. As an adult, Dreyfus found himself perennially drawn to Germany and its language and culture, yet not to the point of remigrating from Australia; and he managed to combine his sense of Germanness with an equally strong sense of himself as a Jew and interest in his Jewish heritage.

The Dellioses and the Dreyfuses of this world make their own decisions, albeit serially contradictory ones. Others were not so lucky, and our volume also focuses

58. Sheila Fitzpatrick, *Mishka's War: A European Odyssey of the 1940s* (Melbourne: Melbourne University Press, 2017).

on those who found themselves moved involuntarily. Deportation was one route, as Jayne Persian and Ruth Balint show. Involuntary departure was also the lot of the refugees who, for complex political reasons, were "swapped" between Australia and the United States in the early twenty-first century, the subject of Clare Higgins' article. Others, whose situation in Australia was a miserable one, like those brought there under the displaced youth scheme described by Karen Agutter, found themselves stuck, without the means, and perhaps the will, to move again.

Third-country departure, including moving on to another part of a national diaspora, is the most challenging process to research because of source problems, but Ruth Balint sets out the parameters in her chapter, exploring the attitudes of Eastern European DPs to Australia in the postwar years. Many would have preferred the United States, and given that these migrants often had relatives who had landed in the American diaspora, we assume that, under the radar of official scrutiny, a proportion of them stayed in Australia only a few years before moving on. The other major third-country attractor for Jewish migrants in this period, Israel, is an interesting and complex case which also deserves further study. European Jews who had settled in Australia and the United States were under some moral pressure to make *Aliyah*. Such onward movement from Australia to Israel did occur, especially after the 1967 war, but, somewhat unexpectedly, it was equaled and often exceeded by an opposite spontaneous movement, that of Jews from Israel joining family members who had settled in Australia.

Individual and family agency is a crucial factor in migrant mobility, but there are also practical prerequisites. Up to the mid-twentieth century, you needed a berth on a ship to leave Australia (before planes reduced that "tyranny of distance"), in addition to the money to buy a ticket (or else the possibility of "working your passage"). Joy Damousi explores the Greek ocean liners that made departures possible during the postwar period. In doing so she considers aspects of departures that are not typically the focus of study: stowaways and the politics of departures in the context of protests against the Greek military junta. As a less desired immigrant, the departure of Greeks did not attract the same attention by policy-makers as the favored British immigrant.

Leaving Australia was not a problem for Greeks who had kept their old passports as well as acquiring Australian/British ones via naturalization, but it was a major problem for the East European "displaced persons" who had arrived as "stateless," without passports. Naturalization, examined in Justine Greenwood's chapter, is usually understood as a mark of migrant assimilation and a desire to become an Australian; successive governments cited naturalization figures as testimony to the success of migrant assimilation. But since it was also the only way a stateless migrant could acquire a passport, as Balint's chapter shows, there is the intriguing possibility that a percentage of those who sought naturalization in the third quarter of the twentieth century wanted it for the opposite reason, namely that it opened the way for their permanent departure from the country. In her concluding overview, Tara Zahra reflects both on the insights offered in the volume and on some paths of future development.

Chapter 1

THE AUSTRALIAN GOVERNMENT RESPONSE TO MIGRANT DEPARTURES, 1947–1973

Justine Greenwood

Historian Nancy Green, in her 2006 article, "The Politics of Exit: Reversing the Immigration Paradigm," outlined the challenges of writing a history of departures, pointing out that "it is more difficult to count those who leave than those who arrive; it is difficult to write a history of absence." One way to surmount such difficulties, Green suggested, was to focus on the attitude of the state to emigration, on how governments have "abetted or fretted about and even obstructed the emigration movement."[1] Green focused her analysis on nineteenth-century Europe, considering how the politics of emigration could oscillate between conceiving emigration as a problem (a weakening of the nation-state through depopulation that needed to be prevented) or as a solution (a way to manage unwanted citizens through providing a "safety valve" for excess population).

Green, in order to "reverse" the immigration paradigm, focused mostly on the perspectives of "sending countries," such as Great Britain, France, Hungary, Germany, and Italy. Broadly speaking, both in the literature and in government policy, departures have been understood as an issue for countries of *emigration*, while countries of *immigration* (United States, Canada, and Australia, for instance) have perceived the challenges of settlement to be their main concern. However, not all those who arrive, chose (or indeed are allowed) to stay. This suggests that another "reversal" is possible. That is, an exploration of the politics of departures in countries of immigration.

This chapter traces that history of double absence in the Australian context. It outlines how Australian politicians and policymakers, from the start of the postwar immigration program in the late 1940s, came to understand that a country of immigration might also have to contend with departures. The departure of migrants became such a cause of concern that two separate governments commissioned reports into the issue, the first of which was handed down in 1967 and the second in 1973 (which provides the end date for this chapter). Although

---

1. Nancy Green, "The politics of exit: reversing the immigration paradigm," *Journal of Modern History* 77 (June 2005): 268.

commissioned relatively closely, they demonstrate how attitudes to departures shifted as the aims of the immigration program came to be re-examined and, relatedly, how migrants themselves were perceived. By the early 1970s, the argument was being made that Australia should be less concerned with permanent immigration (the initial focus of the program) than with attracting highly skilled migrants, and that because these migrants were considered more likely to be very mobile, departures were, therefore, an "inevitable ingredient" of the immigration program.[2]

Here there is an echo of those nineteenth-century debates Green identified: was the departure of these migrants a negative or a positive? Was it amenable to government intervention or was it simply something that was ultimately unpreventable? The responses to these questions shifted considerably across the nearly three decades between the start of the program and the handing down of the final report.

Migration Registration and the Difficulties of Monitoring Departures

Before such debates could take place, the "problem" had to first be identified. It was, perhaps a little ironically, government attempts to monitor the movements of migrants within Australia, for the purposes of settlement, that first revealed some of these migrants were departing. This should not have been particularly surprising or even alarming. However, permanent settlement was a key tenet of Australia's postwar immigration program.[3] To boost the population and, as an extension of that, the economic and defense capabilities of the nation, migrants were required to stay. Thus, migrants were expected to be registered once they arrived in Australia so that details such as their place of address, employment and marital status could be tracked until they obtained citizenship. This, as the following example demonstrates, was not a simple process. It was also an imprecise one. As the below reveals, despite assuming migrants intended to settle permanently, officials had very little idea if migrants would stay or, more concerningly, if they had already departed.

On November 12, 1950, Mr. Alfredo Dell'Oro departed from Melbourne on the SS *Napoli*.[4] The problem was not his return to Italy per se, but rather that the Department of Immigration had no idea that he had left Australia until some seven years after the fact. Technically the Department should have known where

---

2. The phrase is from the 1973 Report, 1: The Parliament of the Commonwealth of Australia, 1973—Parliamentary Paper No. 226, *Immigration Advisory Council Committee on Social Patterns: Final Report: Inquiry into the Departures of Settlers from Australia July 1973* (Canberra: Government Printer of Australia, 1974).

3. Jerzy Zubrzycki, *Arthur Calwell and the Origin of Post-War Immigration* (Canberra: Australian Government Publishing Service, 1995).

4. D4878, DELL ORO A 14/09/1891, 1, National Archives of Australia, Canberra.

Mr. Dell'Oro was at all times because the Aliens Act 1947 required all non-British residents who intended to stay in Australia for a period longer than sixty days to register within the state in which they were domiciled. Upon registration the person would then be given a certificate which had to be produced when required by an immigration officer. The department was also to be notified of any change of address, occupation, or marital status, and ministerial approval was required for a change of surname.[5]

If Mr. Dell'Oro had followed the regulations set out in his Certificate of Registration he should have "surrendered [his] certificate to the Immigration Officer in attendance at the vessel or aircraft at the time of embarkation."[6] Or if he had forgotten his certificate, a replacement form should have been completed at the point of departure.[7] Either document would have then been sent on to the Commonwealth Migration Officer for his particular state or territory so that officials could update his record accordingly.[8] Mr. Dell'Oro's failure to follow the rules (or the failure of the migration officer at the port to enforce them) should not have been that surprising to the department by the mid-1950s. As Markus and Taft explain , "a 1955 report from a Canberra suburb indicates failure to locate individuals … because migrants often fail to notify the Department of their moves." Similarly, a 1957 survey of 2,000 homes in Melbourne found that 53 percent of addresses in the register were incorrect.[9]

Mr. Dell'Oro had, in fact, been mostly compliant. He had arrived in Australia in 1936. In 1939 the National Security (Aliens Control) Regulations was introduced as a wartime measure, with registration coordinated by the military authorities working through the state police forces. Completing the Form of Application for Registration required Mr. Dell'Oro to provide fingerprints as well as a photograph and signature because, as one customs officer put it when the regulations were being formulated, "it is very difficult to identify one Italian from another … photographs could be easily removed and others put in their places."[10] When the issue of "alien registration" was revisited at the beginning of the postwar immigration program, both the Immigration Minister, Arthur Calwell, and his

---

5. Andrew Markus and Margaret Taft, "Postwar Immigration and Assimilation: A Reconceptualisation," *Australian Historical Studies* 46, no. 2 (2015): 241.

6. Wording from a Certificate of Registration. For an example, see NAA: BP25/1, LEONARDI C—ITALIAN, 8.

7. For an example of the form, see NAA: SP908/1, STATELESS/LIU OLGA, 9.

8. For explanation of this process, see NAA: D4878, LEE B Y, 3. From Assimilation Division, Sydney to Chief Migration Officer, South Australia: "In accordance with the usual procedure, if he handed his Aliens Registration Certificate to Customs at the time of his departure, it would have been sent to you."

9. Markus and Taft, "Postwar Immigration and Assimilation," 243.

10. NAA: D4878, DELL ORO A 14/09/1891, 10; Mark Finnane, "Controlling the 'Alien' in mid-twentieth century Australia: The origins and fate of a policing role," *Policing and Society* 19, no. 4 (2009): 13.

Department of Immigration Secretary, Tasman Heyes, strongly opposed the involvement of the police in registering migrants or in requiring fingerprints, arguing that "the Government believed that aliens should not be supervised by police stations because they had come from police states."[11]

Registration, as overseen by the Department of Immigration, was still about surveillance, but, as Labor member, and chairman of the Immigration Advisory Council, Les Haylen, reassured the parliament, it was "in the benevolent sense," migrants would be "watched … so that they can be absorbed into the country."[12] It is hard to say if Mr. Dell'Oro appreciated the subtle distinction between being required to be registered at a post office rather than a police station, as he duly did when the Aliens Act 1947 was introduced. In fact, the witness on his application for a Certificate of Registration in January 1948 was one A. K. Laslett, police officer.[13]

To briefly return to the present day, with the establishment of the Australian Border Force in 2015, law enforcement was brought firmly back into the immigration sphere after an almost seventy-year interlude. The Border Force not only controls the current Movements Reconstruction Database, which records "travellers' name, date of birth, gender and relationship status, country of birth, departure and/or arrival date, travel document number and country, port code and flight/vessel details, visa subclass and expiry date, and the number of movements," but is also now responsible for maintaining all the historical movement records, including those documents that Calwell and Heyes wanted kept out of police hands, the Alien's cards (1947 to 1979).[14]

The Immigration Department, having assumed responsibility for Mr. Dell'Oro's movements, promptly lost track of him. Based on their records, the last time they were certain of his whereabouts was in the same year he was registered, 1948, when he was employed by a Mr. A. A. Nitschke. Almost ten years later, in 1957, the Commonwealth Migration Officer for South Australia wrote to the Commonwealth Investigation Service requesting that they make enquiries as to Mr. Dell'Oro's location because he had not complied with Sections 9 and 10 of the Aliens Act 1947–1952. That is, he had not notified them of his change of address and change of occupation, something they were only made aware of when a letter from their department was "returned to sender."

Enquires by the Investigation Service were able to conclude that Dell'Oro was no longer resident in Australia. Ascertaining this involved talking to his previous employer ("who was unable to give any details of departure but was quite positive that Delloro was now resident in Italy"), the Italian Consular Agent (who confirmed Dell'Oro was issued with a passport in September 1950); and finally, a friend

---

11. Finnane, "Controlling the 'Alien' in mid-twentieth century Australia," 19.
12. Markus and Taft, "Postwar Immigration and Assimilation," 242.
13. D4878, DELL ORO A 14/09/1891, 8.
14. See Australian Border Force, "Crossing the Border, Passenger movement, Movement records," https://www.abf.gov.au/entering-and-leaving-australia/crossing-the-border/passenger-movement/movement-records.

("a Mr. Tarca, who stated that he corresponded with a Delloro in Circo, Italy"). However, when the service checked the shipping lists for Adelaide there was no record for his departure. Luckily for the Investigation Service, Dell'Oro had indicated to the Italian consular office that he intended to leave from Melbourne. A final check with the Department of Immigration office in Melbourne confirmed that an "F. Delloro" departed on the *Napoli*.[15] It took the Immigration Department six months, from November 1957 to May 1958, to be able to update Mr. Dell'Oro's record to "Departed Commonwealth on: 12/11/1950." The money and effort invested in this process, and its utility, was certainly questionable. Speaking more generally, at least one anonymous officer thought that any attempt to register aliens was "an absolute waste of time and resources."[16]

By 1973, it appeared that the Immigration Minister, Al Grassby, agreed with this assessment, announcing that "aliens in Australia would no longer have to report each year their address, job and marital status," although their initial entry into Australia would still be recorded. While this was presented as cutting "red tape" and saving "Treasury funds," the main reason seemed to be extensive non-compliance. As Grassby noted, 54 percent of "aliens ... failed to give their particulars" in 1972.[17] However, the winds of change had been blowing for some time before 1973. Calwell might have promised in 1948 that "Alien Control would be strict," but by 1959 the Act had been adjusted so that aliens no longer had to report any changes in person (posting a form was now acceptable) and the actual Certificate of Registration, which aliens were required to have in their possession at all times, was also abolished.[18]

Still, it is probably not surprising that the immigration minister who introduced multiculturalism would be the one who ended the registration requirements which were predominantly about managing assimilation.[19] When the Aliens Act was introduced, the impetus behind registration had little to do with managing departures. Rather, it was entirely focused on promoting "speedy absorption," largely by attempting to prevent the concentration of ethnic groups in particular areas and industries (although Markus and Taft have disputed whether it even managed to achieve that aim).[20] Movement, if it was considered at all, was assumed to take place domestically. The architects of the Act did not predict that people

---

15. Australian Border Force, "Crossing the Border, Passenger movement, Movement records," 2–4.

16. Markus and Taft, "Postwar Immigration and Assimilation," 243.

17. "Aliens no longer to report," *Canberra Times*, May 29, 1973, 10; "Amend Act," *Australian Jewish News*, June 15, 1973, 10.

18. "Alien control to be strict," *Northern Star* (Lismore), January 14, 1948, 1; "Registration laws amended," *Australian Jewish News*, January 25, 1957, 3; "If you're an alien over 16 you must register with dept.," *Good Neighbour*, September 1, 1959, 7.

19. A. J. Grassby, *A Multi-cultural Society for the Future* (Canberra: Australian Government Publishing Service, 1973).

20. Markus and Taft, "Postwar Immigration and Assimilation," 235.

might arrive and depart multiple times. In the early postwar period this was probably a fair enough assumption. The immigration program was envisaged as offering permanent settlement, and eventually citizenship, to displaced persons who were assumed to have no home to which to return. And even for those who did have countries to which they could more easily return, such as the British, inducements ("sunshine and industry")[21] and disincentives (having to pay back assisted passage fares if one departed within two years of arrival) were imagined as sufficient to persuade migrants to stay.

This meant that the Immigration Department was woefully ill-equipped to keep track of those who did leave, had almost no sense of the scale of departures, and even less understanding of why those who had stated their intention to settle permanently on their arrival had then chosen to depart—and whether there was anything at all that could be done to prevent them leaving. What further complicated things was that the entire registration system relied on individuals to self-report, and to report accurately. Moreover, all the issues with trying to capture internal movements were compounded when it came to tracking overseas departures. Asking someone to provide their new address was a relatively straightforward question compared to asking someone to provide a "purpose of journey," especially when what migrants disclosed to officials might simply be what they thought the authorities wanted to hear (it was much easier to admit to a holiday than a desire to potentially return home permanently). When it dawned on the government that it was not just a handful of individuals like Dell'Oro that they were having problems tracking but potentially thousands of departees, obtaining accurate information from migrants became an even more pressing issue. This, however, as the statisticians tasked with providing a figure for the number of departures soon discovered, was no easy undertaking.

Commonwealth Government Efforts to Collect Departure Statistics

Concerns about the departure of significant numbers of migrants began to be voiced from the mid-1950s. The Labor opposition took the opportunity presented by the Commonwealth Bureau of Statistics' 1954 announcement that "Australia's population gain was the lowest for six years" to attack the Menzies government's handling of the immigration program. ALP senators highlighted the "disturbing" increase in the number of departures, describing it as "a bitter blow at Australia's future, her development and her security."[22]

Taken at face value the figures did seem worrying. The population gain through immigration in 1953 was only 42,883, less than half of that of 1952 and well below the peak of 153,685 in 1950. Poor economic conditions could take some of the

---

21. See Ruth Balint, "Industry and Sunshine: Australia as home in the Displaced Persons' camps of postwar Europe," *History Australia* 11, no. 1 (2014): 102–27.
22. "Population gain 'extremely disturbing'," *Warwick Daily News* (QLD), March 5, 1954, 2.

blame, but statisticians suspected (and the government fervently hoped) that something else was going on.[23] There seemed to be two interrelated problems: firstly, there was almost no distinction made in the statistics between actual migration and the movement of Australian and overseas visitors. The importance of being able to accurately account for the number of people departing temporarily was demonstrated by "the fact that there were now about 250 000 arrivals and 150 000 departures overseas every year."[24] This complication had arisen because of the second issue: information on whether someone was leaving temporarily or permanently was not easily extracted from the main source used to collect such data, entry and exit cards, sometimes referred to as "passenger cards."

The Commonwealth Statistician conceded that the current system of analyzing overseas travelers, having been adopted in 1924, was well overdue an update. But to collect more accurate figures the second problem would have to be solved first. To this end, from July 1, 1958, "entry and exit cards were altered to include birthplace, precise citizenship, and sufficient details to distinguish between settlers, visitors and residents."[25] By 1961 it appeared that the Menzies government had been exonerated. Introducing the distinction between "long- and short-term movement" proved that Australia was not losing up to half of its migrants for the year. Using the new breakdown gave a very different set of numbers: 95,407 people had settled and only 8,240 settlers had left Australia. Relieved by the outcome, Immigration Minister Downer called it a rebuttal to the "number of false assumptions on which recent criticisms of Australia's immigration program had been based."[26]

Unfortunately, vindication was only temporary. While the new classification had rectified one issue (conflating all outward movement as permanent), demographer Charles Price was quick to point out that the new distinction was likely to significantly *underestimate* the number of departures. The new collection method was meant to show "for the first time people who came to Australia with the intention of settling, and settlers who left Australia permanently."[27] The issue, of course, was intention. The statistics that could be collected from the "purpose of journey" on the entry/exit cards only represented the stated intention of the passenger at the time of arrival or departure. The more Price investigated, the more intractable the problem seemed to be. He explained:

> For personal reasons, many former settlers departing permanently may not identify themselves as such on the passenger card. Other passengers, former

---

23. "Population gain 'extremely disturbing,'" 2
24. "British migrants 42.7 per cent of assisted intake," *Good Neighbour*, March 1958, 3.
25. Charles Price, "Australian migration statistics, 1959–65," *Australian Journal of Statistics* 8, no. 3 (1966): 138.
26. "Revision of figures on movements," *Canberra Times*, May 2, 1962, 6; "Figures on migration to be clearer," *Good Neighbour*, June 1, 1962, 3.
27. "Revision of figures on movements," 6.

settlers who genuinely intend to leave on long-term holiday, may subsequently change their plans and stay overseas. Alternatively, many passengers who state that they are long-term visitors may, in fact, be considering permanent migration to Australia, and subsequently settle here.[28]

This, incidentally, is a problem that has still not been resolved. The Australian Bureau of Statistics noted in 2006 that, "passenger cards collect data on the stated intentions of people departing, including country of future residence. However, it should be noted that the stated intention does not always match an individual's actual travel behaviour."[29]

Not being able to quantify the numbers of departures was certainly troubling, but the underlying questions at this point, ones that would lead to the government to commission the Immigration Advisory Council to undertake two inquiries into the departure of settlers from Australia, one in 1967 and in 1973, were: what was the cost of these departures, and did they represent a failure of the immigration program?[30]

The Two Inquiries into "Settler Loss"

The inquiries were both carried out by the Immigration Advisory Council's "Committee on Social Patterns" at the request of the respective Immigration Ministers of the day (Hubert Opperman in 1966 and Jim Forbes in 1971). The first was commissioned in May 1966 and the final report was handed down in October 1967. The second took a little longer, commissioned in September 1971 by the then Liberal government and handed down in July 1973 under the new Labor government. The committee members of both inquiries included a mix of Department of Immigration representatives, academics (mostly from the fields which would produce the new experts of the postwar period, demography,

---

28. Immigration Advisory Council Committee on Social Patterns, "Inquiry into the Departure of Settlers from Australia—Progress Report, October 1972" (Canberra: Government Printer of Australia, 1973), 18.

29. "Permanent Departures Overseas—Where are they Going?," Australian Bureau of Statistics, March 2008, https://www.abs.gov.au/ausstats/abs@.nsf/Previousproducts/3412.0Feature%20Article22006-07?opendocument&tabname=Summary&prodno=3412.0&issue=2006-07&num=&view=.

30. Note that because the Australian government funded assisted passages, the program was expensive. See, e.g., a speech by the Minister for Immigration, Billy Snedden, on August 15, 1968, boasting about an increase in migrant numbers and therefore in funding for assisted passages: "This programme of 160,000 exceeds by 22,475 the 137,525 settlers who arrived in Australia during 1967–68. Almost all of the increase will be in assisted migration. Reflecting this, the budgetary provision of more than $34m for assisted passages exceeds any previous appropriation for this purpose."

psychology, and economics), and members of key Australian institutions (including the Australian Council of Trade Unions, the National Council of Women in Australia, and the Australian Council of Social Services). The terms of reference were near identical for both reports—to ascertain the rate of departure and its causes, and suggest what could be done about it—as, to a large degree, were the findings. Both reports reassured the government that compared to other migrant-receiving countries, the Australian departure rate was low, and furthermore emphasized that departure movement was "an inevitable ingredient of any immigration program," even if the Australian government was reluctant to accept this.[31]

However, there were some differences. As Charles Price, advisor to both committees on the demographic aspects of departures, refined his methods of calculation, he revised his estimates of departure rates upward. By the second report he was arguing for a concept he called "settler loss" as providing the most accurate measure of departures over time. "Settler loss" was a complicated bit of statistical modelling which attempted to account for the problem of "intention" he had previously identified. While in the first report he had estimated the departure rate between 1959 and 1965 to be "not less than 9 per cent," by the second report he calculated "settler loss" to be "nearly 17 per cent" for the same period. By the second report, Price could also give a "cohort analysis." This involved taking all the setter arrivals of, for example, 1966, and estimating how many of these had left Australia by 1971. What this showed was that the longer one traced a cohort, the higher the rate of departures. After six years, nearly 22 percent of the cohort would have left permanently, while by the end of ten years it would be nearly 28 percent.[32] In a separate paper published after these inquiries in 1980, but drawing on the research carried out for them, Charles Price was even able to provide a breakdown of settler loss by country of origin for the period of 1947–70, noting that the "leading countries are Germany and the Netherlands, with the United Kingdom next, a little ahead of Italy, Greece and Malta."[33]

What this seemed to indicate was that there were a lot of people on the move, certainly more than governments wanted and Immigration Department officials had anticipated. To some degree, the usefulness of the reports lay less in providing

---

31. The Parliament of the Commonwealth of Australia, 1967—Parliamentary Paper No. 194, *The Departure of Settlers from Australia: Final Report of the Committee on Social Patterns of the Immigration Advisory Council*, October 1967 (Canberra: A.J. Arthur, Commonwealth Government Printer, 1968); The Parliament of the Commonwealth of Australia, 1973—Parliamentary Paper No. 226, *Immigration Advisory Council Committee on Social Patterns: Final Report: Inquiry into the Departures of Settlers from Australia July 1973* (Canberra: Government Printer of Australia, 1974)—hereafter *1967 Report* and *1973 Report*.

32. *1973 Report*, 3–4.

33. Charles Price, *Overseas Migration to Australia, 1947–1970* (CHOMI REPRINTS, 1980), 12.

an accurate measure of departures and more as an exercise in coming to terms with what was somewhat breathlessly referred to as the "new worldwide mobility."[34] There were certainly elements, or at least the confluence of these factors, that were new. As one article published in the Department's *Good Neighbour* magazine put it:

> A new type of migration has emerged in recent years. It sprang not from fear or dissatisfaction with existing conditions, but from prosperity, high living standards and international competition for skills. Combined with simplified formalities and faster transport, this had led to highly-qualified migrants regarding moves every few years as not abnormal.[35]

However, the postwar planners' focus on permanent settlement and assimilation had also obscured the fact that many migrants, as Jock Collins would later note, "had not intended to settle permanently, while many who did changed their minds."[36] Price, once again reflecting on these patterns in 1980, suggested that, in hindsight, this movement should have been predictable:

> Settler loss seems greatest where prosperity in the country of origin is fairly high, medium where immigrants can return home freely if they wish but where conditions are somewhat less prosperous, and is lowest with the refugee groups.[37]

Yet even among that final group there was still movement. As Price further explained, even for the refugees who arrived between 1947 and 1952, whose mobility was assumed to be limited because they could not readily return to their country of origin, "it was not at all difficult ... particularly if they had friends and relatives in western Europe or the Americas, to move on to settlement in another country," especially for those who were "better qualified."[38]

The attribution of a more positive mobility to those who were classified as "skilled" or "better qualified" emerged in the first report with the inclusion of work by the Canadian migration sociologist Anthony Richmond, who developed the concept of "transilients." Richmond described this group, who he mainly identified as British, as being highly mobile thanks to their transferable employment skills and the ease with which they assumed and relinquished social ties.[39] The second report continued to build the case for attracting more of these "skilled" migrants despite the fact they were thought to be more inclined to depart.

---

34. *1967 Report*, 5.

35. "Committee on social patterns reports expenditure not wasted by return migration," *Good Neighbour*, November 1, 1966, 1.

36. Jock Collins, *Migrant Hands in a Distant Land: Australia's Post-War Immigration* (Sydney: Pluto Press, 1988), 30.

37. Price, *Overseas Migration to Australia, 1947–1970*, 12.

38. Price, *Overseas Migration to Australia, 1947–1970*, 8.

39. Appendix 1, *1967 Report*, 36.

The commissioning of the second report in 1971 came a year after the then Immigration Minister, Phillip Lynch, launched a major review of the Department of Immigration. Noting that it had been twenty-five years since the establishment of the postwar program, Lynch argued that the time was ripe to evaluate the "benefits and cost to Australia of immigration conducted on 'traditional patterns.'"[40] What Lynch meant by "traditional patterns" was the postwar consensus that immigration rates should be high, and that they should comprise a mostly "unskilled" labor force who would not be in competition with Australian-born and trained blue and white collar workers. Lynch implied that the Department of Immigration had become fixated on meeting a numerical target each year when what they should be doing was recruiting "quality over quantity."[41]

This represented a fundamental break with postwar orthodoxy. Using this formulation, the economic usefulness of migrants would no longer be calculated en masse but rather by what each individual could contribute as an "economic unit."[42] In this new way of thinking, departures could be tolerated, and even redefined as a gain. The mobility of "skilled" workers was evidence of Australia's increasing competitiveness in the international marketplace, and of these workers "self reliant and adaptable" personalities.[43] Tellingly, the departure of those migrants classified as "semi-skilled and/or unskilled" was not understood in the same light. Their mobility was more likely to be described as a product of their dissatisfaction with Australian conditions combined with a psychological unsuitability for migration, leading them to make a decision to return home, which was described in some circumstances as, "economically irrational."[44] This was despite there being a whole host of completely rational reasons why these migrants might have departed, including, as the report acknowledged, "difficulty of language, recognition of qualifications" and homesickness.[45]

40. Lynch cited in Bruce Juddery, "Critical time for immigration," *Canberra Times*, July 28, 1970, 8.
41. Lynch cited in Juddery, "Critical time for immigration," 8.
42. Phillip Lynch, Immigration Advisory Council Inquiry, March 14, 1973, House of Representatives, 547. To be fair to Lynch, he did actually concede that "migrants are not just economic units in a program of massive development," but then went on to criticize the Labor government for getting rid of the labor migration scheme and only providing support for family reunion.
43. Note the tendency to equate "skilled" with greater mental stability: *1967 Report*, 24. In terms of thinking of individual migrants as "economic units," there were also attempts to calculate the minimum a migrant would have to stay for the government to recoup costs. See Dr. Forbes, Returning migrants: assisted passages, Wednesday, September 29, 1971, House of Representatives Official Hansard, No. 39, 1616: "I think the House will be interested to know that we have calculated that provided a single migrant stays in this country for 9 months he will return to Australia by indirect and direct taxation as much as is provided to assist him to migrate to this country."
44. *1967 Report*, 8.
45. *1967 Report*, 9.

The Policy Response to Settler Loss

A shift in attitudes towards departures did not mean that the report writers were advocating the government do nothing to prevent migrants from leaving. The inquiries can be seen as part of the coming to fruition of the postwar social science boom.[46] The consultants to the committees—particularly the ascendent trio of economists, demographers, and psychologists—were all people with solutions in search of a problem, ready to prove the worth of their respective disciplines. The results were something of a mixed bag. The economists could not quite agree on the costs and benefits of migration; the demographers realized that quantifying departures could only ever be approximate; and while the psychologists could provide character profiles of individual suitability for immigration, it was usually only *after* the migrant had proven themselves to be unsuitable by departing. Ultimately, the advice they gave to mitigate departures boiled down to two options: select migrants better at the source and support migrants better once they arrived.

Tightening up selection criteria certainly sounded promising on paper. If the right set of personality traits could be delineated, and any tendency to mental illness or emotional instability detected, then settler loss could potentially be eliminated in the source country through the sifting out of any "high-risk persons who lack[ed] the capacity to successfully integrate." The 1967 Committee, while not entirely against introducing more "discriminative selection," did foresee one important issue if it were to be introduced along the lines suggested, explaining that "the rejection of potential immigrants on the basis of their performance in tests of adaptability could cause public comments in source countries and damage potential recruitment."[47] Essentially, source countries were unlikely to appreciate the implication that their citizens were unsuitable recruits for Australia (even if behind closed doors they might admit to wanting to siphon off an excess population). This issue encapsulated a criticism that had long been levelled at the Department of Immigration: that it was so caught up in the "nation-building" aspects of the program, managing assimilation and building public support, it tended to forget that immigration policy was also about "international-relation-building."[48]

If Australia wanted to retain migrants in this era of increased mobility it would have to modify its domestic policies or face the consequences of emigration

---

46. On the establishment of social sciences in the postwar era, see Stuart Macintyre, *Australia's Boldest Experiment: War and Reconstruction in the 1940s* (Sydney: NewSouth, 2015); Hannah Forsyth, "The ownership of knowledge in higher education in Australia, 1939–1966," Ph.D. thesis, University of Sydney, 2012.

47. "Nearly 16pc of migrants leaving but many return," *Canberra Times*, October 31, 1966, 3.

48. See Green, "The politics of exit," 266, on this point: "emigration and immigration policies are also interrelated aspects of international relations."

countries directing their citizens elsewhere.⁴⁹ By the late 1960s, European governments of emigrant countries were reported to be actively dissuading "overseas emigration" in favor of "intra-European emigration." Their reasoning was that Australia, through a combination of distance and policy, made it harder for migrants to sustain their national affiliation to their country of origin, and once there, migrants were thought to be less likely to come back. In comparison, emigration to European nations was said to make it easier for migrants to "retain association with the native country of origin and [ensure] a reasonable chance of return."⁵⁰ Perhaps as a concession to this point, in 1973 the ALP proposed that the oath of affirmation for Australian citizenship should no longer require the applicant to renounce their former allegiance, arguing that for many migrants their country of birth still held "great emotional significance."⁵¹ It would, however, take over a decade for this requirement to be finally removed from the oath.

More immediately, the governments of countries of emigration began, to borrow Nancy Green's phrasing again, to "fret" on behalf of their citizens.⁵² The Italian government in the early 1960s, for instance, pushed for the Australian government to provide better conditions for Italian settlers in Australia, including recognition of trade qualifications, ready access to social service benefits, and greater assistance with passage costs.⁵³ In this instance, the governments did not come to an agreement, resulting in a severe decline in assisted migration from Italy. However, the matter drew attention to the second proposed solution to settler loss: that migrants needed to be better supported once they were in Australia.

The 1967 report offered a novel, and surprisingly compassionate, response to the problem of homesickness, identified as one of the main "non-economic" factors (and the one most attributed to women)⁵⁴ in the decision to return home. The proposed scheme would subsidize the cost of a return air fare for at least one family member. The committee argued the incidental benefits of the scheme would include "helping to attract migrants in the highly competitive climate of

---

49. Of course, the policy that the Australian government actively resisted changing across this period despite pressure from emigration countries in Asia was the White Australia Policy.

50. Australian Parliamentary Mission—Report of visit to—Italy, Federal Republic of Germany, Belgium, Luxembourg, the Netherlands and the United Kingdom, mission led by Hon. G. Freeth, M.P., Minister for Air, June 15 to July 6, 1968.

51. Douglas McClelland, Australian Citizenship Bill 1973, September 11, 1973, The Senate, 417–18.

52. In "The politics of exit," 268, Green states, "We need to confront the ways in which the states and societies of origin aided and abetted or fretted about and even obstructed the emigration movement."

53. Price, *Overseas migration to Australia, 1947–1970*, 6–7.

54. The gendered aspect of homesickness is an interesting aspect of the reports. Husbands very rarely admitted to homesickness, rather it was often referred to as the "wife's homesickness" (8) and a characteristic of "immaturity" (9) or "emotional instability" (19).

international migration, and in holding those who might otherwise depart permanently."⁵⁵ For all its potential, it would appear that the scheme was quietly shelved, as there was no mention of it in the 1973 report.

One concern that was voiced across both reports, although with increased urgency in the second, was that Australia was falling behind other countries in the provision of social services. The 1967 report included interviews with former British migrants who explained that the lack of comparable welfare measures in Australia, in particular the absence of a comprehensive National Health Service like that available in Britain, was a motivating factor in their decision to return home.⁵⁶ In the lead-up to the second inquiry the ALP, citing the recommendations of the previous report and castigating the government for their lack of action, argued that boosting Australia's social welfare program was critical to remedying migrant departures.⁵⁷ Both Nancy Green and Tara Zahra have noted that the establishment of social protections in Italy and across Eastern Europe respectively were, in part, enacted as a response to concerns about the welfare of migrant workers.⁵⁸ In rhetoric at least, the ALP was certainly making a similar connection. As part of calls for the establishment of the second inquiry, a Labor MP cited a report published in the *Dutch Australian Weekly* in parliament: "Australia will never get out of the doldrums—will never regain its name as a really good country to migrate to—if it does realise that it is not the rest of the world which is out of step as far as social services are concerned but Australia and Australia alone."⁵⁹

When the ALP came to power in 1972, the link was strengthened between settler loss and increasing social services targeted at migrants. Al Grassby, as the newly appointed Minister for Immigration, commented on the Inquiry, pointing to his government's implementation of a range of services such as emergency interpreters, citizenship centers, and special programs for migrant children in schools. Grassby also saw the potential to link settler loss to the emerging policy of

---

55. *1967 Report*, 30.

56. *1967 Report*, 24.

57. Leonard Keogh, Appropriation Bill (No. 1) 1971–72 Speech, October 28, 1971, House of Representatives, 2764.

58. Note that the connection to social welfare is slightly different across the two examples. To prevent from leaving: "The rise of a global labor market raised genuine humanitarian and social concerns about the welfare of migrant workers ... Real freedom required stability, security and solidarity at home" (Tara Zahra, *The Great Departures: Mass Migration from Eastern Europe and the Making of the Free World*, New York: W.W. Norton and Co., 2016); To maintain connection with those who had left: "Ultimately, it was in part due to the mass emigration that the Italian protective welfare state even came into being; the government sought first to count and then to aid the emigrants as a way of maintaining ties" (Green, "The politics of exit," 27).

59. Leonard Keogh, Appropriation Bill (No. 1) 1972–73, Wednesday, September 27, 1972, House of Representatives, 2050–51.

multiculturalism. Anticipating his concept of the "family of the nation," central to his articulation of multiculturalism, Grassby argued that migrants could not be expected to want to remain in Australia until "we have fully accepted all migrants into the Australian family, as citizens with equal ranking in all respects."[60] Interestingly, Grassby pushed back against the growing consensus that return- and third-country migration was an inevitable part of the immigration program. In Grassby's formulation, the ALP had been set the "challenge to end settler loss."[61] Whether he actually thought this was possible is questionable, but it did suggest he had his doubts about the desirability of the highly mobile migrant. Grassby's multiculturalism in many ways harked back to the early postwar understanding of migration, in that it would be permanent. He wanted new members of the family to stay and build their lives in Australia.

Conclusion

Did all this "abetting, fretting and obstructing" have any impact on individual migrant decision-making to stay or go? It is a question that the two committees were unable to answer definitively. It's hard not to read a sense of resignation with the whole exercise from at least one of the consultants on the 1967 report. The economic historian Reginald Appleyard, having carried out interviews with departing migrants both pre- and post-departure, noted that the reasons they gave changed so dramatically between those two points that any survey regarding the cause of return migration was likely to be unreliable.[62] We do have a clue in Mr. Dell'Oro's file as to why he left. A handwritten addition reads "wife and children in Italy," suggesting they made their way home first (or, potentially, that they never came to Australia in the first place). Given that in his fourteen years in Australia Mr. Dell'Oro never applied for citizenship, there was probably very little any government could have offered to prevent his departure. Charles Price, having labored over the quantification of settler loss for the better part of a decade, offered perhaps the soundest advice in relation to the whole enterprise:

> Assisted migration is like investing in the stock market—one's best protection against loss is to invest widely and set profits from the many good investments against losses from the few bad ones. In this sense, public money spent on settlers who eventually leave again is part of the price Australia has to pay for obtaining the many who settle successfully.[63]

60. Al Grassby, Immigration Advisory Council Inquiry, March 14, 1973, House of Representatives, 546. In this vision, Grassby was ably supported by the Chair of the 1973 Committee, Professor Jerzy Zubrzycki, who was a key proponent of early multiculturalism.
    61. Grassby, Immigration Advisory Council Inquiry.
    62. *1967 Report*, 8.
    63. Price, *Overseas Migration to Australia, 1947–1970*, 17.

If individual motivations remain opaque, what we can see by beginning to trace the government response to departures from the postwar to the 1970s is the contours of where we are now. Through advances in technology the Australian Border Force has become increasingly sophisticated in its ability to keep track of those "crossing the border." However, their focus is less on monitoring departures and more on trying to prevent "illegal" entry or visa overstaying. Economic arguments, which champion increasing Australia's ability to attract "highly skilled" migrants who leave, are far easier to sustain than those which argue for the improvement of social services for those who are struggling to stay (although, we are yet to fully see what impact the COVID-19 pandemic, which saw many temporary migrants faced with little choice but to go back their countries of origin, might have on government's providing inducements to migrants to return and assistance to stay). Finally, since the early 2000s temporary migrants—as international students, working-holiday makers and temporary skilled workers—have outstripped permanent migration to Australia.[64] Departures are not just an "inevitable ingredient" but are now built into the very structure of Australia's immigration program.

---

64. Jock Collins, "Globalisation, immigration and the second long postwar boom in Australia," *Journal of Australian Political Economy* 61 (June 2008): 262. For a discussion of the role of tourism in reshaping the character of the Australian immigration program, see Justine Greenwood, "Welcome to Australia: Intersections between immigration and tourism in Australia, 1945–2015," Ph.D. thesis, University of Sydney, 2015.

Chapter 2

HOPSCOTCH AUSTRALIA: DISPLACED PERSONS TAKING THE LONG WAY AROUND TO THE REST OF THE WORLD

Ruth Balint

Australia does not often figure in accounts about the postwar resettlement of Displaced Persons (DPs), except in books by Australian historians.[1] This myopia on the part of American and European historians about Australia's role in the migration and resettlement of wartime refugees out of Europe mirrored the same myopia of DPs themselves, who, if they did not already have relatives there had often not heard of Australia or did not always see it as a good option for migration. If they did, it was often as a last resort, after their attempts to reach other countries had failed: America was the promised land. I was struck by this fact when I was researching records created by the International Refugee Organization (IRO), the agency responsible for resettling DPs waiting in camps in Germany, Austria, and Italy who refused to return home to their countries of origin in Eastern Europe. Each DP applying for IRO care and resettlement had to fill in a questionnaire and complete an interview with an IRO officer. One of the last sections on the questionnaire asked DPs to list their preferred destination. Very few listed Australia as a first, second, or even third destination of preference on their forms, and most not at all. And yet, in the end, Australia took an official number of 170,700 (probably closer to 180,000) DPs on their mass resettlement program between 1947 and 1951, second only to the United States in terms of numbers.

Contemporaries on the ground in Europe were fond of commenting on the hierarchy of countries for resettlement in the DP imagination. "Everyone wanted to go to America," wrote Susan Petiss in her memoir of working as a welfare officer

---

1. Exceptions include Jayne Persian, *Beautiful Balts: From Displaced Persons to New Australians* (Sydney: NewSouth, 2017), Sheila Fitzpatrick, *White Russians, Red Peril: A Cold War History of Migration to Australia* (Melbourne: Black, Inc., 2021), and Ruth Balint, *Destination Elsewhere: Displaced Persons and their Quest to Leave Europe after 1945* (Ithaca, NY: Cornell University Press, 2021).

in postwar Germany.[2] One Lithuanian father, examining the options for migration told his family, "America is today, Canada tomorrow, Australia the day after, New Zealand—God knows when!"[3] Such sentiments often followed migrants to Australia, or resurfaced when the reality of Australia's conditions of settlement, including two years of hard labor in remote areas, was bluntly realized upon arrival. The recruitment of laborers from Europe was a central plank of the Australian reconstruction effort after the war, and governed Australia's acceptance of the IRO request to resettle Europe's DPs. Australia was not unique in this respect: none of the resettlement countries were motivated by humanitarianism. Strict entry requirements of age, fitness, and social and ethnic backgrounds governed national intakes among all of the resettlement nations. Malcolm Proudfoot, a US Army officer stationed in occupied Europe who later produced a serious study on the subject of refugees, observed that "in spite of all the protestations of sympathy, the pivot of national immigration policies in almost all the countries was strictly practical and closely related to domestic labour requirements."[4]

It is difficult to quantify how many DPs who arrived in Australia with IRO passage between 1947 and 1952 used Australia as a stepping stone to move on to more desirable locations. But evidence suggests that a considerable number of DPs who came to Australia from postwar Europe left for a third country within the decade, whether through disappointment, a sudden change in circumstances, or because they had always intended to. This yields a somewhat different picture of migrant departure to the more traditional focus on "return," which, in the Australian context, usually meant the British emigrant returning to England.[5] In the nineteenth century, colonial British returnees predominantly followed a "return when rich" ethos.[6] But from the early twentieth century onwards, the British migrant who went back to the United Kingdom left because of disappointment, unemployment, and homesickness rather than because of a

---

2. Susan Petiss and Lynne Taylor, *After the Shooting Stopped: The Story of an UNRRA Welfare Worker in Germany, 1945–1947* (Victoria, BC: Trafford Publishing, 2004), 78.

3. Ben Shephard, *The Long Road Home: The Aftermath of the Second World War* (London: Vintage Books, 2010), 339.

4. Malcolm Proudfoot, *European Refugees: A Study in Forced Population Movements 1939–1952* (London: Faber, 1957), 418.

5. See, for example, the collection of chapters by historians such as Eric Richards, Mark Wyman, and Alistair Thompson, in Marjorie Harper (ed.), *Emigrant Homecomings: The Return Movement of Emigrants 1600–2000* (Manchester: Manchester University Press, 2017).

6. Tony Ward, "Return Migration from Nineteenth Century Australia: Key Drivers and Gender Differences," *Australian Economic History Review*, 61, no. 1 (2021): 82. Ward cites the work of Paul de Seville, *Port Phillip Gentlemen* (Melbourne: Oxford University Press, 1980).

premeditated intention to return.⁷ This trend continued after World War II, much to the consternation of Australian governments keen to attract migrants of British stock over other cohorts. An average of 25 percent of British migrants lured to Australia after World War II by promises of housing and employment left and returned home, prompting an official inquiry into the problem in 1967.⁸ Indeed, it was the high rate of British departees, rather than other groups, that really worried officials, despite the significant numbers of non-Anglo-Saxon departures, many of whom had originally arrived as DPs from postwar Europe.⁹

This chapter explores a history of ambivalence that accompanied the DP journey to Australia. It argues that the phenomenon of DPs who arrived in Australia as part of the mass resettlement scheme and then left again or, in just as many cases, tried to was a significant feature of Australia's postwar migration history. Their voices have until now been obscured in Australian migration history, partly because Australian migration history has traditionally focused on the successes and challenges faced by the migrants who stayed. Another reason is that Australian historians weren't very interested in European migrants. Historians Richard Bosworth and Janis Wilton lamented the insularity of their contemporaries who, they wrote in 1980, were "strangely disdainful" of the study of European migration. "By default," they wrote, "the field has been left to demographers, sociologists, psychologists and other social scientists."¹⁰ The group of social scientists most closely involved with measuring the experiences of the postwar

---

7. Alistair Thomson, "'I Live on My Memories': British Return Migrants and the Possession of the Past," *Oral History* 31, no. 2 (2003): 55–65. In 1960, the annual *Demography Bulletin* issued by the Commonwealth Bureau of Census and Statistics reported that of the 46,595 departures of permanent or long-term residents, 16,219 were to the UK or Ireland, a far higher statistic than for any other country. The next highest number was 9,935 to Italy. "Demography 1960," *Bulletin No. 78* (Canberra: Commonwealth Bureau of Census and Statistics, 1960), 23–6.

8. Commonwealth of Australia parliamentary paper no. 194, "The Departure of Settlers from Australia: Final Report of the Committee on Social Patterns of the Immigration Advisory Council October 1967," Canberra 1968. On the statistic of 25 percent, see Alastair Thomson, "'My Wayward Heart': homesickness, longing and the return of British postwar immigrants from Australia," in Harper, *Emigrant Homecomings*, 106.

9. Note that earlier demography bulletins raised the issue of high rates of departure between 1952 and 1957 as the highest on record and although British migrants remained the highest number of returnees, this figure would include substantial numbers of DPs. Among the total number of departures, it was noted that around one in every five settlers intended to settle in a third country, mostly the United States, Canada, or Israel (*1958 Demography Bulletin*, Australian Bureau of Statistics).

10. Richard Bosworth and Janis Wilton, "A Lost History? The Study of European Migration to Australia," *Australian Journal of Politics and History* 27, no. 2 (1981): 222. Thank you to Dr. Zora Simic for alerting me to this article.

migrants and the processes of assimilation were those linked to the new department of demography at the ANU, established in 1952 with W. D. Borrie as its head. This group included the young Jean Martin, who joined at its inception to complete a Ph.D. under the supervision of Siegfried Nadel, later published in book form as *Refugee Settlers* in 1965.

Wilton and Bosworth singled out Martin for being too focused on the Australian angle of the migrant experience, too blind to the politics of the migrants' pasts.[11] But it is unlikely that Bosworth and Wilton had access at the time of their writing to the trove of primary documents Martin left behind, much of which did not make it into her books, *Refugee Settlers* or *The Migrant Presence*. If they had, they might have tempered their criticisms, for Martin found much to interest her in her interviewees' European pasts as well as their attitudes to Australia. Her archives, now held at the Noel Butlin Archives and the National Library of Australia, give today's historian rare access to the voices of DPs newly settled in postwar Australia. For her research, Martin chose to immerse herself fully in the lives of her interviewees, living for six months in the regional town of Goulburn among the roughly 200 DPs who were settled there after the war.[12] The raw material of her interviews reveals a group of migrants less attached to, less thankful for, and mostly ambivalent about their new country than the grand narrative of multicultural Australia usually suggests. Indeed, if assimilation offered considerable appeal to Martin as a subject of analysis, it was even more novel for East European migrants, who, she found, had mostly never intended to migrate to Australia at the time of being wrenched from their homes, first by war and then by Communism.[13] Instead, "one of the favourite topics of conversation among the Displaced Persons in 1953" was leaving Australia for somewhere else.[14]

The first part of this chapter relies on Martin's interviews together with other better-known primary sources to explore the DP desire for "somewhere else." The second part of this chapter explores some of the routes and strategies some migrants who had arrived as DPs did take to leave Australia in the ten years or so after their arrival. Not all succeeded, and some didn't leave until the end of the Cold War. This longer history of Eastern European departure from Australia in the second half of the twentieth century offers a fruitful avenue for future research.

---

11. Bosworth and Wilton, "A Lost History?", 222, 223.

12. These were mainly non-Jewish DPs, with which this chapter is concerned; the trajectory of Jewish refugees after the war took a different route, and most did not arrive via the IRO.

13. Jean Craig, "Assimilation of European Immigrants: A Study in Role Assumption and Fulfilment," Ph.D. thesis, Australian National University, December 1954, 373.

14. Jean Martin, *Refugee Settlers: A Study of Displaced Persons in Australia* (Canberra: ANU Press, 1965), 76.

DP Ambivalence to Australia

A section in Martin's Ph.D. thesis is called "Attitudes to Australia." Among her earliest and most frequent observations was that fate or happenstance characterized most DP journeys to Australia.[15] Her interviewees regaled her with accounts of being detoured at the last possible moment from their original migration plans for other countries, to Australia. One Hungarian couple, for example, were hoping to go to Brazil or Argentina, "but they would have to wait even longer to go there so they came to Australia."[16] Another young man, who had spent his teenage years as a forced laborer in Germany during the war, described how "the first possible place that turned up was Aus, and he came here," although his real desire had been to go to America.[17] One woman told Martin that first she had wanted to go to France:

> But just before she was due to go, they canceled all further immigration for the time being. Then she chose England, and the same thing happened in that case. So then there was Aus [sic]—she raised her hands in mock horror, it was the last place she would ever have thought of going and it seemed too far away ... She could never tell me what it was like the day she sailed from Italy—she felt completely desolated.[18]

As Martin quickly learned, the decision to join the Australian resettlement scheme was influenced less by the attraction of the country than by factors on the ground in Europe, including the need to leave before resettlement places dried up, and the relative ease, if one was healthy, of being accepted for Australia. "Sometimes, the Displaced Persons deliberately chose Australia as their alternative," she found, "but more often they came to this country because other opportunities for resettlement had failed to materialise, or because it was of no consequence to them where they settled if they could not return home."[19]

This antipathy towards Australia was something the film director Roy Maslyn Williams also encountered first-hand in his tour of the DP camps in 1949. He had gone there to make a documentary for the Commonwealth Film Unit, as part of an official publicity campaign to promote the DP scheme to a skeptical public back home. The film was meant to trace the journey of a refugee family from the end of the war to their successful arrival in Australia, but as Williams soon realized, no one wanted the starring roles. "From the point of view of many DPs Australia is the gambler's shot when attempts to get to America have failed," he wrote to his

---

15. "Most of the subjects had an ambivalent attitude towards Australia" she writes. Craig, "Assimilation of European Immigrants," 378.

16. "JIC 124," Jean Martin papers, Series 7912, Box 4, Male JIC 300–35, National Library of Australia (hereafter NLA).

17. "JIC 329," Jean Martin papers, Series 7912, Box 4, Male JIC 300–35, NLA.

18. "JIC 121," Jean Martin papers, Series 7912, Box 5, File 321, 121, 326, NLA.

19. Craig, "Assimilation of European Immigrants," 374.

producer Stanley Hawes. "I heard of one IRO official last week who threatened an uncooperative DP that if he did not behave, she would have him registered for Australia." He didn't find willing participants easily: "As one intelligent DP put it to me, 'It is Australia or Siberia or starvation.'"[20]

Like Williams, Australian migration agents also struggled to fill their quotas of suitable DPs. "The Selection Teams in 1949 and 1950 were under constant pressure to fill the ships which always seemed to be waiting at Bremen, the port of embarkation," reported Keith Turbayne, one of the two Australian intelligence officers stationed in Germany after the war.[21] Australian migration officials had arrived in Europe in 1947 tasked by the new Immigration Minister, Arthur Calwell, with recruiting young, fit, and "assimilable" single men and women. Mort Barwick arrived in Germany in 1949 with minimal instructions about the kind of person to admit on the scheme: "provided they were of reasonable standard and in your opinion could assimilate into your community, then it was a question of, if you were satisfied, select them."[22] But it soon became evident that Australia would have to work hard to fill its DP migrant quota, competing against other countries with far stronger, more popular profiles than its own. Even before Calwell toured the refugee camps of Germany and became aware of the "splendid human material" to be found among the DPs, reports were filtering back to Canberra about the danger that other Western governments might skim "the whole of the cream" if Australia did not act quickly.[23]

This official scramble for young, fit laborers and child-bearers was felt first-hand by Martin's interviewees. "They didn't tell her anything about Australia," Martin jotted down after a discussion with a Latvian interviewee about her encounter with Australian migration officials. "The Australian rep wasn't at all helpful—he just made sure they were healthy and that was all he was interested in."[24] One woman had wanted to go to the United States, she told Martin, "but Mr. B [a selection officer] advised her not to . . . he told her that it would not be so easy for a woman nearly 40 [with] a child in America . . . [W]ithin a few weeks of her first contact with Mr. B she was on a ship to Australia."[25] Such "accidental" decisions were remarked upon "over and over" again.[26]

---

20. Stanley Hawes Collection, Box 54, 35864, National Film and Sound Archive, Canberra.

21. "Report Written by Keith Turbayne 27 February 1964, European Migration to Australia 1949–1951," CRS A6122, NAA.

22. Harry Martin, *Angels and Arrogant Gods: Migration Officers and Migrants Reminisce, 1945–1985* (Canberra: Australian Government Publishing Service, 1989), 17.

23. Andrew Markus, "Labour and immigration 1946–49: the displaced persons program," *Labour History* 47 (November 1984): 78. Ruth Balint, "Industry and Sunshine: Australia as Home in the Displaced Persons' Camps of Postwar Europe," *History Australia* 11, no. 1 (April 2014): 106–31.

24. "JIC 119," Jean Martin papers, Series 7912, Box 4, Male JIC 300–35, NLA.

25. "JIC 115," Jean Martin papers, Series 7912, Box 5, File 115, NLA.

26. Fitzpatrick, *White Russians, Red Peril*, 151.

Perhaps the most common sentiment expressed by Martin's interviewees in the 1950s was a longing for the United States. This desire for America was one that was commonly remarked upon by welfare officers in Europe. Kathryn Hulme, the director of the Polish DP camp Wildflecken, recalled the efforts she and her IRO colleagues made to remind DPs about countries other than the United States, after America finally opened its doors a crack in late 1948. "Despite the pitfalls in the US scheme visible to all," she wrote, "so many DPs wanted to switch to it from their sure bets like Belgium, Australia and Canada, that we began to publicise letters from satisfied customers in those countries to take the mass mind off the gold-paved streets of Neuyorke Amerika."[27] Such yearnings for America didn't dissipate for DPs who ended up in Australia, and it seems may have become further exaggerated after their arrival. As Tara Zahra has shown, America's association with freedom, and the right to mobility, was in part created by Eastern Europeans who had looked to America since the beginning of the century as a place to make money and live freely.[28] The aftermath of World War II hardened this division of East and West into associations of "free" and "unfree." The "free world" became understood in terms of its opposite, the Communist "slave world" behind the Iron Curtain.[29] Refugees spoke frequently about their desire for freedom, continuing an older conversation about the right to emigrate, a conversation that had been developing since the turn of the century in the context of mass migration from Eastern Europe to the "new world." "I don't ask for care," wrote Arnolds M. to the IRO from a DP camp in Germany. "I request only the rights which will give me the possibility to emigrate from Germany and to build a new life in a free country."[30]

But unhappiness with Australia's work conditions soon complicated its position on the spectrum of "free" and "unfree" countries in the DP imagination. The two-year labor contract each DP had to sign, and the reality of the harsh working conditions migrants faced once they arrived, led to frequent reports of "slave conditions" filtering back to DPs still in Europe.[31] An officer in Bonegilla, the Australian resettlement center, wrote to the Department of Immigration warning that some migrants were writing to family and friends in Europe warning them not to come. He blamed the Communists. "There is a strong Communist campaign through the camps to discourage people from coming to Australia, with the promise that they will commit themselves to slavery" he wrote, warning that "people who have already come to Australia are writing to confirm the facts of

---

27. Kathryn Hulme, *The Wild Place* (London: Frederick Muller Ltd., 1954), 198.

28. Tara Zahra, *The Great Departure: Mass Migration from Eastern Europe and the Making of the Free World* (New York and London: W.W. Norton and Company, 2016), 20.

29. Zahra, *The Great Departure*, 20.

30. IRO review board decision for Arnolds M., AJ43/471, Archives Nationale, Paris (hereafter AN).

31. Sheila Fitzpatrick, "The Motherland Calls: 'Soft' Repatriation of Soviet Citizens from Europe, 1945–1953," *Journal of Modern History* 90 (June 2018): 327.

slavery and advising their friends, in any case, to give up hopes of coming to Australia."[32]

By comparison, the lives of friends and relatives who had successfully emigrated to the United States was a frequent topic of conversation among Martin's interviewees. "Success stories about relatives or friends who had settled somewhere else—usually in the United States—circulated freely from one immigrant to another," she wrote, "adding to the favorable images of these countries already existing in the minds of many Displaced Persons and aggravating their discontent with conditions in Australia."[33] One man told Martin that he received letters from people who had gone to the United States, "and no one makes you speak English or tries to force you to become American straight away—and they don't talk about 'new Americans.'"[34] He resented being forced to become Australian "too quickly," particularly as Australians continued to look down on immigrants.[35] New arrivals in America were free to work wherever they wanted, another man informed Martin. "He has friends who went to America with nothing," Martin elaborated, "and already they have their own businesses, they own five cars—they have everything they want."[36]

Getting a visa for America was a more difficult, bureaucratic, and restrictive process than for Australia. Like Australia, each DP applicant in Europe had to be given a clean bill of health and be of working age.[37] Unlike Australia, however, each applicant was required to find a sponsor in America to financially support them and their family upon arrival. As one recent arrival to Goulburn told Martin, "[I]f it was easy and anyone who wanted could apply for admission to the United States there would not be many immigrants left in Australia—they would all go to America."[38] Some began the process of trying to get to the United States as soon as they had arrived in Australia, or not long after. "7 said that she knew of a number of migrants who had already applied for their passages to the United States from Australia but, shrugging her shoulders, 'it cost a lot of money to get to the United States and in any case you had to wait for admission' (the implication was that she would like to go there but it was impossible for them in their present circumstances)."[39]

---

32. "Memo to The Secretary, Department of Immigration," author and date illegible, NAA: CP815/1, 021.134 Attachment. It is important to note that the metaphor of slavery was used by a number of critics of IRO resettlement practices. See Gerard Daniel Cohen, *In War's Wake: Europe's Displaced Persons in the Postwar Order* (Oxford: Oxford University Press), 112–13.

33. Martin, *Refugee Settlers*, 76.

34. "JIC 304, 116, 316," N132/125, NBA.

35. Craig, "Assimilation of European Immigrants," 410.

36. "JIC 346," N132/125, NBA.

37. It is important to note here that Jewish DPs who wished to come to Australia did have to find financial sponsors to guarantee accommodation and support, unlike non-Jewish DPs.

38. Jean Martin papers, N132/125, NBA.

39. "JIC 7," Jean Martin papers, N132/132. NBA.

One man "quite openly" expressed his desire to go to the US, and had applied for a visa and filled in all the necessary papers, and was now waiting to go.[40] However, not all were convinced that America was a better option. One woman told Martin that although she had a lot of friends who had gone to the United States, "she thinks it is better for them here. Later on, her husband also came back to this question and he said that probably the United States was good for rich people but for people who came here with nothing like themselves Australia was a far better country."[41] It seemed clear that for those with professional qualifications, America offered recognition and better possibilities, while in Australia, it was brawn rather than brains that was valued. A friend of one of Martin's interviewees was a doctor, who had been sent to work in an abattoir. "What sort of country is this that would do that to a man? Then he got in touch with the American consulate, and they let him go to America, and he could practice as a doctor there, and everything was fine for him."[42]

Egon Kunz researched the experiences of professionally trained, higher educated DPs who came to Australia on the two-year labor contract, and found that the majority experienced "degradation" and a severe loss of status. He compared the work experiences of DP professionals in Australia with those in America. One in three who went to the United States was employed in a professional or semi-professional capacity by the end of their first year, while in Australia, only one in eleven was able to use their qualifications. "This suggests that displaced persons with high qualifications had [a] three to four times better chance for an early recovery of their status in the USA than in Australia."[43] Stories in the press reinforced Kunz's argument that the better educated believed the United States was a better destination. One journalist for the *Newcastle Morning Herald* spoke to Jonas, a Lithuanian immigrant, who told him about an Estonian doctor, once a professor, who was "now chopping wood in Canberra, but has been offered a post at a Chicago University. When he has completed his two year contract in this country, he will be glad to leave for America."[44] As Martin concluded:

> The subjects compared themselves, as immigrants to Australia, with immigrants in the U.S.A., claiming in particular that Americans were much more hospitable than Australians towards strangers, that there was more opportunity for private enterprise, and hence more chance of financial success, and that there were no obstacles in the way of practising the profession or trade in which the immigrant had been trained in Europe.[45]

---

40. Jean Martin papers, N132/125, NBA.
41. "13," Jean Martin papers, N132/126, NBA.
42. JIC 305, Jean Martin papers, N132/125, NBA.
43. Egon F. Kunz, *Displaced Persons: Calwell's New Australians* (Sydney: ANU Press, 1988), 160.
44. S. A. Barney, "Going Tough For Some Migrants," *Newcastle Morning Herald*, December 3, 1959, 5.
45. Craig, "Assimilation of European Immigrants," 410.

Australia may have been an accidental choice for many, but equally, it may only have ever meant to have been temporary. Michael Kovacs, who gave questionnaires to 200 recently arrived migrants in the early 1950s for his doctoral thesis, found that "few of them embarked on their emigration with a determination not to return to their mother countries; in fact, most of them were regarding themselves as 'temporary' emigrants, instead of permanent immigrants."[46] Martin also found that, with few exceptions, most "showed some attachment to their home countries" and some couldn't tolerate the idea of being permanently settled here.[47] Instead, many hoped to be able to return after a few years, once the Communists had left. "She could do nothing and make nothing of her life here, but after the war she would return to help with the rebuilding of her own country."[48] Many confessed to using Australia as a way station to wait out the Communist regimes in their countries, although as time passed the possibility of this happening became less real. One couple had left behind their workshop, their house, and other properties in Czechoslovakia in 1949, determined to return when the Communists left. "However, after he said all this, he shrugged his shoulders hopelessly and said, but I expect we will die here anyway."[49]

Ten years later, Martin followed up with thirty-one of her original interviewees. "By this time, the question, 'Would you return home now if you could?' had become meaningless to all of them; to a few it sounded like a cruel joke."[50] The Latvian patriot who had wanted to return to rebuild her country had left for the United States. Two of Martin's single male interviewees had done the same. Another seven were seriously contemplating it. The wish to return home to Eastern Europe, however, diminished as time progressed. Kovacs also found that the prospect for IRO immigrants of returning home "where the approximate prewar order had been restored seems less practicable with every year; consequently for many of them their residence in this country has been slowly losing the character of temporariness," even if leaving Australia for somewhere else continued to be "an ever recurring topic of conversation."[51]

Leaving Australia

It wasn't easy for migrants to leave Australia in the 1950s. It was expensive, shipping was scarce, and one needed the right papers. "Dissatisfied migrants have been pestering the masters of foreign vessels for return passages to Europe," the *Herald*

---

46. Michael L. Kovacs, "Immigration and Assimilation: An Outline Account of the IRO Immigrants in Australia," M.A. thesis, University of Melbourne, 1955, 202.

47. Martin, *Refugee Settlers*, 75, 65.

48. Martin, *Refugee Settlers*, 75–6.

49. Jean Martin papers, Series 7912, Box 5, file 140 and 340, NLA. See also Box 4, Male JIG 336, for interview with 351 and 151

50. Martin, *Refugee Settlers*, 76.

51. Kovacs, "Immigration and Assimilation," 367.

reported in 1952. Ludwig Roth, chief officer of the German freighter the *Wilhelm Bornhoffen*, claimed that in the one week the ship had anchored at Melbourne's South Wharf, the captain had been approached by at least fifty people to allow them to work return passages to Europe.[52]

Unlike some other countries at this time that allowed non-citizens to have passports, for Australia nationality and citizenship were necessary to claim a passport for travel, and this process was cumbersome. Non-British residents had to have been resident in Australia for five years (as opposed to one year for British subjects), to have lodged a "Declaration of Intention to Apply for Naturalisation" two years prior, to have published their intention to become a citizen in two local newspapers, and to have acquired three certificates of character written by Australian citizens. It also required a knowledge of English and a formal renunciation of allegiance to the country of origin. Consequently, the uptake was slow. Before 1952, less than half of Australia's postwar migrants had registered an intention to naturalize, and nearly 80 percent hadn't pursued it.[53] Among the reasons for the low take-up found by Immigration Department research in the 1950s and 1960s was the reluctance to give up their allegiance to their own countries, uncertainty about wanting to stay in Australia permanently, and social marginalization.[54]

Officials assumed that those who did take up naturalization represented a measure of migrant satisfaction and assimilation, but Egon Kunz found that naturalization offered many a way to leave Australia rather than to stay.[55] Among his sample of 2,148 males, Kunz found that four out of every ten migrant former university students who lined up for naturalization immediately after becoming eligible "did so in order to obtain a passport by which to leave Australia forever." This form of "transit naturalisation," he wrote, "was more frequent among the better educated than among the less qualified, more among the young than the old, and more among the single or childless married couples than among those with families."[56] Martin also quickly learned that taking out Australian citizenship was seen as expedient because it offered a passport, rather than being a statement of loyalty to their new homeland.[57] Many had arrived without papers, and naturalization offered a legitimate way to travel. "[Subject] is waiting to get his

52. "Migrants Beg Return Trips," *Herald*, March 17, 1952, 8.

53. Jane Douleman and David Lee, *Every Assistance and Protection: A History of the Australian Passport* (Canberra: Federation Press, 2008), 178.

54. Klaus Neumann and Gwenda Tavan, *Does History Matter? Making and Debating Citizenship, Immigration and Refugee Policy in Australia and New Zealand* (Canberra: ANU Press, 2009).

55. Kunz, *Displaced Persons*, 220–1; see also James Jupp, *Arrivals and Departures* (Melbourne: Cheshire-Lansdowne, 1966), 130.

56. Kunz, *Displaced Persons*, 221.

57. Martin, *Refugee Settlers*, 74.

naturalisation papers now," Martin wrote after one interview with a Czech man who had survived Auschwitz, as "he wants those so he will be free to move around."[58] A number of Martin's interviewees conversely thought that naturalization would be a barrier to leaving. "As an indirect explanation of his own lack of interest in getting naturalised," she noted in an interview, "S said that he wanted to travel around—as long as he was not married, he wanted to go and see different places—the islands, anywhere."[59]

Another of the more radical strategies used by DPs to leave Australia was deportation via refusal to work. It wasn't long before disgruntled DPs figured out that deportation was one way of orchestrating a return to Europe, without having to pay the expense of the journey or secure the relevant visas themselves. As Kunz observed, disillusioned DPs who wanted to leave Australia had few alternative options. The rules of their work contract meant they couldn't leave legally during the first two years; the cost of a sea trip was beyond most DPs; and many did not have valid travel documents. "It is not surprising," Kunz wrote, "that under these circumstances there were some DPs who felt sufficiently desperate to employ the only sure means to clear all these hurdles in one move; they provoked their deportation."[60] Juozas K., for example, had constantly refused to do the work he was allocated "and requested his own return to Germany. Threatened to commit a misdemeanor in order to force the Department to take action against him." The tactic worked, and he was returned to Germany as a deportee that year. By this time, many DPs had become aware of deportation as a cheap mode of travel. A report on Australian deportees found, for example, that "a check of the USDP records reveals that thirteen deportees from Australia applied for emigration to the US. Four of these were accepted and have sailed ... The US Authorities are aware that some people, for various reasons, emigrate to either Canada or Australia with a view to subsequent movement to the US."[61] One case reported in the press was that of a Polish couple who camped on the steps of the Department of Immigration in Sydney with all of their belongings. After seventeen months of separation, while the husband toiled in the cane fields of Queensland, they had had enough and wanted an immediate deportation, telling reporters they were "sick of Australia and they would prefer Russia."[62]

Deportations of DPs reached their peak in 1950, when around forty-two DPs were sent home because they were "unsuitable as migrants," over half of these for refusing to work.[63] By 1951, the practice of sending DPs back to their countries of

---

58. Jean Martin papers, Series 7912, Box 4, File Male JIG 336, NLA.
59. "JIC 307," Jean Martin papers, Series 7912, Box 5, 107, 307, NLA.
60. Kunz, *Displaced Persons*, 220.
61. "Deportees—memo to the Chief Migration Officer by Captain Turbayne, 23 January, 1951," A6980, S250240, NAA.
62. Kunz, *Displaced Persons*, 220.
63. Persian, *Beautiful Balts*, 108.

last residence (Germany, Italy, or Austria) had run into serious problems. The Combined Travel Board, which controlled movement in and out of the three zones of occupation in Germany, had started refusing to issue entry visas if the potential deportee had been in Australia for eighteen months or more, or if it was felt that Australia's reasons were too flimsy to warrant deportation. Italy had also begun refusing to accept DPs who had previously spent time in its DP camps, or to grant transit visas through their borders for DPs en route to Austria or Germany. In response to Australia's attempt to deport the epileptic Josef B. back to Italy, for example, the Italians determined that it did "not seem relevant for the Italian Government to assume responsibility for the behaviour of IRO refugees in the countries of resettlement."[64] Italy also refused to take back Josef L., a Hungarian with a "very poor employment record and history of drunkenness," who refused to marry an eighteen-year-old woman who was pregnant by him. In any case, Josef L. absconded while waiting for the deportation to occur, and nothing more was heard of him.[65]

Australia, which had traded on IRO goodwill to accept their returnees on a case-by-case basis, now faced the fact that by mid-1951 there was a "noticeable hardening of attitudes in the IRO" towards resettlement countries trying to return unwanted DPs. The IRO, which up until this time had assisted Australia in arranging the return of their undesirable DPs, had "not only lost interest in assisting Australia in the return of undesirables, but also [begun] to raise objections on their own behalf to such returns," in the words of one Australian senior immigration official on the ground in Germany.[66] This was part of a more general policy developed by the organization, suddenly faced with an unexpected influx of hundreds of returnees in 1948, following the passage of the US Displaced Persons Act in 1948. The IRO made it clear that it could not resettle people twice, except perhaps with transport on a reimbursable basis. "All governmental and intergovernmental calculations on the life-span of the IRO, on immigration, and on finance were based on the assumption that these refugees would not need further material assistance," wrote the IRO's official historian, Louise Holborn.[67]

When the practice ground to a halt, it left a number of deportees stuck in legal limbo. William O, for example, waited in a jail cell while immigration officials tried to navigate his return. "This man is anxious to return to Germany," noted an internal memo to the Immigration Secretary Heyes, "and complains periodically

---

64. Memo from E. L Charles for the secretary entitled "Re-entry of former displaced persons into Italy," September 14, 1951, A6980, S250240, Calwell, NAA.

65. "Josef L.," A6980, S250240, NAA.

66. Memo from E. L. Charles for the secretary, "Deportees," June 29, 1951, A6980, S250240, NAA.

67. Louise Holborn, *The International Refugee Organization, A Specialized Agency of the United Nations, Its History and Work 1946–1952* (London: Oxford University Press, 1956), 379–80.

to gaol authorities here that he is being detained in Australia against his will."[68] Harijs K., a twenty-three-year-old Latvian DP, had arrived in Australia in 1949 and was sent to work in Canberra where he lasted six months, after which "he complained the work was too heavy for him." He was sent to Sydney, where he ended up in the psychiatric institution Broughton Hall. After six months, he was discharged, only to show up again before finally being discharged again on November 7, 1950. His case file stated:

> Many attempts were made to have him accept employment but to no avail. The Commonwealth Employment Service was forced to declare him unemployable. He was returned to Bonegilla on 22nd October, 1951 where he has remained ever since. He has flatly refused to work and his return to Germany has become an obsession with him. He will not believe that this Department is unable to return him to Germany . . . [yet] all efforts to obtain K's readmission to Germany failed.[69]

Immigration briefly toyed with the idea of returning DPs to their countries of origin, bypassing the IRO altogether, but gave up this idea when the Department of External Affairs vetoed the plan, arguing that sending DPs back to countries behind the Iron Curtain would invite international censure and political embarrassment. After the IRO's departure from Europe in 1952, immigration officials tried to insist that the Federal Republic of Germany was bound by an agreement to accept their undesirable DPs, but when they were asked to produce the agreement, they could not, as none existed.[70] To their considerable surprise, it transpired that all that Calwell had been able to secure in 1947 was a verbal agreement with a British official that the return of unsuitable migrants to the British zone could "probably" be arranged with IRO support.[71] In the end, most of those still held in detention were simply released back into the community after it became clear that returning them to Europe was impossible.

Not all deportees were happy with their return. Peter Edwards, an Australian migration officer, recalled "a little club in the waiting room of about half a dozen to a dozen, unsuccessful migrants who'd come back to Germany. They had been disillusioned with Australia but after they'd been back in Germany for a while, they were far more disillusioned with Germany than they were with Australia and

---

68. Memorandum from a Commonwealth migration officer to the Secretary of Immigration, May 25, 1949, A6980, S250240, NAA.

69. "Harijs K.," A6980, S250240, NAA.

70. Memorandum no. 70/53, for the Secretary of Department of External Affairs, March 3, 1953, A6980, S250240, NAA. See also Alfred Kuen, "The Disowned Revolution: The Reconstruction of Australian Immigration, 1945–1952," Ph.D. dissertation, Monash University, 1997, 239.

71. Kuen, "The Disowned Revolution," 237.

wanted to go back very quickly."⁷² Deportation continued to be available as a device to export those regarded as politically suspect from 1953, though no longer through the Immigration Act, but through the Crimes Act.⁷³ Following this brief postwar flurry of deportations of undesirable DPs, the only people the deportation provisions in the Immigration Act were ever used for again were illegal migrants.

Australia is fond of employing statistics of migrant resettlement in the postwar era to represent the moment when the nation began to open up to the world and "Europeanize" its British population. The trope of migration as a one-way street has been a difficult one to dismantle in Australian migration scholarship.⁷⁴ But as Martin found in her early encounters with DPs, many felt that Australia was accidental, temporary, and a stepping stone to elsewhere. Ambivalence characterized their attitude to their new country. "Very few of the Displaced persons conceived of Australia either as a land of golden opportunities, or as a bastion of freedom and democracy."⁷⁵ By contrast, the pull of America or of homelands in Europe was a central theme of DP conversations for decades following their arrival, even if in the end, many decided to remain.

---

72. Martin, *Angels and Arrogant Gods*, 27.

73. Philip Deery, "Dear Mr Brown: Migrants, Security and the Cold War," *History Australia* 2, no. 2 (2005): 40–2.

74. An exception to this general rule can be found in the scholarship on the phenomenon of the "boomerang poms," British migrants who returned to the UK, only to "boomerang" their way back to Australia. See, for example, Thomson, "'I Live on My Memories.'" Another more recent exception is Sheila Fitzpatrick, "Soviet Repatriation Efforts Among 'Displaced Persons' Resettled in Australia, 1950–53," *Australian Journal of Politics and History* 63, no. 1 (2017): 45–61.

75. Craig, "Assimilation of European Immigrants," 375.

Chapter 3

FAR RIGHT SECURITY RISKS? DEPORTATIONS AND EXTRADITION REQUESTS OF DISPLACED PERSONS, 1947–1952

Jayne Persian

In July 1947, the Minister for Immigration, Arthur Calwell, gained an important concession in his negotiations with the International Refugee Organization (IRO) for admission of Central and Eastern European displaced persons (DPs) to Australia. It was agreed that "no difficulties would be raised to the return to Germany of migrants who had proved unsuitable in Australia." Unfortunately for Calwell, and his successor, Harold Holt, this agreement was informal and not committed to writing, and both the IRO and Germany placed obstacles in the way with regard to its practice. This chapter will examine the deportation policies and extradition requests surrounding displaced persons who were accused of being war criminals, focusing particularly on the rhetoric surrounding Australian deportation policy and the actual practice of deportations for those deemed a security risk or, indeed, whose extradition was requested by a foreign government.

Displaced Persons

The definition of "displaced persons" that emerged amongst the Allied military authorities before World War II ended in Europe predominantly related to the non-German people they supposed would be found in Germany and Austria. A working definition, formulated by the Supreme Headquarters, Allied Expeditionary Force (SHAEF), commanded by the United States general, Dwight D. Eisenhower, included concentration camp inmates, forced agricultural and factory workers, and civilian evacuees fleeing west from the oncoming Soviet Army. The category also included "former members of forces under German command," that is, non-German soldiers in military units withdrawing westwards.[1] It has been estimated

---

1. SHAEF Planning Directive: Refugees and Displaced Persons (DPs), June 3, 1944, Prisoners of War/Displaced Persons Division: Registered Files (PWDP and other Series), Control Office for Germany and Austria and Foreign Office, Foreign Office (FO) 1052/10, Post-War Europe Series I: Refugees, Exiles and Resettlement, 1945–1950, Gale Digital Collections.

that in May 1945 up to 10 percent of the 7.8 million troops wearing German uniforms were not German.[2] DPs thus included in their ranks those who had made up the machinery of genocide in Eastern Europe, including participation in SS units, regular army units incorporated into German armies, independent armies, and paramilitary and irregular organizations.[3] Others were far-right ideologues, either members of collaborationist political parties and/or governments, and propagandists.

After SHAEF ceased functioning in July 1945, all of these displaced persons came under the care of American, British, and French military authorities in the western zones, and Soviet military authorities in the east. The United Nations resolved that nothing should be done to "interfere in any way with the surrender and punishment of war criminals, quislings and traitors."[4] However, the detection of war criminals and their arrest and surrender was the sole responsibility of the relevant governments and occupation authorities. Unlike the swift punitive actions carried out in the east, the British military authorities, for example, soon championed Baltic ex-combatants so that they were given DP status en masse.[5] Others were used in intelligence work (against the Soviets) by both the Americans and British and were then given security clearance for DP status. Moreover, in the western zones, Germans and Austrians were the main judicial priority; there were never very good lists of collaborators in the east.[6]

The United Nations Relief and Rehabilitation Administration (UNRRA) originally set out to assist displaced persons to repatriate. When confronted with a "last million" who refused to return home,[7] the International Refugee Organization was established to facilitate resettlement to any country that would take them. The official historian of the IRO, Louise Holborn, noted that "as the Cold War developed there was a growing appreciation of the fact that many persons might technically have collaborated with the Germans and yet were in refugee status," that is, they were refugees from the Soviet bloc because they had a valid political objection to repatriation, and so were deserving of international assistance.[8] This did not negate the principle that war criminals were not supposed to receive DP status, and thus the opportunity to resettle. However, the IRO did not have a security apparatus of

---

2. David Cesarani, *Justice Delayed: How Britain Became a Refuge for Nazi War Criminals* (London: Phoenix Press, 2001/1992), 35.

3. George Ginsburgs, "The Soviet Union and the Problem of Refugees and Displaced Persons, 1917–1956," *American Journal of International Law* 51, no. 2 (1957): 356.

4. Louise W. Holborn, *The International Refugee Organization: A Specialized Agency of the United Nations: Its History and Work, 1946–1952* (London, New York, and Toronto: Oxford University Press, 1956), 207.

5. Cesarani, *Justice Delayed*, 50.

6. Cesarani, *Justice Delayed*, 37, 90, 164.

7. George Fisher, "The New Soviet Emigration," *Russian Review* 8, no. 1 (1949): 8.

8. Holborn, *The International Refugee Organization*, 192.

its own and was quite explicitly not responsible for actively hunting war criminals.[9] Dependent as it was upon "the authorities of the countries [they operated in], on official lists and on other available sources,"[10] the view of the IRO was that "security [was] necessarily the primary concern of the receiving country."[11]

Rather than focusing on security, the Australian government was more concerned with solving its population and workforce deficit, and so with the race, age, and physical health of any potential migrants. Once the inaugural Minister for Immigration, Arthur Calwell (1945–9), realized that displaced persons were cheap, and that he could stipulate almost any selection criteria—this would be the country's first mass intake of non-British migrants—he signed an agreement with the International Refugee Organization on July 21, 1947. This intake eventually numbered 170,700, made up of Poles, "Balts" (Estonians, Latvians, and Lithuanians), Yugoslavs, Ukrainians, Hungarians, Czechoslovaks, and Russians.[12]

For the Australians, security checking involved two steps after the initial IRO screening for eligibility for displaced person status: an interview conducted by Australian Selection officers, and a final check by the Combined Travel Board of the Allied High Commission before issue of a travel permit.[13] The Australian Selection Mission in Naples boasted of their fast-processing capability, admitting that "we are not so elaborate as [the US mission]. Instead of a lengthy security check, a[n] ... intelligence blacklist is used. If the refugee's name is not on the list, he is assumed to be acceptable."[14] This intelligence blacklist was the one used by the British and contained around 2,000 names; the British policy was that "the matter of checking of DPs does not merit a high priority." In contrast, officers from the United States checked potential migrants "against the complete Intelligence Division records." Captain H. W. Miller, one of the two security officers appointed by the Australian authorities in mid-1949, described Australia's simplified process

---

9. Holborn, *The International Refugee Organization*, 207.

10. Draft letter to Chiefs of Missions whose governments accept refugees as immigrants, February 1, 1949, Bureau de Michaël Macking, chef de la Section historique, Organisation internationale pour les réfugiés, AJ/43/457 (hereafter, IRO), Archives Nationales (France) (hereafter, France).

11. Interoffice Memorandum from F. C. Blanchard to M. L. Hacking, Chief, Mandate Branch, March 14, 1949, IRO, France.

12. For a comprehensive review of this scheme, see Jayne Persian, *Beautiful Balts: From Displaced Persons to New Australians* (Sydney: NewSouth Publishing, 2017).

13. Andrew Menzies, "Review of Material Relating to the Entry of Suspected War Criminals into Australia," Parliamentary Paper No. 90/1987, The Parliament of the Commonwealth of Australia, 39.

14. Fred M. Hechinger, "Australia puts United States Displaced Persons Mission to Shame," *Washington Post*, August 10, 1949; Article in Washington Post—10 August 1949—Australia puts United States Displaced Persons Mission to Shame, 1949–1950, Department of Immigration, Central Office, A434, 1949/3/8754, NAA.

as "a selfish and, from a British Commonwealth viewpoint, very short-sighted security appreciation."[15]

Before 1950, Australian selection officers did not even have access to the International Refugee Organization's Eligibility Manual, which provided histories and discussions around the various problematic nationality backgrounds. A perturbed selection officer, H. J. Grant, was forced to specifically request access to this document in order to "strengthen security."[16] With regard to displaced persons from Yugoslavia, for example, who could have been Croatian, Serbian, or Slovenian perpetrators and/or fascist ideologues, Arthur Calwell made it clear that "we had only to distinguish between Communists and non-Communists."[17] In practice, it seems to have been only Jewish DPs who were suspected of Communist sympathies.[18] Further, there was no "systematic exchange of information between Australian migration offices in Europe."[19]

Two Australian security officers—Captain H. W. Miller and Captain K. G. Turbayne—were eventually added to this mix in a consultative capacity, one in the British zone and one in the American zone.[20] They carried out checks with the

---

15. "Routine Checking of Lists of Names of DPs for Immigration to Australia," Captain H. W. Miller to Chief Migration Officer, October 13, 1949 [Australian Military Mission Berlin], Migration—Security—General, 1949–1953, Australian Military Mission to Allied Control Council for Germany and Austria/Allied High Commission/Federal Republic of Germany, A9306, 355/1 (hereafter [Australian Military Mission Berlin], Migration—Security—General), National Archives of Australia (hereafter, NAA).

16. "IRO Eligibility Manuals," from Taylor, acting Chief Migration Officer to Head, Australian Military Mission, November 4, 1949 [Australian Military Mission Berlin], Migration—Security—General, NAA.

17. Ministers visit to Europe—Report on, 1947, Department of Immigration, Central Office, A438, 1949/7/1067 (hereafter, Ministers visit to Europe—Report on), NAA.

18. See [Australian Military Mission Berlin] Security Officers' Reports, 1949–1952, Australian Military Mission to Allied Control Council for Germany and Austria/Allied High Commission/Federal Republic of Germany, West Berlin, A9306, 355/3 (hereafter [Australian Military Mission Berlin], Security Officers' Reports), NAA; Ruth Balint, "A Jewish Refugee Racket," in Ruth Balint and Julie Kalman, *Smuggled: An Illegal History of Journeys to Australia* (Sydney: NewSouth Publishing, 2021), 33.

19. Letter from G. V. Greenhalgh to Acting Head, Australian Military Mission, May 27, 1950, [Australian Military Mission Berlin] Migration—Security—General, NAA.

20. There was no security officer in Italy until late June 1951. "Selection Teams" Administrative Instruction No. 29—Confidential: Security Checks," Australian Military Mission, Berlin—Proposed Change in Status and Consequent Reorganisation for Immigration Purposes, 1949–1950, Department of Immigration, Central Office, A438, 1949/7/706; Menzies, "Review of Material Relating to the Entry of Suspected War Criminals into Australia," 80; see also [Australian Military Mission Berlin] Migration—Security—General, NAA.

principal agencies[21] as well as Canadian and American rejection lists. If deemed necessary, checks were also made with secondary agencies[22] as well as ground and neighborhood checks "where possible" and individual "interrogations."[23] This whole process could take up to six months.[24] As well as time limitations, they were hampered by the complexity of the task over large areas—they relied mostly on contacts within the Allied militaries and other resettlement missions, especially the Canadians; they were also hindered by "incessant trouble over [access to reliable] cars."[25] In any case, they admitted that "in order to maintain [the] flow [of displaced persons to Australia], it [would] be impracticable to impose a tight individual security interrogation on each applicant."[26] Their work ended up including investigating a fair proportion of cases who had already traveled to Australia;[27] in some instances they recommended "surveillance and, if necessary, deport[ation]."[28]

The Threat of Deportation

In July 1947, Arthur Calwell, as well as mandating that the Australian government could select displaced persons "individually" after interview and *not* on a group basis, gained another important concession in his negotiations with the International Refugee Organization regarding the recruitment and admission of

---

21. "Berlin Document Centre, Intelligence Division and Counter Intelligence Corps."

22. "Int. Org and CIC Austria, German police records, French and Belgian Surete, Swiss Police, British and US Army Int., Field Security Section, Allied Regional Int. Offices, and local contacts."

23. Letter from K. G. Turbayne to Chief Migration Officer, July 12, 1949, [Australian Military Mission Berlin] Migration—Security—General, NAA.

24. Letter from K. G. Turbayne to Chief Migration Officer, July 12, 1949, [Australian Military Mission Berlin] Migration—Security—General, NAA.

25. Notes for Brigadier F. G. Galleghan from M. R. Booker, undated, Sir Frederick Gallagher, Galleghan Papers, 1917–1972, MLMSS 2474, State Library of New South Wales (hereafter, SLNSW); Letter from K. G. Turbayne to F. G. Galleghan, June 17, 1949, [Australian Military Mission Berlin] Security Officers' Reports, NAA.

26. "Appreciation of the situation," K. G. Turbayne and H. W. Miller, May 24, 1949, [Australian Military Mission Berlin] Migration—Security—General, NAA. From the sparse available evidence, it seems that Turbayne and Miller generally rejected on security grounds 5–10% of applicants they reviewed. See [Australian Military Mission Berlin] Migration—Security—General, NAA; Menzies, "Review of Material Relating to the Entry of Suspected War Criminals into Australia," 19.

27. Letter from G. V. Greenhalgh to Acting Head, Australian Military Mission, May 27, 1950, [Australian Military Mission Berlin] Migration—Security—General, NAA.

28. Letter from Captain H. W. Miller to Chief Migration Officer, March 20, 1950, [Australian Military Mission Berlin] Security Officers' Reports, NAA.

displaced persons to Australia. In preliminary discussions, Brigadier R. N. Thicknesse of the British Control Commission assured Calwell that it "was unlikely that Australia would get people who desire to return to Europe—[they] will have definitely made up their minds to start life afresh in a new country and they will not wish to return." However, Calwell argued that "it was not unlikely that we would get some nasty people who would prove unsatisfactory, and if we had this weapon that they would be returned, it would help considerably."[29] It was agreed that "no difficulties would be raised to the return to [the British zone of] Germany of migrants who had proved unsuitable in Australia," although they could only be returned within an eighteen-month period.[30] Unfortunately for Calwell, and his successor, Harold Holt (1949–56), this agreement had not been committed to writing and the IRO as well as the countries of departure—Germany, Austria, and Italy—were placing obstacles in the way with regard to its operation.[31] By March 1952, Department of Immigration officials complained that "this whole question is at the moment in a very confused state." They were "urgently trying to find trace of the agreement" and "could only conclude that such an agreement never existed."[32]

To further strengthen his hand with regard to security, Calwell introduced the Aliens Deportation Act, which became law in January 1949. This gave the government unprecedented powers of deportation, no matter how long the migrant had been resident in Australia, on the grounds of poor conduct or character.[33] Of course the problem with deporting displaced persons was that they were by definition displaced, stateless, or at least, unrepatriable.[34] The IRO was winding up operations in Western Europe, and the countries of departure certainly didn't want them.[35] It would be

---

29. Ministers visit to Europe—Report on, NAA.

30. Deportations from Australia—Deportations of Displaced Persons, 1951–1973, Department of External Affairs [II], Central Office, A1838, 1477/2/45, Part 1 (hereafter, Deportations from Australia—Deportations of Displaced Persons), NAA; Ministers visit to Europe—Report on, NAA.

31. See Deportation of Displaced Persons—Policy, NAA.

32. Deportation of Displaced Persons—Policy, 1949–1955, Department of Immigration, Central Office, A6980, S250240 (hereafter, Deportation of Displaced Persons—Policy), NAA.

33. Glenn Nicholls notes that this "strengthening of the Commonwealth's deportation power in fact went further than his successors needed." It was never used by Harold Holt and was in fact replaced in 1958 by the Migration Act. Glenn Nicholls, "Gone with hardly a trace: deportees in immigration policy," in Klaus Neumann and Gwenda Tavan (eds.), *Does History Matter: Making and Debating Citizenship, Immigration and Refugee Policy in Australia and New Zealand*, Australian and New Zealand School of Government (Canberra: ANU Press, 2009), 13.

34. See Jayne Persian, "Displaced Persons and the Politics of International Categorisation(s)," *Australian Journal of Politics and History* 58, no. 4 (2012): 481–96.

35. See Deportation of Displaced Persons—Policy, Department of Immigration, Central Office, A6980, S250240, NAA.

politically and morally unconscionable for Australia to return them to their home countries in the Eastern Bloc—migrants argued that deportations to Yugoslavia, for example, would be "a death sentence."[36] However, deportations did apparently happen in a "very few cases where an Iron Curtain country agreed to accept" deportees; one man committed suicide en route.[37] While it was recommended that these types of deportations only be for "capital/security offences," one prepared list of deportees "for 'Iron Curtain' Countries," circa July 1951, included thirteen to be deported for employment reasons and four for criminality.[38]

There are unfortunately no reliable numbers for displaced persons who were deported from Australia in this period. In an answer to a parliamentary question in June 1950, Holt said that forty of the 128,000 DPs who had arrived had been deported.[39] More broadly, between 1950 and 1961, 2,951 migrants from all backgrounds, including British, were deported—1,436 of these were deserting seamen; 914 were deported for criminal activities; 297 on the grounds of physical and mental illness; and 303 on "other grounds." There is no record of the individual countries to which these migrants were returned.[40] It does seem that most deportations of DPs for "character," health, or security reasons occurred before 1954, when Australia ratified the Convention Relating to the Status of Refugees (1951), which prevented Australia from deporting refugees unless they threatened national security or public order.[41]

Of the more than forty displaced persons who were deported, contemporary publicity highlighted a "refusal to work" within their two-year indentured labor contracts.[42] So, deportation was used as a threat to keep the DPs in line: they would accept "approved work" or, as threatened by Calwell, "they, too, will be deported as soon as that can be arranged," and deportations were to be publicized "through migrant publications as an example."[43] However, the publicity given to these deportations misfired when an increasing number of dissatisfied DPs began

---

36. "Deportation 'Is Death Sentence'," *The Advertiser* (Adelaide), November 27, 1953.

37. See Deportations from Australia—Deportations of Displaced Persons, NAA; Glenn Nicholls, *Deported! A History of Forced Departures from Australia* (Sydney: University of New South Wales Press, 2007), 100; Note, October 24, 1951, Deportation of Displaced Persons—Policy, NAA.

38. Deportation of Displaced Persons—Policy, NAA.

39. "Only 40 DPs Deported," *Daily Telegraph* (Sydney), June 15, 1950.

40. Ann-Mari Jordens, *Alien to Citizen: Settling Migrants in Australia, 1945-75* (St. Leonards, NSW: Allen & Unwin, 1997), 196.

41. Klaus Neumann, *Refuge Australia: Australia's Humanitarian Record* (Sydney: UNSW Press, 2004), 101.

42. "Thousand Migrants have Broken Work Contracts," *Sydney Morning Herald*, March 7, 1951.

43. Telegram from Dempsey, Canberra, to Chief Migration Officer, Melbourne, July 4, 1950, Deportation of Displaced Persons—Policy, NAA.

demanding deportation to escape from their contract and gain an inexpensive return trip to Europe. Yugoslav DP Enoch M. informed the Department of Immigration that "nothing would suit him better than to be returned to Europe."[44] Czech DP Rudolf H. not only refused to work and stated his wish to be sent back to Europe, but also attempted to influence other DPs into not submitting to the labor contract.[45]

From the beginning of 1949, then, employment officers were prohibited from threatening displaced persons with deportations. So, when a DP working in Tasmania pleaded to be taken "back to Germany," he was told by officials that this was impossible as it was too expensive. Similarly, Russian DP Kuzma I. was rebuffed when he requested deportation. Kuzma's wife had been committed to a mental health facility and he himself had walked out on his contracted employment and had been diagnosed as "being of low mentality as well as probably psychotic." The department replied that "it is regretted that there are no funds available to this Department which could be used to assist you, but there is no objection to you and your family leaving Australia at any time by your own arrangement and at your own expense."[46]

However, courts continued to call for migrant deportations, including of one Polish woman, a resident of Benalla migrant camp, who was threatened with deportation for alleged prostitution as late as 1953.[47] Other reasons for initiating deportation in this period included serious physical ailments and/or mental instability, a history of homosexuality, suicide attempt, and serious criminal activity, ranging from habitual theft, knife crimes, indecent exposure, and domestic violence to rape and murder.[48]

Although apparently theoretically agreeing to the return of unsuitable migrants, in practice the International Refugee Organization was nonplussed by requests to return displaced persons, and particularly those who were to be returned on the grounds of political unsuitability. In 1949 the Chief of the Mandate Branch drafted a letter to all resettlement countries assuring them that "we endeavour ... to see that we do not put up war criminals for selection" and that "this matter of [undesirables, i.e. Communists] should not be exaggerated; it does not often

---

44. For the main text I am using first names and the first letter of surnames for individual displaced persons whose names are not already a matter of public record. Displaced Persons—Notifications of Deportations, 1949-1951, Department of Labour and National Service, Central Office, MP1722/1, 49/23/13355 (hereafter, Displaced Persons—Notifications of Deportations), NAA.

45. Letter from T. H. E. Heyes, Secretary, Department of Immigration, to General C. M. E. Lloyd, Chief of the UNIRO in Australia and New Zealand, April 24, 1950, "Deportations," Egon Kunz papers, 1970–1980, 497–130, Australian National University Archives.

46. Persian, *Beautiful Balts*, 108–10.

47. "Deportation Warning to Migrant," *Benalla Ensign*, June 4, 1953.

48. See Deportation of Displaced Persons—Policy, NAA; Displaced Persons—Notifications of Deportations, NAA.

arise."⁴⁹ In a letter to IRO Headquarters, a frustrated Care and Eligibility Division admitted that "we have been completely unsuccessful in our efforts to secure from the Resettlement Missions the reasons why individuals or families are turned down for security reasons."⁵⁰ In other words, if the United States, for example, rejected a potential migrant for security reasons, it did not share those reasons with either the IRO or with other resettlement missions.

In April 1949 the International Refugee Organization warned the Australian government that because of the "administrative difficulties occasioned by deportation action . . . with little or no notice," displaced persons would have to be held "in gaol during the course of negotiations with the military government of the occupying power concerned." The cable emphasized "gaol, repeat gaol."⁵¹ A few months later, they complained that "too little information on the case is usually provided by the Authorities in Australia." The Australian reasons for deportation were, though, broadly "in the first place health; in the second place security; and in the third place bad behaviour."⁵² This is noteworthy because by this reckoning, more of the forty-plus deportations must have been on security grounds than the Australian government was publicly admitting.

By mid-1951, the International Refugee Organization was categorically refusing to facilitate the repatriation of deported displaced persons; some deportations had to be attempted twice.⁵³ In one case, a frustrated Combined Travel Board instead recommended "strong counselling" for Lithuanian DP Pranas A., an unaccompanied youth who had absconded from his work contract, and refused to facilitate his deportation.⁵⁴ Even in 1954, though, those who had committed serious crimes in Australia were being threatened by government officials that "when relations between the countries improve [and here they are referencing the Soviet Bloc], [the recalcitrant DP] will be deported."⁵⁵

In 1951, Harold Holt stated that there had only been one displaced person sent back to Europe "for political reasons; he was a communist organiser"—that was

49. Resettlement in Australia 1947–50, AJ43/401, IRO.
50. Resettlement in Australia 1947–50, AJ43/401, IRO.
51. Resettlement in Australia 1947–50, AJ43/401, IRO.
52. Letter from M. L. Hacking to Dr V. Gross, Protection (Coordination and Liaison Division), July 14, 1949, IRO, France.
53. Persian, *Beautiful Balts*, 109–10; Resettlement in Australia 1947–50, AJ43/401, IRO.
54. "Re-entry of Displaced Persons into Germany—Authorities," Memorandum from T. H. E. Heyes, Secretary, Department of Immigration, to Secretary, Department of External Affairs, July 1951, Deportation of Displaced Persons—Policy, NAA; and Deportation of Displaced Persons—Policy, NAA.
55. "Nationals of Iron Curtain Countries convicted of Serious Crimes—Question of Deportation," Circular, T. H. E. Heyes, Secretary, Department of Immigration, to the Commonwealth Migration Officers, All States and Darwin, undated, c. 1954, Deportation of Displaced Persons—Policy, NAA.

probably former Soviet officer and suspected Communist Gregor L.[56] We now know that Soviet agents and Communist sympathizers were present amongst the DPs in Australia,[57] and that the government knew this and were prepared to subject such migrants to "surveillance and, if necessary, deport[ation]."[58]

We do not have a definitive list of those who were actually deported or even those whom the government attempted to deport—some of these men (and they are mostly men) were listed as "whereabouts unknown" or "absconded"; at least one died in an all-too-common motor accident in 1951.[59] In his 1986 governmental review, Andrew Menzies reported that there were "at least four cases where DPs were removed from Australia on security grounds after their arrival"; he acknowledged that there "may have been additional instances."[60] We do know from the deportation files that as well as Gregor L., who was deported for "security reasons," a Czech, Bohumil H., was suspected of "communist sympathies," and a Hungarian, József K., was "a known security risk," although his politics were not specified. A family—husband, wife, and two children—were also subject to deportation orders on "security grounds."[61]

There is evidence that the question of the deportation of Estonian Verner P.— who arrived in Australia on a landing permit rather than through the IRO scheme—was considered, causing "some confusion within the department."[62] In late 1949 Captain K. G. Turbayne, one of the security officers in Europe, had received information from "a usually reliable source" that Verner had commanded a Russian submarine during the Soviet occupation and was an alleged NKVD

---

56. "False Reports of Nazis Here," *Sunday Telegraph*, April 1, 1951; Sheila Fitzpatrick, *White Russians, Red Peril: A Cold War History of Migration to Australia* (Carlton, Victoria: Black Inc., 2021), 233; Ruth Balint, *Destination Elsewhere: Displaced Persons and their Quest to Leave Postwar Europe* (Ithaca, NY: Cornell University Press, 2021), 122–6.

57. See Fitzpatrick, *White Russians, Red Peril*.

58. In 1953 the Cabinet perused a report that concluded that even membership of the Communist Party "should not be regarded as sufficient to justify recourse to the deportation provisions of the Immigration Act." "Istvan and Marta Szegfy, sailed for Australia on Goya 23/11/49," letter from Captain H. W. Miller to Chief Medical Officer, March 20, 1950, [Australian Military Mission Berlin] Security Officers' Reports, NAA.

59. See Displaced Persons—Notifications of Deportations, NAA; Deportation of Displaced Persons—Policy, NAA; "Migrant Dies After Smash," *West Australian*, November 15, 1951.

60. Menzies, "Review of Material Relating to the Entry of Suspected War Criminals into Australia," 85.

61. See Deportation of Displaced Persons—Policy, NAA.

62. Memorandum from Liaison Officer, Department of Immigration, to Headquarters Section Sydney and Officer in Charge Qld, April 13, 1951, Puurand, Hans Verner— Nationality: Estonian—arrived Melbourne on Derna November 5, 1948, 1948–1956, Department of Immigration, Queensland Branch, BP25/1, PUURAND H V ESTONIAN (hereafter, Puurand), NAA.

agent, as well as subsequently acting as Chief of Intelligence Section of the German Baltic Fleet under German occupation.[63] Australian authorities were pragmatic in noting the "opportunists and turncoats" among the Balts during the occupation years, making sure to tell Verner, who had offered his intelligence services, that "he is just an ordinary alien to whom asylum in Australia has been granted as a privilege; and that this privilege will cease if he engaged in any of his old political antics or tries to act as anybody's agent."[64] He was, in any event, cleared for naturalization in 1955.[65]

There were later rumors that Ferenc N., a Hungarian who had been a parliamentarian under the Szálasi regime, had been deported.[66] Although his brother Károly, known as "Bombing-N." because he was implicated in the bombing of a synagogue in Budapest in 1939, definitely was not deported.[67] It is more likely that Ferenz, as reported by Mr. C. C. Aronsfeld at the Wiener Holocaust Library in London, simply voluntarily returned to Europe, in 1956.[68]

One Latvian displaced person, Jānis Balodis,[69] approached officials at Bonegilla in 1951 to confess that his real name was Erich K. and that he was an Austrian who had served in the German Air Force and ground units. This admission occurred because K. wanted to be able to apply for a landing permit for his wife, in her name (Mrs. K.). Holt directed that he be deported because of "gross misrepresentation by an Austrian national who has entered Australia illegally," in order to set "an example to others who may make similar attempts."[70] Similarly, Latvian DP Georg A. was

63. Letter from K. G. Turbayne, Australian Military Mission (Migration Office), to Senior Security Officer, Australian Embassy, The Hague, January 8, 1952, Puurand, NAA.

64. Note, redacted, July 1952, Puurand, NAA.

65. Memorandum from Regional Director, Qld to Headquarters, ASIO, June 8, 1955, Puurand, NAA.

66. "List of Suspected Leaders of Hungarian Nazis in Australia," undated [c. 1961], Australia, 1940–1962, 1658/10/5, The Wiener Holocaust Library, United Kingdom (hereafter, Wiener Library).

67. Evan Smith and Jayne Persian, "European and Australian Fascisms: The case of Ferenc Molnár and National Socialism in Cold War Australia," in Evan Smith, Jayne Persian, and Vashti Jane Fox (eds.), *Histories of Fascism and Anti-Fascism in Australia and New Zealand* (Routledge Studies in Fascism and the Far Right, 2022), 143.

68. Letter from C. C. Aronsfeld, Wiener Library, to Monty Schaffer, Victorian Jewish Board of Deputies, March 11, 1960, Correspondence with Victorian Jewish Board of Deputies, 1951–1963, 3000/9/1/1463, Wiener Library.

69. Apparently, "Jānis Balodis" was frequently used by displaced persons in the same way as "Bill Smith" in English-speaking countries. "Canberra Court: Behaviour in Bus," *Canberra Times*, August 16, 1950.

70. "Erich Koller (alias Janis Balodis)," Letter from T. H. E. Heyes, Secretary, Department of Immigration, to W. K. Leadbeatter, Acting Chief of the UNIRO in Australia and New Zealand, June 1951, Displaced Persons—Notifications of Deportations, NAA.

accused of "gross misrepresentation" after admitting that he was actually Hans D., an Austrian. He had served in the German Army and had bought papers from a Latvian student, substituting his photograph on the documents "at the last minute."[71] Of Herman W., a German veteran who also entered as a Latvian and was discovered upon arrival "that he could not speak Latvian," it was merely noted that he had "entered illegally and there is little that can be said in his favour."[72] Whether he was deported is unclear. These are notable examples because we know that many DPs entered Australia under false names and *were not* deported—in fact, they were able to become naturalized—even after they applied to change their names, admitting misrepresentation on their migration documents.[73]

Interestingly, there is firm evidence for two deportations of Germans who were not part of the International Refugee Organization scheme but who both arrived in Australia on the same ship on landing permits organized by the Executive Council of Australian Jewry (ECAJ). One, Egon Lerch, was a German who had served in the German Navy and traveled to Australia with his Jewish wife. He was denounced on board as having been a commandant of a concentration camp. The second, Herbert Bandmann, was the brother of a German woman married to a Jewish man in Australia, who had sponsored his ECAJ landing permit. Bandmann had also served with the German Army and was deported on the basis of misrepresentation because, as Calwell argued publicly, "no one who fought against the Allied cause was permitted to be here."[74] Privately, Calwell lamented that "some of the Jewish people and their Organisations had not played the game" and "had let him down."[75] These cases had more to do with the embarrassing publicity potential of drawing attention to the controversial postwar Jewish migration scheme, in an atmosphere of virulent anti-Semitism, than with migrants who had fought against

71. Letter from T. H. E. Heyes, Secretary, Department of Immigration, to W. K. Leadbeatter, Acting Chief of the UNIRO in Australia and New Zealand, July 13, 1951, Displaced Persons—Notifications of Deportations, NAA.

72. Letter from T. H. E. Heyes, Secretary, Department of Immigration, to W. K. Leadbeatter, Acting Chief of the UNIRO in Australia and New Zealand, July 5, 1951, Displaced Persons—Notifications of Deportations, NAA.

73. See, for an example of how common this practice was, PAVLOV, Nikolai [Russian born 1923]; wife Anna—born 1927 [nee Kiseleva]; children George [born 1952], Vladimir [born 1956] and Alexe [born 1957], 1952-1974, Department of Immigration, Queensland Branch, J25, 1968/18023, NAA; PAVLOV, Nikolaj [aka ALFERTSCHIK, Nicolai], 1951-1959, Department of Immigration, Victorian Branch, MT874/1, V1956/32393, NAA. These are two different Nikolai Pavlovs who are requesting changes of name and/or particulars.

74. "They Fell In Love In A Setting of Nazi Hate," *The Herald* (Melbourne), May 22, 1947; see BANDMANN Herbert Reinhold—Nationality: German—Arrived Sydney per Johan de Witt March 16, 1947; Departed Commonwealth on April 07, 1948, 1939-1972, Department of Immigration, Victoria Branch, B78, GERMAN/BANDMANN HERBERT REINHOLD, NAA.

75. Ministers Visit to Europe—Report on, NAA.

the Allies. Indeed, when it became clear that many Baltic displaced persons had fought with the German Army, the Australian public was assured that this "was on the Russian front and not against the British or Americans."[76]

In 1949, the Sydney Council to Combat Fascism and Anti-Semitism began to conduct investigations and collect statutory declarations implicating, from personal knowledge, displaced persons who were either recognized as former Nazis or members of pro-Nazi organizations in Eastern Europe, or who had voiced Nazi sentiments while in Australia. This evidence was sent directly to the Minister for Immigration—Calwell, and then Holt.[77] At the same time, a Jewish woman in Sydney with contacts in Hungary supplied the official newspaper of the Communist Party of Australia, *Tribune*, with various accusations to publicize.[78]

One Jewish displaced person said that in the migrant camps in Australia "there is so much anti-Semitism and Nazi talk that at times it seems like being under Hitler again." Another reported, "I went through the terrible war, and I find myself again, in a camp with fascists. They still seek our extermination. Their animal instincts follow me like black clouds." He characterized the non-Jewish DPs as "Jew-haters with a black past" and asked plaintively, "How am I better than my father and brother and the whole family who were murdered through Hitler, and who knows through which of my present camp inmates they were killed."[79]

Calwell dismissed allegations of this type as a "farrago of nonsense." Publicly, he warned that if non-Jewish displaced persons were stopped from migrating under the DP scheme due to this negative publicity, then so too would Jews be stopped from migrating to Australia.[80] His successor, Harold Holt, said in 1950 that "several migrants had been deported following security reports. But in almost every case where allegations of active Nazism had been made, they had been proved false."[81] In private meetings with members of the Executive Council of Australian Jewry, though, he was reported to have given the impression that a number of deportations had resulted from their complaints.[82]

---

76. "Came From Behind The Iron Curtain," *Sunday Times* (Perth), March 29, 1949.

77. See Mark Aarons—General Australian War Crimes, Box 9, SLNSW.

78. "Alleged Ex-Nazis and Fascists at Displaced Persons Camps in NSW and Vic," Memorandum to Director, Sydney, May 14, 1950, Anti-Communist Activities in Australia, Series 1: Mark Aarons—General Australian War Crimes, MLMSS1062/Box 1 (hereafter, Mark Aarons—General Australian War Crimes, Box 1), SLNSW.

79. Statement of Michael Einleger, Hostel Walanove, Rooty Hill, undated, Mark Aarons—General Australian War Crimes, Box 9, SLNSW.

80. Philip Mendes, "Jews, Nazis and Communists Down Under: The Jewish Council's Controversial Campaign Against German Immigration," *Australian Historical Studies* 33, no. 119 (2002): 78–9; see also Letter from T. H. E. Heyes, Secretary, Department of Immigration, to Sir John Storey, Melbourne, November 6, 1950, Mark Aarons—General Australian War Crimes, Box 1, SLNSW, and various items of correspondence in Mark Aarons—General Australian War Crimes, Box 9, SLNSW.

81. "Few Nazis Get In As Immigrants," *The Sun*, November 23, 1950.

82. "Nazis Here As Migrants, Say Jews," *The Herald* (Melbourne), November 22, 1950.

In March 1951, the Executive Council of Australian Jewry sent a file containing forty names and substantiating evidence to Holt; these had been provided by famed Nazi-hunter Simon Wiesenthal. Rabbi Louis Rubin-Zacks of Perth met with his local member Paul Hasluck arguing that while "it was virtually impossible to provide 'legal evidence' on these matters, acceptable to a court of law, 'prima facie' evidence was overwhelming."[83] At a public meeting at Perth Town Hall to protest the proposed mass German migration of 1952, the Rabbi noted, correctly,[84] that "it is common knowledge that for the price of the equivalent of a few pounds, any person in Europe today may purchase forged documents that will pass the closest scrutiny of any 'screening' procedures."[85]

In 1951, Holt replied to Ben Green, the President of ECAJ, that his accusations were "of a sketchy and hearsay nature." Dr Andrew Laszlo, for example, who had been convicted in Hungary for his collaborationist activities but released on appeal, had been investigated by the Australian authorities and found to be a "sincere Christian worker"; there was "no subversive sentiment" discernible in the activities of the Hungarian Officers' Club in Sydney and, importantly, "no evidence of un- or anti-Australian attitude[s]."[86] This became the key test, the only thing that the Australian Security Intelligence Organisation (ASIO) was interested in: were those accused of war crimes during the war likely to be a *current* threat to Australia? The answer was, almost always, "no," and so we see almost all of those investigated by ASIO passed for naturalization with the comment that they posed no security threat to Australia. The Director-General of ASIO, Sir Charles Spry, also admitted that "any action to repatriate migrants due to an adverse background in Europe or to their activities here after arrival is confined to extremely bad cases."[87] He advised his Senior Security Officer in The Hague in 1952 that once "an alien has evaded the security screen," "a strong case is essential before deportation proceedings may be approved."[88]

In his letter to the Executive Council of Australian Jewry, Holt admitted that one of the accused, Stanisław Rzedzieki, was being deported but that this was "not because there is proof of the loose statement said to have been made by him that he was an SS man, but because of his general unsuitability and the doubt which

---

83. "Interview with Mr. Paul Hasluck, MHR," Letter from L. Rubin-Zacks, Perth Hebrew Congregation, to Ben Green, President, Executive Council of Australian Jewry, March 28, 1951, Mark Aarons—General Australian War Crimes, Box 9, SLNSW.

84. Persian, *Beautiful Balts*, 23–5.

85. "Mass German Migration: Record Public Meeting Registers Protest," *Westralian Judean* (Perth), February 1, 1951.

86. Letter from Harold Holt, Minister for Immigration, to Ben Green, President, Executive Council of Jewry, March 28, 1951, Mark Aarons—General Australian War Crimes, Box 9, SLNSW.

87. Menzies, "Review of Material Relating to the Entry of Suspected War Criminals into Australia," 52.

88. Menzies, "Review of Material Relating to the Entry of Suspected War Criminals into Australia," 55.

exists regarding his successful assimilation into the Australian community."[89] Rzedzieki, a Pole, had been convicted of assault five times within a month; the Police Prosecutor told the Footscray Court that he was "a menace to the community" and that "he has boasted that he was a Storm trooper."[90]

Extradition Requests

Australia received at least eight extradition requests between 1950 and 1961 from Yugoslavia, Estonia, and Latvia, which were all refused.[91] The first extradition request occurred in March 1950 when Yugoslavia requested the extradition of Branislav I., accused of being Assistant Minister of Transport in the Nedić government and son-in-law of Milan Nedić. Branislav was then a Serbian block supervisor at Bonegilla, who had already been investigated by Australian authorities because he was reported to exhibit a "tendency to fascism."[92] However, the Australian government replied to the Yugoslav government that it had "not been possible to identify this person," and there are some indications that Branislav was being used for intelligence work against Communist organizations in Australia.[93] In 1955 he was naturalized, with no objection from the Australian Security Intelligence Organisation.[94]

In 1951, Yugoslavia—again—requested the extradition of two alleged war criminals: Serbian Milorad Lukic, who allegedly worked for the Gestapo denouncing pro-nationalist Yugoslavs in a prisoner of war camp in Nuremberg, and Montenegrin Mihailo Rajkovic, an ex-judge who was similarly charged with working with the Gestapo to denounce Yugoslavs at a prisoner of war camp in Albania.[95] In Australia, Lukic and Rajkovic were well known to the Australian Security Intelligence Organisation as informants who infiltrated pro-Communist Yugoslav groups and were, according to ASIO's Director-General, "unceasing in

---

89. Letter from Harold Holt, Minister for Immigration, to Ben Green, President, Executive Council of Jewry, March 28, 1951, Mark Aarons—General Australian War Crimes, Box 9, SLNSW.

90. "Migrant Gets Month's Gaol," *The Herald* (Melbourne), July 13, 1950.

91. Branislav I. (1950), Milorad Lukic (1951), Mihailo Rajkovic (1951), Mica M. (1954), Bogoliub R. (1955), Jozef K. (1958), Anton B. (1958), Erwin Viks (1961).

92. Various items of correspondence, Mark Aarons—General Australian War Crimes, Box 1, SLNSW.

93. See Branislav IVANOVIC, 1950–1957, Australian Security Intelligence Organisation, Central Office, A6126, 1126, NAA.

94. See War Crimes—Ivanovic Branislav Brana—War Criminal, 1950, Department of External Affairs, Central Office, A1838, 1550/18, NAA.

95. Letter from Consulate General of the Federal People's Republic of Yugoslavia, Sydney, to Minister, Department of External Affairs, May 8, 1951, War Crimes—Alleged Yugoslav War Criminals—Lukic and Rajkovic, 1951–1952, Department of External Affairs, Central Office, A1838, 1550/20 (hereafter, Lukic and Rajkovic), NAA.

their campaign against communism."⁹⁶ In any event, there was never any intention to extradite such cases, as was made clear in a memorandum of advice upon receipt of the request which directed that "even if the investigation discloses that there is some truth in the ... allegations," Australia would continue to follow the British line that "it is time to bring to an end the punishment of minor war criminals." The legal and consular advice was that:

> The few persons handed over to the Yugoslav Government [by the British military] were those who "by the nature of their official positions, rendered such signal service to the enemy that it would be difficult, if not impossible, to justify a refusal to consider surrendering them". Lukic and Rajkovic do not appear to be in this category.⁹⁷

When Estonian Erwin Viks was targeted for extradition in 1961, and the Baltic community in Australia reacted in uproar, Attorney-General Garfield Barwick announced that "the time has come to close the chapter." He argued that on the

> ... one hand, there is the utter abhorrence felt by Australians for those offences against humanity to which we give the generic name of war crimes. On the other hand, there is the right of this nation, by receiving people into its country, to enable men to turn their backs on past bitternesses and to make a new life for themselves and for their families in a happier community.⁹⁸

Historians, and victims, may be forgiven for being surprised that the Australian government ever considered this chapter open. This chapter has presented some supposition for security deportations based on far-right activity, but there is little evidence of this occurring. Further, when Eastern Bloc countries requested extraditions of alleged war criminals, Australia consistently refused to hand these migrants over.⁹⁹ As later charged by investigator Mark Aarons, Australia had proved a sanctuary for fugitives of the far right.¹⁰⁰

---

96. Letter from Director-General of Security, Attorney-General's Department, to Secretary, Department of External Affairs, July 11, 1951, Lukic and Rajkovic, NAA.

97. "Yugoslav 'War Criminals' in Australia," from Legal and Consular to Secretary, Department of External Affairs, June 4, 1951, Lukic and Rajkovic, NAA.

98. "Extradition of Migrant," Sir Garfield Barwick, Acting Minister for External Affairs and Attorney-General, March 22, 1961, House of Representatives, 23rd Parliament, 3rd Session, http://historichansard.net/hofreps/1961/19610322_reps_23_hor30/#subdebate-20-00hyeg4Z%^.

99. It wasn't until after the end of the Cold War, in 2012, that Hungarian Charles Z. narrowly escaped extradition proceedings with an appeal to the High Court, who ruled that the offence of "war crime" did not exist under Hungarian law in 1944 and so Australia was under no compulsion to extradite. See Ruth Balint, "The Ties that Bind: Australia, Hungary and the Case of Károly Zentai," *Patterns of Prejudice* 44, no. 3 (2010): 281–303.

100. Mark Aarons, *Sanctuary! Nazi Fugitives in Australia* (Port Melbourne, Victoria: William Heinemann Australia, 1989).

Chapter 4

REPATRIATION OF POSTWAR MIGRANTS FROM
AUSTRALIA TO THE SOVIET UNION: THE
AUSTRALIAN VIEW

Ebony Nilsson

When Natalia Stashevska arrived at Sydney's Mascot airport on November 20, 1950, there was an officer of the Australian Security Intelligence Organisation (ASIO) not far behind her. He noted that she carried only light luggage and was in the company of an unknown man, who farewelled her in Russian and kissed her as she boarded the aircraft.[1] Security men had also covertly checked her bags but found nothing suspicious. Natalia was flying to Hong Kong, where MI5 would pick up her trail, and then on to Shanghai, but her ultimate destination was the Soviet Union. She was leaving Australia for good, trading life under Western capitalism for Soviet Communism, and there would be security officers watching her each step of the way.

Two years later, ASIO's Director-General, Charles Spry, was sufficiently concerned about the increasing number of Soviet migrants making this same choice—repatriation to the Soviet Union—that he drafted a memo for the Department of Immigration.[2] Spry identified three security issues which arose from these departures: espionage, propaganda, and subversion. Repatriates' potential value for espionage was clear, as individuals with fresh experience of Western language, life, and culture; subversion was always more nebulous, with Spry referring vaguely to the potential "disloyalty" of migrants considering return.[3] But beyond individuals, repatriates were simply a bad look. The idea that Soviet citizens—refugees who had fled Communism, no less—would experience

---

1. National Archives of Australia (hereafter NAA): A6126, 1413, "STASHEVSKY, Natalia": Natasha Stashevsky—Departure from Sydney, Australia by Air for Hong Kong, November 21, 1950, f. 51; Courtenay Young, MI5 Liaison Officer to Director Sydney, November 1, 1950, f. 49.

2. NAA: A6980, S250323, "Assimilation of Soviet Nationals in Australia": C. C. F. Spry to T. H. E. Heyes, October 28, 1952, f. 4–6.

3. NAA: A6980, S250232: Spry to Heyes, f. 5.

capitalism and want to *return* played right into the Soviet Union's hands, bolstering its propaganda narrative and undermining the West's. Though the number of repatriates was only ever small, they were a significant concern for ASIO and constituted a distinct section of the organization's work.

World War II had left millions of Eastern Europeans displaced and the fate of those who refused to return to Soviet territory was considered amid growing Cold War tensions. When Russian émigrés began to leave China in the late 1940s, as Chinese Communist forces gained the upper hand, they too were often seen as Cold War refugees.[4] The countries which agreed to resettle them, including Australia, generally sought laborers to fuel postwar reconstruction. But their new workers also fitted neatly into Cold War narratives: life in the East was unbearable and its citizens were "choosing freedom" in the West. At least 50,000 migrants of Soviet origin arrived in Australia following World War II.[5] Cases of failed migration, where these "displaced persons" (DPs) sought to voluntarily return to the Soviet Union, thus presented an issue in terms of both security and optics.

Migration and security are, of course, deeply connected—but we usually associate this with inward migration. States police their borders to restrict the entry of individuals who might compromise the security of their social, political, and cultural (or racial) milieux. In Australia, an island nation with a long history of immigration restriction, such a connection is obvious. But as the issue of Soviet repatriation shows, departures have also been conceived of as a security issue. The postwar drive to populate Australia with white, assimilable workers and citizens was closely connected to notions of national security. As Immigration minister Arthur Calwell's oft-repeated slogan—"populate or perish"—succinctly put it, with a birthrate that could not climb quickly enough, the perceived alternative to migration was demise. If these migrants began to leave, then Australia was potentially at risk.[6] This assumption underpinned many of ASIO's assessments; officers' vague statements about the threat of subversion referred, often, to repatriates subverting not democracy or elected government, but Australia's immigration program and its assimilationist ideals.

---

4. The International Refugee Organization granted protection to some of these "White Russians" as the Communist victory became clear, though Australia was somewhat more reticent about resettlement. See Sheila Fitzpatrick and Justine Greenwood, "Anti-Communism in Australian Immigration Policies 1947–54: The Case of Russian/Soviet Displaced Persons from Europe and White Russians from China," *Australian Historical Studies* 50, no. 1 (2019): 41–62.

5. Sheila Fitzpatrick, *White Russians, Red Peril: A Cold War History of Migration to Australia* (Melbourne: Black Inc., 2021), 263–72.

6. On the security rationale for postwar immigration, see Andrew Markus, "Labor and Immigration: Policy Formation 1943–5," *Labour History* 46 (1984): 22–32; Klaus Neumann, *Across the Seas, Australia's Response to Refugees: A History* (Melbourne: Black Inc., 2015), 81–2.

Failed migration among postwar refugees has received relatively little scholarly attention.[7] In part, this is because most did, indeed, settle permanently in Australia: the return rate for Eastern European migrants between 1947 and 1980 was a rather low 9.5 percent (and was likely even lower for the DP group).[8] But this lacuna also exists because departures are more difficult to trace in the archive than arrivals. An arriving non-British migrant triggered a deluge of paperwork. Arrival papers and registration certificates—with their biographical details and pasted-down portrait photographs—are often the fare of family historians so readily available in archives and, increasingly, online. But a departing migrant left significantly fewer traces—if they had a passport and entry visa for their destination, they needed little more than a tax clearance and a ticket. They will sometimes appear on the other side, in their destination country, as Sheila Fitzpatrick's chapter in this volume shows.

The Department of Immigration made some attempts to capture the repatriates in aggregate, compiling figures on return rates. But it was keen to keep the actual dissatisfied migrant considering return at arm's length.[9] ASIO, on the other hand, put significant time into monitoring such people. Fitzpatrick's chapter shows that the Soviets saw it as self-evident that their DPs would want to return; ASIO, equally, thought it self-evident that they would want to stay. Thus, these anomalous migrants were thoroughly, and individually, investigated. By the late 1960s, repatriation occupied a whole section of ASIO's B1 (counter-subversion) branch, under three key areas: potential repatriates, "repatriation workers" (migrants thought to be convincing others to return), and repatriates attempting to come back to Australia.[10] ASIO's administrative approach to repatriation during the early Cold War remains shrouded in classification—but Spry's memo and individual case files on migrants who considered return point to monitoring of the

---

7. Some important contributions have been made recently by migration historians. On Soviet repatriation, see Sheila Fitzpatrick, "Soviet Repatriation Efforts among 'Displaced Persons' Resettled in Australia, 1950–53," *Australian Journal of Politics and History* 63, no. 1 (2017): 45–61; on DPs' onward migration, see Jayne Persian, *Beautiful Balts: From Displaced Persons to New Australians* (Sydney: NewSouth Publishing, 2017), 108–11; and on deportation of DPs to Europe, see Ruth Balint, *Destination Elsewhere: Displaced Persons and their Quest to Leave Postwar Europe* (New York: Cornell University Press, 2021), 126–8.

8. Jock Collins, *Migrant Hands in a Distant Land: Australia's Post-war Immigration* (Sydney: Pluto Press, 1988), 30. The category of "Eastern Europe" included Poland, the Baltic States, Yugoslavia, Hungary, Russia, Ukraine, and a mysterious "other."

9. Heyes, the department secretary, responded to Spry's concerned memo by setting up a meeting with ASIS (ASIO's overseas security counterpart), but warned both that there was little the department could do for individual migrants. NAA: A6980, S250323: T. H. E. Heyes to C.C.F. Spry, November 21, 1952, f. 7.

10. NAA: A6122, 2079, "History of ASIO by Bob Swan—Volume 13": Functions and Responsibilities of B1 Branch Headquarters, Duty Statements—July 1968, f. 129.

same three areas.¹¹ They also tell us about the lives of migrants whose resettlement failed, the expectations Australian security officials had about their behavior, and how departure was sometimes seen to be as much a threat to national security as arrival. This chapter uses these individual case files to reconstruct Australian intelligence officers' approach to departures to the Soviet Union during the 1950s.

Potential Repatriates

ASIO was concerned with the threat posed by individual repatriates not just for Australia's sake but as part of the broader project of Western democracy. If, as intelligence agencies suspected, the Soviets had planted spies among the DP population prior to their resettlement, repatriation was a way to bring these agents in from the cold. ASIO posited that such agents' experiences of Western life and languages could be of particular use in future assignments—making repatriates an issue of collective security.¹² ASIO knew, by way of its British and Canadian counterparts, that Igor Gouzenko, a Soviet cipher clerk who defected to Canada in 1945, had divulged Soviet plans to target Eastern European migrants under the cover of repatriation efforts, in order to create a sympathetic fifth column.¹³ As Sheila Fitzpatrick's chapter in this book shows, the reality in Australia was a little more complicated, with intelligence men like Anatoli Gordeev apparently sent only to do repatriation work. ASIO did not have this information, however, and worked to assess potential repatriates' convictions and motives, to ascertain if they were being recruited.

If one was looking for espionage, all manner of activities were likely to appear suspicious, and ASIO dutifully recorded what officers observed with surveillance or were told by informants. Natalia Stashevska, whose final trip to the airport was watched step by step, had become close with the representative of TASS, the Soviet

---

11. Volume 1 of the *Official History* explains that of nine field officers in NSW's B1 Branch in 1953, three were tasked with investigating "subversive activities among aliens." It's possible that this included repatriation, but Horner doesn't provide further detail. See David Horner, *The Spy Catchers: The Official History of ASIO, 1949–1963*, vol. 1 (Sydney: Allen & Unwin, 2014), 207. Though screening of incoming migrants receives substantive attention in Horner's volume (see pp. 250–68, 268–9), repatriation is not mentioned at all. Volume 2, which surveys the following decade, has a handful of pages dealing with repatriation, but they focus almost solely on the actions of Soviet intelligence officers, rather than the repatriates themselves. See John Blaxland, *The Protest Years: The Official History of ASIO, 1963–1975*, vol. 2 (Sydney: Allen & Unwin, 2015), 206–8.

12. Fitzpatrick, "Soviet Repatriation Efforts," 54–5.

13. NAA: A6122, 2739, "Official Representation of USSR in Australia prior to 1955—Survey of Contacts made by Embassy Personnel in New South Wales 1950–1952": [Redacted], B2 Section, Report for Regional Director (RD), Survey of Contacts Made By Soviet Embassy Personnel in Victoria, 1950–2, f. 1.

news agency. The TASS men were indeed working for Soviet intelligence, though ASIO didn't yet know this for sure.[14] When Stashevska began making plans to leave, ASIO immediately suspected her recruitment, likely as a courier.[15] But she was also a single woman alone in a new city and these older Soviet couples appear to have acted as chaperones and substitute parents for a young Russian missing her own family.[16] ASIO knew, because it had bugged the TASS representative's apartment, that Stashevska had told her Soviet friends she was desperately unhappy in Australia and wanted to return to the Soviet Union with her parents.[17] ASIO didn't comment on whether it thought she was genuinely unhappy but, along with MI5, deemed espionage a likely explanation for her plan to repatriate and the Soviet company she kept.[18]

Nikita Pivnijev, a Russian DP who planned to repatriate with his Yugoslav wife and their son, was also suspected of acting as a courier, by an informant who had rented a room in the family's house and discovered a covered fireplace where she believed documents had been secreted and then removed.[19] Some ASIO officers remained wary of this informant (who reported to Special Branch police, rather than them). Pivnijev's adult son, Viktor, also raised alarm bells in ASIO due to his work as a technical assistant in the Postmaster General's Department and alleged interest in "military camouflage" and "aerial photography."[20] Thus, several ASIO officers flagged espionage as a possibility for this repatriate family, too. Jakob Zelensky, a young Ukrainian DP, was more brash about his intentions. He told Vladimir Petrov, a Soviet diplomat and intelligence officer (who would defect in 1954), that he wanted to return to the Soviet Union so that he could fight with the Red Army in Korea, where he would "kill Yanks and bloody Australians."[21] Perhaps more alarmingly for ASIO, he told Petrov that he could assist Russia because he knew "the aerodromes in Melbourne and in Tasmania also."[22] Officers recorded

---

14. Horner, *The Spy Catchers*, 55, 319.

15. NAA: A6126, 1413: [Redacted] to B2, October 26, 1950, f. 47–8.

16. NAA: A6126, 1413: R. Gamble Report, May 4, 1950, f. 22; [Redacted] to B2, October 26, 1950, f. 48; Report for Principal Section Officer (PSO) B2, November 17, 1950, f. 50; RD NSW Report, January 4, 1951, f. 58–9.

17. NAA: A6126, 1413: R. Gamble Report, June 16, 1950, f. 33; R. Gamble Report, July 12, 1950, f. 35.

18. NAA: A6126, 1413: Courtenay Young to Director Sydney, November 1, 1950, f. 49.

19. NAA: A6119, 7451, "PIVNIJEV, Victor Volume 1": Special Branch Report, S/Constable Walsh, January 22, 1957, f. 14.

20. NAA: A6119, 7451: Director B1 to DDG Ops, March 15, 1957, f. 40; Undated B2 Report, Callers at Public office, March 1, 1957, f. 47; R. H. T. Gamble for RD Vic to ASIO HQ, March 15, 1957, f. 48.

21. NAA: A6126, 1416, "ZALENSKI, Jakiw": RD NSW Report, October 31, 1951, f. 33. The Red Army did not fight in Korea, but Jakob evidently thought that it might.

22. NAA: A6126, 1416: RD NSW Report, October 31, 1951, f. 33.

this and appear to have taken it at face value, not assessing whether Zelensky really *did* know anything useful (which appears doubtful).[23]

Such overtures to Soviet officials were not typical; migrants more often emphasized poor working or living conditions in Australia.[24] Soviet officials were inclined to accept such explanations, but ASIO's officers were not. Instead, they often suspected manipulation. In Zelensky's case, ASIO agreed with its informant's view that the young Ukrainian had been talked into repatriating by Soviet officials and held "a personal grudge against Australians, brought about by the fact that he was bashed up by some chaps in Melbourne."[25] Zelensky had struggled under the two-year indentured work contract required of the DPs, falling on hard times after breaking a wrist. He explained to an immigration official that the Tasmanian mine where he was injured was "200 years behind European working conditions" and he was astonished that "conditions in Australia could be so bad." But this official, too, put his malcontent down to the influence of "communist agitators."[26]

ASIO's assessments more often attributed repatriation to the influence of Soviet officials than to issues with Australia's immigration program. For example, officers deemed that another young Ukrainian, Petr Bronski, had come under the influence of Gordeev, the Soviet repatriation official.[27] Bronski told ASIO in an interview that he felt "he could not be assimilated," and had "been happy in Australia until about three months previously when he discovered that he could not settle permanently in a foreign community."[28] On the latter point, an ASIO officer appears to have editorialized: "i.e. until Gordeev's visits he had been quite happy."[29] The field officer also noted Bronski's "nervous agitation" and hypothesized that Gordeev had pressured the young DP, perhaps even threatening his family in the Soviet Union. The latter seems less likely, given Soviet policy at the time was geared toward encouraging repatriates rather than coercing them.[30]

---

23. Zelensky had not worked at any locations of military significance (NAA: A6126, 1416: J. M. Gilmour Report for PSO B2, January 2, 1952, f. 24), nor did he apparently supply any such information when he did repatriate (Fitzpatrick, "Soviet Repatriation," 60).

24. See Sheila Fitzpatrick's contribution to this volume.

25. NAA: A6126, 1416: G. R. Richards, RD NSW, to Director General (DG) ASIO, January 9, 1952, f. 23; NAA: A6119, 3635, "Bialoguski, Michael Volume 1 (Operation Fairmile)": J. M. Gilmour Report for PSO B2, February 26, 1952, f. 189.

26. NAA: A6126, 1416: J. M. Gilmour Report to PSO B2, January 2, 1952, f. 24.

27. For a detailed examination of Gordeev's repatriation work, see Fitzpatrick, "Soviet Repatriation Efforts."

28. NAA: A6122, 2739: [Redacted], B2 Section, Report for RD, December 22, 1953, f. 22.

29. NAA: A6122, 2739: Report for RD, December 22, 1953, f. 22.

30. Sheila Fitzpatrick, "The Motherland Calls: 'Soft' Repatriation of Soviet Citizens from Europe, 1945–1953," *Journal of Modern History* 90, no. 2 (2018): 324. Further, Fitzpatrick has shown that Gordeev's methods don't appear to have involved coercion: see "Soviet Repatriation Efforts," 45–6.

Spry wasn't entirely insensible of, or unsympathetic to, the difficulties faced by some DPs. In writing to the Department of Immigration about his concerns regarding repatriation, he first discussed Soviet pressure on refugees, but went on to describe "the harm that can be done by placing highly qualified refugees in low class jobs and in inadequate houses."[31] Here he gave the case of a Ukrainian doctor working as a laborer (though his sympathy did not always extend to refugees he considered of a lower caliber than doctors). Spry was attentive to the fact that "special measures" might be needed to assist some migrants—he pushed that the solution to the issue of repatriation lay in "an adequate assimilation scheme" (which presumably implied that Immigration's efforts were falling short of the mark).[32] But ASIO's officers did consider that migrants had some degree of personal responsibility in assimilating. One assessment concluded that Juris Pintans, a Latvian who repatriated in 1960, "never displayed any interest in becoming assimilated and he apparently made no effort to secure accommodation for his family away from the migrant camp," which counted as a black mark against his name.[33] Nikita Pivnijev, the Russian with the suspect fireplace, received a similar black mark. Though reports noted his inability to gain work in his previous field of engineering with a degree of sympathy, the family's "complete lack of assimilation (and their love for the U.S.S.R)" produced a "very grave doubt" about them for ASIO.[34]

Just as Spry did not think that ASIO had any role to play in supporting migrants' assimilation, neither did the organization appear to have tried to convince repatriates to stay, nor impede their leaving. Field officers just watched Natalia Stashevska depart and passed their observations on to MI5. In Juris Pintans' case, it seems they even missed it, only noting his emigration after the fact.[35] ASIO directed the Immigration Department to keep it updated on Jakob Zelensky's repatriation plans, but didn't get in the way of his being issued identity documents, though Immigration offered to hold up the process.[36] ASIO officers did interview some of the potential repatriates, such as Petr Bronski and his colleague Nadejda Berilko. But these interviews were primarily about gathering intelligence on Soviet officials' activities in Australia.[37] Perhaps ASIO officers didn't think it was in their

---

31. NAA: A6980, S250323: Spry to Heyes, f. 5.

32. NAA: A6980, S250323: Spry to Heyes, f. 5. Heyes certainly seems to have taken this as an implicit critique of the department's work.

33. NAA: A6119, 7049, "PINTANS, Juris Peteris Volume 1": Report for [Redacted], November 5, 1970, f. 149.

34. NAA: A6119, 7451: C. C. F. Spry to Secretary, Department of Immigration, March 1958, f. 82.

35. NAA: A6119, 7049: Travel Control Office (TCO) Report for Senior Field Officer (SFO), March 22, 1960, f. 130.

36. NAA: A6126, 1416: J. M. Gilmour Report to PSO B2, January 2, 1952, f. 24; RD ACT Report for DG ASIO, January 23, 1952, f. 18.

37. NAA: A6122, 2739: Report for RD, December 22, 1953, f. 17.

job description to convince repatriates they were wrong, or perhaps they didn't have to. A number of returning migrants reported that others were already doing so: a Bulgarian, Andon Stironoff, reported his boss at the Sydney Water Board trying to scare him off with stories of what happened behind the Iron Curtain, and others mentioned the warnings of Immigration officials.[38] The security service, meanwhile, simply watched, collected intelligence, passed it on to other Western agencies, and let others issue warning speeches about the Iron Curtain.

Repatriation Workers

Apart from migrants who intended to repatriate themselves, ASIO was concerned by those who encouraged their friends, neighbors, and colleagues to return. Western governments expected that Soviet officials were attempting to encourage or force repatriation, after their efforts in Europe's DP camps.[39] And having lived in the camps, most DPs gave Soviet officials a wide berth, fearing the possibility of forcible repatriation, kidnapping, or even assassination.[40] But migrants active within their own communities as "Iron Curtain Repatriation Workers"—more familiar and less fearsome faces—could potentially have more success, or so ASIO worried. This fell not under espionage, but that hazier notion of subversion. "Repatriation workers" were, ASIO thought, potential saboteurs lurking within migrant communities, threatening their assimilation, the success of Australia's immigration program, and thus, its security.

Juris Pintans, the Latvian repatriate who was apparently disinterested in assimilation, was one alleged "repatriation worker." Pintans, struggling to get ahead in Australia, began corresponding with the Soviet-backed "Return to the Homeland" Committee. Run out of East Berlin and staffed by Red Army officers, the committee produced magazines and radio broadcasts aimed at encouraging repatriation; its messaging emphasized the amnesty extended to all repatriates, the corruption of the West, and improved conditions in the Soviet Union.[41] Pintans

---

38. "More Migrants to Go Back to Russia," *Tribune*, April 9, 1952, 8; W. J. Brown, "More Migrants Go Home to Soviet and Security," *Tribune*, December 3, 1952, 4; "Still More Migrants Decide to Go Home," *Tribune*, April 23, 1952, 8.

39. "Official denies 'pressure,'" *The Herald* (Melbourne), October 17, 1953, 9; "Secret Dossiers Kept in Canberra?" *The Mail* (Adelaide), October 24, 1953, 9; "Security Men Ordered to Find Out—Are Reds at Work on Our Migrants," *The Argus*, May 7, 1956, 7; "No Known Body Urging Migrants Back to Russia," *Canberra Times*, May 9, 1956, 2; "You Need Not Fear Threats!" *Good Neighbour*, August 1, 1957, 8.

40. Persian, *Beautiful Balts*, 163–5.

41. Simo Mikkonen, "Mass Communications as a Vehicle to Lure Russian Émigrés Homeward," *Journal of International and Global Studies* 2, no. 2 (2011): 47; Jean Martin, *Community and Identity: Refugee Groups in Adelaide* (Canberra: ANU Press, 1972), 16.

initially asked for materials for himself and his family, but gradually his requests became evangelical.[42] He asked the committee to send their pro-Soviet periodicals to other DPs, providing the names and addresses of at least forty individual migrants, including other Latvians, but also Russians, Ukrainians, Lithuanians, Estonians, and a Byelorussian.[43] ASIO thus assessed that Pintans was "loyal to the Soviet Union only."[44] Interestingly, the committee was actually KGB-linked and the information it gathered was sometimes used for operations.[45] Pintans' information could have assisted with building lists of émigrés and understanding what anti-Communist émigrés were publishing in Australia, though not much more.[46] But it does not appear that Pintans knew about this link to the KGB and nor, for that matter, did ASIO. Though Pintans wanted to repatriate his own family, this was not his primary goal for his neighbors. Instead, he wrote to the committee that he sought to help fellow migrants see through anti-Soviet propaganda lest their anti-Communism harm *Australia's* labor movement.[47] It was fine with him if they stayed in Australia—so long as they didn't impede its Labor Party or trade unions. But it's doubtful he met with any success in encouraging repatriation or a more positive view of the Soviet Union. Australia's migrant camps, where Pintans lived, were typically bastions of anti-Soviet sentiment and staunch nationalism and he was consistently ostracized for his pro-Soviet views.[48] ASIO viewed Pintans' efforts as a threat, however, with little examination of their success or failure.[49]

42. NAA: A6119, 7049: J. Pintans to "Return to the Homeland" Committee, January 12, 1957, f. 7.

43. NAA: A6119, 7049: Letters from J. Pintans to "Return to the Homeland" Committee, January 30, 1958, f. 40; February 2, 1958, f. 33; February 7, 1958, f. 36; February 15, 1958, f. 46; April 11, 1958, f. 64; May 10, 1958, f. 65; June 4, 1958, f. 76; June 26, 1958, f. 81; July 15, 1958, f. 85; July 25, 1958, f. 88; August 21, 1958, f. 95; September 9, 1958, f. 100; September 21, 1958, f. 106; October 20, 1958, f. 107; March 25, 1959, f. 116; DG to RD NSW, April 8, 1958, f. 41; DG to RD NSW, Mr. J Pintans, September 17, 1958, f, 103.

44. NAA: A6119, 7049: ASIO Minute Paper, January 18, 1962, f. 140.

45. Simo Mikkonen, "Not By Force Alone: Soviet Return Migration in the 1950s," in Sharif Gemie, Scott Soo, and Norman LaPorte (eds.), *Coming Home? Conflict and Return Migration in the Aftermath of Europe's Twentieth Century Civil Wars* (Newcastle upon Tyne: Cambridge Scholars Publishing, 2013), 191.

46. NAA: A6119, 7049: J. Pintans to "Return to the Homeland" Committee, September 9, 1958, f. 100.

47. NAA: A6119, 7049: J. Pintans to "Return to the Homeland" Committee, May 10, 1958, f. 65, and August 4, 1958, f. 92.

48. Christopher Keating, *Greta: A History of the Army Camp and Migrant Camp at Greta, New South Wales, 1939–1960* (Sydney: Uri Windt, 1997), 71.

49. NAA: A6119, 7049: DG ASIO to RD NSW, December 3, 1958, f. 109; SFO to RD NSW, June 29, 1959, f. 123.

Alexander Antropoff, an earlier Russian arrival from Shanghai, was also in ASIO's sights because of activities related to the "Return to the Homeland" Committee. The former wharf laborer and trade unionist was mentioned in the committee's periodical in 1958 as having assisted a friend who had been "placed in a lunatic asylum" following his application to return to the Soviet Union.[50] The friend—who did eventually repatriate—needed financial assistance and someone to undertake responsibility for him when he was discharged from the facility, and Antropoff assisted on both counts.[51] ASIO jumped on this reference: it had already suspected that Antropoff was "supplying information" to the committee, "if not acting in some capacity on their behalf in Australia."[52] Unlike the Pintans case, however, ASIO does not appear to have had any evidence that Antropoff was actually in contact with the committee. ASIO's sources suggested he had ambiguous connections with both pro- and anti-Communist migrants, making him well placed to encourage repatriation.[53] He apparently had a letter from one Mrs. Nikolaeff, a Muscovite who wrote to him "extolling conditions in the Soviet Union," which he would show to migrant customers who visited his furniture shop.[54] Similarly vague reports were made about Nikita Pivnijev drunkenly boasting that he had regular contact with, and worked as an agent for, the head of the Repatriation Committee.[55] One imagines in both cases that given migrant communities' prevailing anti-Communism (and the fact that someone in their audience saw fit to report on them), these overtures, boasts, and letters were not welcomed by many. But ASIO was concerned nonetheless: the already-naturalized Antropoff was being praised in a Soviet newspaper and helping friends who wanted to return, while Pivnijev was trying to convert his neighbors.[56] Both were potentially undermining Australia's immigration program—hardly the settled, assimilated behavior expected of "New Australians."

Abraham Frankel was perhaps a better candidate for ASIO's "repatriation worker." ASIO was concerned by reports that Frankel was spending significant amounts of time with officials from the Soviet Embassy and particularly with Yanis Plaitkais, who had taken over repatriation efforts when Gordeev departed. Surveillance officers noted that Frankel was "constantly in Plaitkais' company

---

50. "Konchilis' gody skitanii," *Za Vozvrashchenie na Rodinu* 9, January 27, 1958, 4.

51. NAA: A6119, 2881: Report by [Redacted], Field Officer (FO), to SFO, July 25, 1958, f. 11.

52. NAA: A6119, 2881: [Redacted] to SFO, July 25, 1958, f. 11.

53. NAA: A6119, 2881: [Redacted] to SFO, July 25, 1958, f. 11.

54. NAA: A6119, 2881: File Note, October 20, 1959, f. 18; Report by [Redacted], FO, to SFO, October 15, 1959, f. 15.

55. NAA: A6119, 7451: Report No. 11055, Victoria: Nick Pivnieff (phonetic), August 8, 1957, f. 52.

56. NAA: A6119, 7451: Geoffrey G. Walsh, Report for Officer in Charge, Special Branch, February 2, 1957, f. 37.

when the official was interviewing repatriates" in Melbourne.⁵⁷ He also knew Petrov, who did some repatriation work and would bring sweets for Frankel's children when they met.⁵⁸ Based on observations of Frankel's apparently "conspiratorial" meetings with the Soviet men and their knowledge of his other pro-Soviet associates, ASIO decided that he must have been obtaining the names of potential repatriates at a Melbourne Russian Club and then passing them on to the embassy.⁵⁹

Some DPs did give the Soviet officials names and introductions. As Fitzpatrick's chapter in this volume describes, this could be quite a help for the Soviets, who struggled to make contact with DPs.⁶⁰ Further, the Soviet men had to deal with the frequent (if occasionally hapless) presence of ASIO officers whenever they left Canberra.⁶¹ Gordeev feared trouble with the Australian authorities if he visited migrant camps and hostels—a concern that was probably warranted.⁶² The idea that Soviet officials were pressuring refugees to return flared several times in the media and on the floor of parliament during the 1950s.⁶³ Between ASIO's

---

57. NAA: A6122, 2739: Report for RD, December 22, 1953, f. 22.

58. NAA: A1838, 1453/4137, "Entry into Australia—Frankel Family": Interview with Mr. Frankel, September 28, 1961, f. 149. Petrov was not officially tasked with repatriation duties (as Gordeev was) but his intelligence duties included keeping an eye on Soviet émigrés and encouraging repatriation—which he did, often—and appears to have been a kind of natural extension of this work. Horner, *The Spy Catchers*, 319.

59. NAA: A6122, 2739: Report for RD, December 22, 1953, f. 22; NAA: A1838, 1453/4137: C. C. F. Spry, DG ASIO, to Secretary, Department of Immigration (DOI), August 4, 1961, f. 134.

60. See also Fitzpatrick, *White Russians, Red Peril*, 219.

61. Horner, *The Spy Catchers*, 286–7. This surveillance was conducted quite consistently up until 1954, when the Soviet Embassy closed down in the wake of the Petrov Affair. Soviet officials would not return until 1959.

62. Fitzpatrick, *White Russians, Red Peril*, 213; Horner, *The Spy Catchers*, 285.

63. The first flashpoint was in 1953: "Reds urged Russian girl to go back home," and "Official denies 'pressure,'" *The Herald* (Melbourne), October 17, 1953, 9; Hansard, House of Representatives, Question for Harold Holt, Minister for Immigration, by Jo Gullett, Member for Henty, October 20, 1953: http://historichansard.net/hofreps/1953/19531020_reps_20_hor1/#subdebate-19-0. A planned investigation into the matter was perhaps usurped by Petrov's defection, but the issue reappeared in 1956–7 in relation to the Return to the Homeland Committee's activities: Hansard, House of Representatives, Question for Harold Holt, Minister for Immigration by Dan Mackinnon, Member for Corangamite, February 29, 1956: http://historichansard.net/hofreps/1956/19560229_reps_22_hor9/#subdebate-9-0; "Red Agents' Pressure on New Austlns," *Central Queensland Herald*, March 8, 1956, 12; "Security men order to find out—Are Reds at work on our migrants?" *The Argus*, May 7, 1956, 7; Hansard, House of Representatives, Question for Harold Holt, Minister for Immigration by Frank Timson, Member for Higinbotham, May 8, 1956: http://historichansard.net/hofreps/1956/19560508_reps_22_hor10/#subdebate-5-0; "No Known Body Urging Migrants Back to Russia," *Canberra Times*, May 9, 1956, 2; "Offer to Protect Migrants," *The Argus*, July 3, 1957, 1.

attentions, the possibility of a diplomatic incident, and migrants' frequent reticence to speak with them, a little local assistance was indeed rather helpful for the Soviets.

Frankel, for his part, would later tell the Australian authorities that he hadn't helped any officials, just his friends. Once it became known in the migrant community that Frankel was considering repatriation for himself and his family, other Russians came to him for help—he said his English was good, so he assisted them in making travel arrangements and completing necessary paperwork.[64] With regard to Plaitkais and Petrov, Frankel claimed he had only ever showed them street addresses they had written down, where the Soviet men would go and speak with other migrants.[65] Of course, Frankel was likely playing down his involvement for the benefit of the Australian officials. But it does seem that most of his "repatriation work" involved not evangelizing but rendering assistance—to his friends who asked for help with forms, and to Soviet officials with lists of names who didn't know their way around Melbourne (but perhaps also benefited from a local's introduction).[66] But this was immaterial to ASIO. Spry didn't mince words when assessing Frankel for the Department of Immigration, writing that Frankel's activities "amounted to sabotage of your Immigration programme."[67]

The Question of Re-entry

ASIO's final concern about migrants departing for the Soviet Union was that they might later try to return to Australia. Immigration Minister Harold Holt had issued a warning to migrants considering repatriation in 1956: that "a migrant who returned to his homeland as a result of propaganda and once again changed his mind would find it easier to go to his own country than to return to Australia, though he had been naturalised here."[68] This proved true, for the immigration "saboteur" Abraham Frankel, and others. Applications for re-entry were dealt with by Immigration, where the Minister had the final say, but ASIO was consulted at each turn. The security service's general view on readmittance was a resounding "no." But in the case of families with Australian-born children, who had some right of return, the issue became significantly more complex. ASIO's primary concern

---

64. NAA: A1838, 1453/4137: Interview with Mr. Frankel, September 28, 1961, f. 150.

65. NAA: A1838, 1453/4137: Interview with Mr. Frankel, September 28, 1961, f. 149–50.

66. An Australian diplomat in Moscow would later assess Frankel—based on a lengthy interview—in much the same way. He thought Frankel's repatriation work could be "explained by his proclivity to be regarded as one to whom people looked for advice and assistance." NAA: A1838, 1453/4137: W. L. Morrison, First Secretary Australian Embassy Moscow, to Secretary, Department of External Affairs (DEA), October 4, 1961, f. 155.

67. NAA: A6980, S201205, "FRANKEL Abraham—part 1": C. C. F. Spry to Secretary, DOI, September 8, 1958, f. 32.

68. "No Known Body Urging Migrants Back to Russia," *Canberra Times*, May 9, 1956, 2.

in assessing returnees was the possibility that they would conduct espionage, but alongside this were concerns about migrant assimilation and the integrity of Australia's immigration program.

When Spry first came to substantively assess the issue of Soviet re-entry in 1958, he was more concerned about the Soviet authorities' motives than the reasons of migrant applicants. He thought it quite possible that the applicants were sincere (i.e., that they really didn't enjoy living in the Soviet Union), but that the Soviets would only let them leave if there was something in it for the USSR.[69] Spry guessed that "the price of an exit permit" might be the applicant's agreeing to undertake espionage or subversive activity upon their return to Australia—with any extended family in the Soviet Union used as collateral, ensuring the act was carried out.[70] This could perhaps have been the fate of the Mikhailoff family, whose case even the typically dispassionate Spry thought a "rather pathetic one."[71] They were Russians from China. Olga Mikhailoff developed a kind of "cancer phobia" and, seeing friends diagnosed with the condition after migrating, believed something in the Australian water caused it. She decided she, her husband, and their teenage daughter had to repatriate, which almost tore the family apart—but in 1957 they departed together. Spry really did seem somewhat sympathetic to the Mikhailoffs; though he described Olga as "continually pester[ing]" her husband about return, the daughter was "thoroughly assimilated; she was doing very well at school . . . and very happy to be in Australia."[72] He seemed to think her an ideal type of "New Australian"—the kind who could actually increase Australia's security. But with the family desperate to return to Australia and Olga's brother still a resident in a Soviet collective farm, ASIO deemed it likely that the Mikhailoffs could be coerced into espionage and recommended rejection.

Spry was less sympathetic regarding the Pivnijev family. They repatriated in April 1957, returning to Soviet Russia, but after just seven months began petitioning British authorities for permission to return to Australia. Spry recognized that Nikita Pivnijev's discontent in Australia had been partly the result of having to work as a laborer, despite having engineering qualifications, but noted that the whole family had developed "strongly pro-communist and pro-Soviet ideas."[73] Spry didn't assess Pivnijev's son, twenty-three-year-old Viktor so favorably as the Mikhailoff girl: Viktor was "an intelligent man of intellectual tastes, much given to argument and theorising."[74] This, combined with his apparent technical abilities, and prior work as a translator for a Soviet team at the 1956 Olympics, made the young Pivnijev a prime candidate for espionage.[75] Spry seemed more circumspect

---

69. NAA: A6980, S201205: C. C. F. Spry to Secretary, DOI, April 11, 1958, f. 21.
70. NAA: A6980, S201205: Spry to Secretary, April 11, 1958, f. 20.
71. NAA: A6980, S201205: Spry to Secretary, April 11, 1958, f. 21.
72. NAA: A6980, S201205: Spry to Secretary, April 11, 1958, f. 21.
73. NAA: A6980, S201205: Spry to Secretary, April 11, 1958, f. 22.
74. NAA: A6980, S201205: Spry to Secretary, April 11, 1958, f. 22.
75. NAA: A6119, 7451: E. V. Wiggins to Director B2, March 14, 1958, f. 77.

regarding the family's pleas that they hated the Soviet Union, given the views they had apparently displayed in Australia. And as with the Mikhailoffs, Spry thought it highly likely that they might be convinced or coerced into working for the Soviets. Indeed, the family's somewhat lower profile in Australia (as compared with the Frankels) actually worked against them: they would be an even better choice for Soviet intelligence, having attracted less attention previously.[76] Further, Spry noted the possibility that these were "pilot cases" by which the Soviets could establish a precedent with Australian immigration; more "repentant repatriates" would follow and, among them, spies.[77]

With the Frankel family, however, Spry acknowledged that Australia's position was more difficult. Abraham Frankel, the "repatriation worker," had departed with his wife Tania and three Australian-born children: Genia (aged twelve), Boris (ten), and Maia (just two). The family—soon disillusioned with the Soviet Union—blamed Abraham's decision to return to the USSR on wily propaganda and persistent letters from his sister.[78] As they boarded a Soviet-bound ship, Abraham told a reporter, "I wasn't forced—I'm homesick."[79] But Abraham had left for Palestine with his parents as a boy and had only brief, childhood experiences of Soviet Russia. His keen desire to return was motivated by his long involvement with pro-Soviet groups in Australia, including as a member of the Australian Communist Party.[80] This concerned Spry: given Frankel's involvement with both Australian Communists and Soviet officials, Spry thought him an "obvious candidate" for the category of Soviet spy.[81] Perhaps, the Director-General mused, this had been the plan for Frankel all along: use repatriation to return him to base, train "him in some particular role," and then send him back to Australia.[82] Spry acknowledged that, given how openly Frankel had involved himself with Australian leftists, he probably wasn't much good for espionage now, but could work on subversion: encouraging repatriation, promoting Soviet culture and life, and perhaps "talent-spotting" for Soviet intelligence on the side. Because—and here Spry highlighted the most devious part of this potential plan—with his Australian-born children, the Soviets probably thought that Australia could not refuse Frankel.[83]

---

76. NAA: A6119, 7451: DDG Ops, re. Pivnijev, March 20, 1958, f. 79.

77. NAA:A6980, S201205: Spry to Secretary, April 11, 1958, f. 19–20.

78. NAA: A1209, 1959/491, "Boris and Genia Frankel—Assistance to return to Australia": B. Frankel & G. Frankel to R. Menzies, undated, f. 1.

79. "I wasn't forced—I'm homesick; Russian Returns after 18 Years," *The Argus*, May 8, 1956, 5.

80. NAA: A1838, 1453/4137: T. Frankel to Minister for External Affairs, April 28, 1960, f. 87; Interview with Mr. Frankel, September 28 1961, f. 151.

81. NAA: A6980, S201205: Spry to Secretary, April 11, 1958, f. 20.

82. NAA: A6980, S201205: Spry to Secretary, April 11, 1958, f. 20.

83. NAA: A6980, S201205: Spry to Secretary, April 11, 1958, f. 20.

And could they refuse Australian-born children? Spry thought not. He wrote that they were "Australians by birth, and have a right to be here."[84] Further, he conceded (almost compassionately) that "we should not, if we can safely avoid it, leave young Australians to grow up in the environment of Soviet Russia."[85] He thought they should allow the children back, accompanied by their mother, but that Abraham was too great a security risk (now not mentioning the risk of family left behind becoming Soviet collateral). The Department of Immigration decided to reject the entire family, even though the children had citizenship, to avoid separating them.[86]

The Frankel children and their mother did, eventually, make it back to Australia. The two teenaged children, Boris and Genia, made a solo trip to Moscow and managed to sway the opinion of the British Ambassador, who made representations to Prime Minister Menzies on their behalf.[87] The Ambassador, Sir Patrick Reilly, saw the Frankel children as "patently young Australians," telling Menzies that "unless the children are consummate actors, they have certainly now had a strong inoculation against communism and to the best of my judgement they should prove loyal citizens of Australia, where their hearts seem undoubtedly to lie."[88] This diplomatic pressure—and concerns about optics within the Department of Immigration—saw Spry's original advice win out.[89] The children and their mother were repatriated to Australia, though Abraham had to stay behind in Soviet Ukraine.[90] The family fought for another three years to have Abraham readmitted to Australia. ASIO consented to this only after Frankel was interviewed, on their own brief, by a senior diplomat at the Australian Embassy in Moscow. Spry continued to grumble that he was "not over impressed" with Frankel's answers, but eventually withdrew his security objection.[91]

84. NAA: A1209, 1959/491: W. G. A. Landale, DEA, to Secretary, DOI, April 22, 1959, f. 8; Spry to Secretary, April 11, 1958, f. 12.

85. NAA: A1209, 1959/491: Spry to Secretary, April 11, 1958, f. 12.

86. NAA: A1209, 1959/491: H. McGinness, Acting Secretary DOI, to DG ASIO, June 18, 1959, f. 18.

87. NAA: A1209, 1959/491: Sir Patrick Reilly, British Ambassador to the Soviet Union, to Richard Casey, Minister for External Affairs, April 2, 1959, f. 2–5. The Australian Embassy in Moscow did not reopen until diplomatic relations resumed in 1959—hence the Frankel children had to visit the British Embassy.

88. NAA: A1209, 1959/491: P. Reilly to R. Menzies, April 3, 1959, f. 6.

89. NAA: A6980, S201205: A. W. Bazley, Secret Memo for Acting Secretary, DOI, May 29, 1959, f. 74; H. McGinness, Assistant Secretary, Secret Memo for Acting Secretary, DOI, June 2, 1959, f. 86; R. R. Downer, Memo for T. H. E. Heyes, Secretary, DOI, July 27, 1959, f. 94.

90. NAA: A1209, 1959/491: A. R. Downer, Minister for Immigration, to R. Menzies, August 18, 1959, f. 28; Prime Minister's Department to Australian High Commission London, March 11, 1960, f. 35.

91. NAA: A6980, S201206, "FRANKEL Abraham—part 2": C. C. F. Spry to Secretary, DOI, November 21, 1961, f. 276.

The Frankel case became a point of reference for ASIO just a few weeks later, when it considered Juris Pintans' petitions for re-entry. Pintans, the letter-writing "repatriation worker," had returned to Soviet Latvia in 1960 with his wife and five children, two of whom were Australian-born. The Pintans family, too, struggled with Soviet life.[92] In 1961, Juris traveled to the Australian Embassy in Moscow with his eldest daughter (who was not Australian-born), demanding that his two younger, Australian-born children be repatriated, as he waved their birth certificates at the embassy secretaries.[93] Unlike the sympathetic Sir Patrick Reilly, Australian officials asked Pintans and his daughter to leave. The First Secretary wrote to Canberra rather skeptically; he thought that their "story did not hang together ... [they] were reasonably dressed and far from the verge of starvation."[94]

Spry, having only recently signed off on Abraham Frankel's return, gave the same initial assessment he had used with the Frankels. The two youngest Pintans children, Australian-born, had a right of return, so ASIO would approve of them, their siblings, and their mother being resettled, but not their father. He developed a new argument for this, too, writing that "there is grave risk that the two Australian born children would be brought up in Russia as communists and might easily be returned by the Soviet Union to Australia as espionage agents when they reach maturity."[95] Better that the children return immediately and grow up as Australians, than return later as Communist spies. Their father, however, had spent his chance: ASIO assessed that he had "failed after 7 years to settle] down to life in Australia ... [and so] there seems no likelihood that he would ever become a loyal and contented Australian citizen if given another opportunity to do so."[96] But Immigration, as in the Frankel case, chose to reject the whole family outright rather than split them up.[97] The Pintans family would never return to Australia.

The differing outcomes were probably a product of contingency—particularly the reopening of the Australian Embassy in Moscow, just after the Frankel children's visit. But ASIO's assessments were consistent. In both cases, Spry considered that the Australian-born children's right to return couldn't be ignored. Further, since they were young, he thought they could probably be brought up as assimilated, loyal Australians if hastily returned. But Juris and Abraham were a different story. In the case of both fathers, their past actions made them an ongoing security risk.

---

92. Latvijas Valsts arhīvs (Latvian State Archive, hereafter LVA): Fond 1986, Criminal cases of persons accused of particularly dangerous anti-state crimes by the Committee for State Security (KGB) of the Latvian SSR, Series 1, Latvian Register of Politically Repressed Persons, Item 44701, Minutes of Court Hearing, March 16–17, 1962, Supreme Court LSSR; Report of Colonel Vasil'ev, Deputy Chief of KGB 2nd Department, LSSR, December 6, 1961.

93. NAA: A6119, 7049: H. S. North, Embassy Second Secretary, to Secretary, DEA, December 8, 1961, f. 137.

94. NAA: A6119, 7049: North to Secretary, December 8, 1961, f. 136.

95. NAA: A6119, 7049: Note for File, February 9, 1962, f. 145.

96. NAA: A6119, 7049: ASIO Minute Paper, January 18, 1962, f. 141.

97. NAA: A6119, 7049: P. R. Heydon to DG ASIO, April 30, 1962, f. 146.

ASIO was never particularly good at dealing with changes in migrants' political views, usually suspecting that it was some kind of ruse.[98] Australia needed immigrants for security, but only those who proved their ability to assimilate, becoming loyal, preferably naturalized, Australians the first time around.

* * *

In the postwar period, immigration and national security became increasingly entwined in Australia. For its vast open spaces—surely attractive to the Communist powers lurking on Australia's doorstep in South East Asia—Australia needed migrants (preferably white ones). It needed them to populate land, but also factories, railways, farms, hospitals, and new industrial sites. As a domestic intelligence organization, ASIO played a key role in screening and then monitoring these new arrivals, ensuring that their activities and associations aligned with Australia's anti-Communism. But migrant departures were also a security risk. ASIO was particularly concerned about the possibility of espionage when it considered Soviet repatriates. Departures for the East could mean Soviet spies being brought in (with information and new experience) but could also represent a failure of Australia's immigration program. Returnees often mentioned their difficulties with the two-year work contract, or other Australian conditions, and ASIO was, to some extent, receptive to these. But its officials were also likely to judge that migrants desiring to return had been duped by Soviet officials and propaganda. And, sometimes, they probably had been. Though they had struggled with Australian conditions, a few families struggled with Soviet ones too, and tried to re-enter Australia. But ASIO was not usually inclined to give second chances. The security service deemed migrants who had repatriated too great a security risk, even if their circumstances made a compelling case for compassionate treatment. Soviet repatriates with Australian-born children were more difficult, but they could be returned without the offending family member—in these cases, their fathers—if it seemed they could become the loyal citizens Australia needed.

Ultimately, at least in Spry's view, the desire to repatriate was a failure of assimilation. In some circumstances—particularly during the early 1950s—he saw this as the Department of Immigration's responsibility, and something it could mitigate with special provisions and support for Soviet migrants desiring to return. The department disagreed—or didn't feel it had the capacity for this task. As the 1950s progressed, ASIO's assessments tended to shift the onus onto the migrant. With time and opportunity to assimilate, perhaps the responsibility now lay with them. And if they continued to be discontented, to discuss return, and to agitate those around them, at some point this could become subversion: sabotage against Australia's migration efforts. Australia needed to maintain public confidence in its immigration program, among migrants (to ensure they stayed, and that more arrived) and the community at large (to ensure it accepted them). So ASIO watched, recorded, and assessed departures, all in the pursuit of security.

98. Ebony Nilsson, "The Enemy Within: Left-wing Soviet Displaced Persons in Australia," Ph.D. dissertation, University of Sydney, 2020, 205.

Chapter 5

REPATRIATION FROM AUSTRALIA OF POSTWAR RUSSIAN MIGRANTS: THE SOVIET PERSPECTIVE

Sheila Fitzpatrick

At the end of World War II, there were over five million Soviet citizens—POWs, wartime forced laborers, voluntary border-crossers—in Germany and other parts of the former Reich, and the Soviet Union wanted them all home. Mandatory repatriation, conducted in 1945 in cooperation with the Western Allies, got most of them back, but a residue of close to half a million remained, unwilling to repatriate.[1] Most of them were in displaced person (DP) camps in the Western occupation zones, many disguising their origins—with Allied connivance—to evade forced repatriation.

UNRRA—the United Nations Relief and Rehabilitation Agency, in charge of displaced persons at the end of the war—was uncertain what to do with those who refused to repatriate. But when the International Refugee Organization (IRO) took over from UNRRA in mid-1947, it had a plan: resettlement outside Europe in countries like the US, Australia, Canada, and Latin America. This provoked outrage in the Soviet Union (not a party to IRO, which was basically US-financed, though it had been a member of UNRRA), which regarded the resettlement as theft of its citizens.[2] The whole thing became one of the early issues of conflict in the Cold War. On IRO's part, it involved recasting the DPs from being victims of "war and fascism" to being "victims of Communism" (since, although displaced by the war, the countries of Eastern Europe from which they came, and to which they did not wish to repatriate, were now Communist).

---

1. This introductory discussion draws on Sheila Fitzpatrick, *White Russians, Red Peril: A Cold War History of Migration to Australia* (Melbourne: Black, Inc., 2021), ch. 1. Figures from V. N. Zemskov, *Vozvrashchenie sovetskikh peremeshchennykh lits v SSSR, 1944–1952 gg.* (Moscow and St. Petersburg: Tsentr gumanitarnykh initsiativ, 2016), 127; V. N. Zemskov, "Rozhdenie 'vtoroi emigratsii', 1944–1952," *Sotsiologicheskie issledovaniia* 4 (1991): 21.

2. See Sheila Fitzpatrick, "The Motherland Calls: 'Soft' Repatriation of Soviet Citizens from Europe, 1945–1953," *Journal of Modern History* 90, no. 2 (2018): 327–8, 349–50.

When Australia signed on to be a resettlement place for DPs in 1947, its primary interest was in acquiring labor and population rather than acquiring anti-Communist migrants. But, like all the other resettlement countries, it implicitly required an affirmation of anti-Communism (demonstrating that the applicant was a political rather than economic refugee) to get through the selection process. These affirmations were no doubt usually genuine, although the fact that they were, in effect, mandatory to obtain a ticket out means that we cannot take them entirely at face value. The mood in the DP camps was strongly anti-Communist, partly because the Soviet definition of "Soviet citizen" (i.e., a person liable for repatriation) included those from the Baltic states and western Ukraine whose countries had been forcibly incorporated into the Soviet Union by the terms of the Nazi-Soviet Pact of 1939. The DP camps also included many at risk of being punished as Nazi collaborators who had added reason to fear and dislike the Soviet Union.

The Soviet Union continued its repatriation efforts (now largely based on persuasion) after the breakdown of Allied cooperation, and even after the resettlement of DPs outside Europe. For this purpose, in late 1951 the Soviet Union sent out two agents under diplomatic cover, Anatoly Gordeev and Dmitry Pavlov, to encourage resettled DPs who were former Soviet citizens to repatriate and offer them free passages.[3] Their repatriation efforts found little resonance in the Russian émigré community, as a whole strongly anti-Communist, with an influential activist minority associated with NTS (the National Labour Union, a conspiratorial international émigré organization dedicated to the overthrow of the Soviet regime), and clustered around the Orthodox Church. But there was a small pro-Soviet minority of Russians and Russian speakers (Jews, Latvians, Ukrainians, etc.) that dissented, forming its own much smaller community around centers like Sydney's Russian Social Club.[4] Here the repatriation agents were able to meet DPs who were sympathetic to the Soviet Union, though in most cases not to the point of wanting to return there.

In these same years, starting in the late 1940s and continuing until the late 1950s, Australia took in a separate stream of Russian migrants—the "White Russians" and Russian-speaking Jews who had spent the interwar years in China and left with the Communist takeover there in 1949.[5] Historically anti-Communist, this group had nevertheless had a different recent relationship with the USSR: during World War II, many "China" Russians became patriotic supporters of the Soviet fight against the Germans, and many also had friends and families who,

---

3. See Sheila Fitzpatrick, "Soviet Repatriation Efforts among 'Displaced Persons' Resettled in Australia, 1950–1953," *Australian Journal of Politics and History* 63, no. 1 (2017): 45, 51.

4. Ebony Nilsson, "The 'Enemy Within': Left-Wing Soviet Displaced Persons in Australia," Ph.D. dissertation, University of Sydney, 2021.

5. For more detailed discussion of the "China" Russians, see Fitzpatrick, *White Russians, Red Peril*, Part II.

faced with departure from China in one direction or another in the late 1940s and 1950s, had chosen repatriation and returned to the Soviet Union. The Soviet undercover agents who arrived in Canberra in late 1951 targeted only DPs from Europe. But in subsequent years, some "China" Russians also decided to repatriate from Australia for various reasons. By this time, an informal community of China repatriates had formed in various towns of resettlement in the Urals and Siberia.[6] This implied a different equation with regard to repatriation from that of the European DPs, who had severed their ties with relatives back home, faced danger as suspected Nazi collaborators if they returned, and had no equivalent community in the Soviet Union to ease re-entry.

This chapter focuses primarily on repatriation of DPs from Australia in the late 1940s and early 1950s, drawing on material in Russian (formerly Soviet) archives, primarily reports from undercover repatriation agents. This unusual perspective offers an intriguing comparison with that of Australian intelligence surveyed in this volume by Ebony Nilsson. My chapter will also address the question of repatriation to the Soviet Union of "China" Russians, on the basis of individual cases, most of which were the subject of memoirs or articles in the Russian-language community historical journal, *Avstraliada*—again, a perspective that offers an interesting comparison to that of the ASIO view described in Nilsson's chapter. The Soviet perspective on non-returning, actively anti-Communist DP migrants is unfortunately not accessible through either of these sources. But Soviet intelligence services undoubtedly did their best to plant agents and informers among them, and such fragmentary information as is available is included in my discussion.

The Soviet Repatriation Mission of 1952

The task facing Gordeev and Pavlov was complex for a number of reasons. In the first place, their intelligence agency (the GRU) was at odds with the competing Soviet security service, the MVD/MGB, whose undercover agent Vladimir Petrov (the Soviet diplomat who defected in 1954) had handled repatriation before their arrival; and Petrov was instructed not to share information with them. In the second place, they were operating in Australia in a context of the burgeoning Cold War, which meant that the Australian authorities regarded them with suspicion and placed various restrictions on them. Gordeev was uncertain whether he was allowed, as a Soviet diplomat, to visit the migrant camps, but in any case he was too afraid of the Australian police to do so.[7]

---

6. See Laurie Manchester, "Repatriation to a Totalitarian Homeland: the Ambiguous Alterity of Russian Repatriates from China to the USSR," *Diaspora* 16, no. 3 (2007).

7. GARF (Gosudarstvennyi arkhiv Rossiiskoi Federatsii/State Archive of the Russian Federation): 9526/6s/888, ll. 87 (Gordeev to Moscow [April–May, 1952]); GARF: 9526/6s/836, l. 124: "Kratkii obzor po repatriatsii peremshchennykh sovetskikh grazhdan za 1950 g." [1951].

The migrants were also suspicious. The rumor in the DP camps—incorrect, as it turned out—had been that, whatever promises were made to lure them back, repatriates were sent to the Gulag as soon as they crossed the border.[8] Any contact with the Soviet Embassy or Soviet personnel was regarded as dangerous in the Australian Russian community, partly from memory of Europe, where DPs feared kidnapping or other pressure to repatriate, and partly out of (justified) fear that any such contact would bring them to the unfavorable notice of the Australian authorities.

Making contact with resettled DPs who might be persuaded to repatriate was a big problem for Gordeev. He did not have access to Australian immigration lists of arrivals, so had to painstakingly assemble his own list, never more than a few hundred. His instructions were to follow-up on resettled Soviet DPs whose Soviet families had discovered their addresses and written to them (sometimes on their own initiative, sometimes coached by the authorities) asking them to return, but the results of this were meagre. The local mainstream Russian community was obviously not going to cooperate and read out Soviet appeals from the pulpits. One of the few places that the Soviet agents could actually meet DPs was at the left-wing Russian Social Club (RSC) in Sydney. This was already a hangout for Petrov and others from the embassy, and Gordeev seems not to have been encouraged by his colleagues to frequent it, but he did anyway, usually late at night, and made a few contacts.

Those most willing to talk to him were young single men of Soviet sympathies, often too young to remember the actual USSR, but at odds with their fathers' willingness to leave and/or remain in the West, feeling themselves rootless and unhappy in Australia.[9] With some of these, however, there was a problem of citizenship. Repatriation was only available to persons whose Soviet citizenship had been confirmed from Moscow; and it could be a problem if—as often happened—the DP had come to Australia under another nationality, such as Polish. Serge Volodar, the son of Russian emigrants born in Yugoslavia, failed to quality, as did Kuzma Muratidi, born of a Soviet Greek family from Crimea that had been deported to Central Asia during war and, after the war, allowed to emigrate to Greece (thus losing their Soviet citizenship) before migrating to Australia in 1950.[10]

---

8. See discussion in Fitzpatrick, "The Motherland Calls," 343–6. Of the more than 4 million repatriated to the Soviet Union by March 1946, only 7 percent were sent to the Gulag, while almost 60 percent were returned directly to their prewar homes. At the same time, repatriates undoubtedly faced discrimination on their return, both from the authorities and their neighbors.

9. See, for example, Gordeev's conversations with DP migrants George Marfutenko and Vyacheslav Schinkewitsch in GARF, Moscow: 9526/6s/888, l.79, 85, 87, 143–4; 206–14 (Marfutenko) and ll. 172–3, 206–14, 220 (Schinkewitsch); also Jascha Zelensky (below).

10. GARF: 9526/6/888, ll. 148–50 (Volodar), 153–5 (Muratidi).

The results of Gordeev's mission were disappointing: a mere twenty-four repatriates from Australia in 1951–2, nine of them dependents.[11] This constituted less than half of 1 percent of the 50,000 Soviet DPs estimated by the Soviet authorities to have been resettled in Australia.[12] (The comparable results from North America, however, were even worse.)[13] Of the fifteen non-dependent Australian repatriates, all but two were functionally single, and all but two were male, mainly in their late twenties. "Single," however, was a relative term, which should not be taken to mean that the repatriants had never been married. One of the men admitted to leaving a wife in Germany and another had a wife back in the USSR. Of the two "single" women in the group, one had had two recent husbands (perhaps bigamously).[14] Two family households—at fifty-year-old widower taking his four young sons back to the Soviet Union and a man in his early forties, repatriating with wife, mother, and two children—together made up almost half of the total group.

The repatriates were all, necessarily, Soviet citizens, but in the multinational Soviet Union, citizens also officially possessed a nationality. "Russians" were the largest group among the Australian repatriates, followed by "Ukrainians." But this categorization was also complicated. Due to the complexities of DP life (where identifying as a Russian could be disadvantageous), some of the Russians had identified at times as Ukrainian and several had arrived in Australia calling themselves Poles. Even their earlier Soviet lives were not entirely straightforward with regard to nationality: one "Russian" had been born in Latvia to a Russian father and Ukrainian mother; another, born in Kazakhstan, had spent most of his

---

11. The following repatriations from Australia are recorded for 1951–2 in Soviet sources: Nadezhda Berilko, Russian, born 1924; Petr Bronsky (Nikanorov), Ukrainian, born 1922; Vasily Petrovich Gvozdetsky, Ukrainian, born 1925; Nikolai Vasilevich Ialynychev, Russian, born 1925; Iosif Zinovevich Ivanov, Russian, born 1913; Pavel Ivanovich Kapustin, Russian, born 1910 (repatriating with wife, mother, and two children); Vladimir Rodionovich Knagis, Latvian, born 1911; Pavel Klementevich Komar, Ukrainian, born 1901 (repatriating with four sons); Aleksandr Lekhner (no further information other than that he had been living in Sydney and unemployed for a considerable time); Elena Fedorovna Nesterovskaya (Mauers), Russian, born 1920; Grigory Efimovich Salnikov, Jewish, born 1919, whose repatriation was processed by the embassy in London; Ionas Nikodimovich Shaulinskas, Lithuanian, born 1922; Evgeny Shevelev, Russian, born 1924; Alfonsas Stankus, Lithuanian, born 1927 (1929?), who shipped out for repatriation in 1952 but disappeared en route in London; and Iakov Fomich Zelensky, Ukrainian, born 1929: data from GARF 9526/6s/ 888, 889, 1101. ASIO reported thirteen unnamed Soviet citizens repatriated in the period January–October 1952, with twelve more cases in the pipeline: Memo of Col. Spry (ASIO) to Tasman Heyes (Department of Immigration), October 20, 1952: NAA: A6980 S250323.

12. Zemskov, "Rozhdenie," 71.

13. GARF 9256/6s/1101 [file covering repatriations worldwide January 1951–December 1952].

14. See below on the twice-married Elena Nesterovskaya.

working life in Ukraine; while one of the "Latvians" had been born in Russian St. Petersburg.[15]

A range of reasons were offered for return in the repatriates' conversations with Soviet officials. These, of course, cannot be taken at face value: undoubtedly other motives were suppressed for one reason or another, and—out of the mix of motives that people normally have for any complex action—the ones most acceptable to the Soviets would surely be emphasized. Only one of the repatriates presented himself as an active Soviet patriot. This was twenty-three-year-old Jascha Zelensky (also rendered as Zilensky), a contact of Vladimir Petrov at the left-wing Russian Social Club, whose statements of belligerent Soviet patriotism pleased Petrov, who said "You are a good Soviet citizen already."[16] One of several young Russian DPs who blamed their fathers for leaving the USSR voluntarily during the war, Zelensky had evidently come to Australia with his parents, but broken off contact with them. He told Gordeev (who took over from Petrov as organizer of his repatriation) that anti-Communist Russians made life impossible for anyone who was thought to be planning to return to the Soviet Union—"you have to hide your intention to go home from your fellow countrymen," otherwise they will beat you up. Working as a loader in the warehouse of a Sydney hospital and living with eighteen people in one room in the hospital barracks, he said he earned scarcely enough for his food, but other employment was hard to find.[17] After his departure in March 1952, seen off by Gordeev and a Russian DP friend and arriving in Murmansk some weeks later, the rumor spread in the Australian Russian community that he had in fact been killed in Melbourne (unclear by whom) and never reached home. Gordeev had to write urging Moscow to get him to write to reassure his friends in the Russian Social Club that he was safe and well.[18]

Repatriates focused on dissatisfaction with Australia in explaining their decision to return to Soviet officials. Conditions of work during the contract labor phase were a particular source of grievance. Young Ukrainian peasant Vladimir Gvozdetsky was sent to work on a sugar plantation, forced to live in a tent where he was eaten by mosquitos, stricken by TB and stomach ulcers, and mocked by children; he was desperately unhappy and ready to kill himself.[19] Iosif Ivanov, a Russian from Riga nearing forty, had been "unemployed for a substantial period"

---

15. Berilko and Bronsky were Russians who had called themselves Ukrainians; Bronsky—as well as Kapustin, Shevelev, and Nesterovskaya—had at some point claimed to be Polish. Ivanov and Shevelev were the Russians born in Latvia and Kazakhstan; the Latvian Knagis had been born in Russia.

16. GARF: 9526/6s/836, l. 296; GARF: 9526/6s/888, ll. 79, 81, 154–5, 224; GARF: 9526/6s/1101; NAA (National Archive of Australia): A6119 1386 (report by Phillip Crane, December 10, 1951, on Petrov's party); NAA: A6122, 2799: Russian Social Club NSW, vol. I (quotation from ASIO report—thanks to Ebony Nilsson for drawing my attention to this).

17. GARF 9526/6s/888, ll. 154–5, 331–2.

18. GARF 9526/6s/890, l. 79.

19. GARF 9526/6s/888, ll. 180, 223, 320–3; 9526/6s/1101.

in Australia.[20] Widower Pavel Komar was unhappy both in his assigned manual job and in later work on a farm; and he wanted to take his four sons, aged eleven to sixteen, home.[21]

A desire to reunite with family was often given as a motive by voluntary repatriates from Europe (many of whom were women),[22] but in the Australian group (almost all men) only Natalia Berilko seemed concerned about family back home: she was worried that her emigration had caused political difficulties for her mother in Kharkov.[23] Peter Bronsky (Petr Bronskii/Bronski), who had been her fellow-worker at Kew Mental Hospital, was a former POW and DP in a Munich camp in Germany. He was first contacted by Gordeev as a friend of another Russian DP contact in Melbourne in July 1952, three years after his arrival in Australia. To ASIO, he was a Ukrainian born in Poland, as stated on his DP and Australian entry documents; to the Soviets he was a Russian who also went by the name Petr Nikanorov.[24] Paraguay had been his first choice of destination, which may partially explain the problems of assimilating he described to ASIO in an interview.[25] He was helpful to Gordeev in Melbourne by introducing him to some more Soviet DPs (who prudently did not give Gordeev their last names),[26] but was still hesitating about repatriation: "In conversation he said he had written a letter to his relatives and his decision on return to the native land depends on their answer."[27] When he actually departed—on the *Genoa*, with Berilko, in December 1952, farewelled at the dock by Gordeev and Pavlov—both repatriates seemed "happy and excited," according to ASIO's report.[28]

The migrants most resentful of their contract job assignments were often educated people who despaired (not wholly without reason) of ever getting back into their previous professions. Dmitry Uglicki (Uglitsky) and his wife Zinaida fell into this category: both born in 1907, they were university graduates who had held responsible professional jobs in Voronezh before and during the German occupation, and at the end of the war had departed with the Germans because they feared accusations of collaboration when the Soviets returned. They put in their repatriation application in 1950, while living in Broadmeadows Migrant Camp and still working off their contracts, but later withdrew it and stayed in Australia.

20. GARF 9526/6s/890, l. 63.

21. GARF 9526/6s/888, ll. 217–18 (interview).

22. See Sheila Fitzpatrick, "The Women's Side of the Story: Soviet 'Displaced Persons' and Postwar Repatriation," *Russian Review* 81 (April 2022): 284–301.

23. GARF 9526/6s/888, l. 81; NAA, A6122 2739: ASIO Victoria report of December 1953.

24. Bad Arolsen archives, ITS file on Bronsky, Peter (thanks to Jayne Persian for this information); NAA 11599, 28, 4102763: "Bronsky (Bronski), Peter."

25. ITS file on Bronsky, Peter.

26. GARF 9526/6s/890, l. 74.

27. GARF 9526/6s/890, l. 86.

28. NAA: A6122 2739.

(Zinaida would later get a Ph.D. and work in the University of Melbourne's Russian Department.)[29] The Kapustins were a similar case, except that they actually did repatriate, citing a belief that their children, aged eleven and nine, would have a better future in the Soviet Union (presumably a reflection on Australia's cultural level as they perceived it).[30] Even ASIO Director Colonel Spry had some sympathy with their plight, noting in letter to Immigration Secretary Heyes:

> When asked why he wished to return to the USSR, KAPUSTIN said, "I cannot live all my life on a concrete floor. I cannot work all my life as a labourer." For the past two years, KAPUSTIN and his family have been residing in a large unused poultry feed-shed and he is employed as a joiner. It is understood that he graduated as a Doctor at Kiev University in 1941 and that his wife is an industrial chemist.[31]

Mental illness in various guises was part of the story of a number of repatriation cases. This must be seen in the context of a fairly high rate of psychiatric disturbance among DPs recorded both in Germany and after arrival in Australia, and the fact that such states would be liable to produce both statements of a desire to repatriate and repudiations of such statements, often within a short space of time. But the Soviets had their own way of seeing the high incidence of psychiatric hospitalization episodes, namely as a sign that Australia was trying to prevent repatriation by punitive psychiatric arrests (ironically, something the Soviets themselves would be accused of a decade or so later with regard to dissidents). This suspicion received worldwide dissemination in March 1952 when the Soviet government newspaper *Izvestiia* published an article entitled "Present-day American Slave Traders," alleging that the capitalist states wanted Soviet DPs as "slave labour," and used psychiatric hospitalization as one of their tools for retaining control over any migrant who might show a wish to repatriate, citing the Australian case of Nikolai Bezugly (aka Morgan). Like the Uglitskys, Bezugly/Morgan put in an application for repatriation and been accepted by the Soviet authorities, but after being hospitalized for schizophrenia he apparently changed his mind. The Soviets were suspicious about this and had their embassy raise the question with the Australian government. After investigation, Australia reported back that "Mr. Morgan" was in Royal Park Mental Hospital, suffering paranoid delusions and sometimes violent, and was unlikely to recover.[32] (It is not clear what happened to his wife, who had also wished to repatriate, and their young children.)

---

29. GARF 9526/6s/888, l. 228; GARF 9526/6s/890, l. 83; GARF 9526/6s/888.
30. GARF 9526/6s/890, l. 70.
31. NAA, A6980, S250323: Spry to Heyes, October 28, 1952.
32. GARF: 9526/6s/888, l. 222: G. Mikhailov and G. Semenov, "Present-day American Slave-Traders," translation from *Izvestiia*, March 23, 1952, in NAA: A6980 S250323; GARF: 9526/6s/836; NAA: A462 867/2/29, "Mr. Bezugly (aka Morgan)." GARF, 9526/6s/136, l. 125; GARF: 9526/6s/888, l. 83.

Two male repatriates, Latvian Vladimir Knagis and Lithuanian Alfons Stankus told stories that fitted the Soviet template. Knagis cited pressure put on him by Australian authorities to get psychiatric treatment, after he got in trouble with the police, as the main reason he decided to repatriate (and thus escape their clutches),[33] while Stankus claimed to have been forcibly consigned to a mental hospital, from which he escaped, as well as beaten and taunted on the streets by Australians. Stankus, incidentally, was the only repatriate who departed Australian shores but failed to arrive in the Soviet Union—he skipped out of his London hotel in transit between the two boat trips, returning briefly with an English bobby to pick up his things before vanishing into the blue.[34] A Latvian repatriate chronicled by Ebony Nilsson had a spell in a mental hospital *after* his repatriation, when he proved a troublemaker to the Soviet authorities.[35]

Adventurers—people who had used displacement as a stepping-stone for seeing the world and were now ready to come home—were another identifiable category of repatriates.[36] As might be expected, most of them were young single men. Ivan Gladyshev, using a false name in Australia (Aleksandr Nikolaevich Granin, according to Gordeev), had arrived in Germany as a forced laborer around the age of twenty, been repatriated and drafted into the Soviet Army, and then deserted from a posting in Germany "to do a bit of travelling." He managed to see Germany, Switzerland, Luxemburg, France, Belgium, Holland, Denmark, Sweden, Norway, and, as a member of the French Foreign Legion, North Africa, before getting himself to Australia as a DP (which he wasn't) in 1951. He told Gordeev about a White Russian club in Adelaide "conducting active anti-Soviet and anti-repatriation propaganda." He also said migrant workers in Australia were deprived of rights, including medical coverage, and claimed to have been fired from his job in the summer of 1952. Gordeev, not usually censorious, thought he was a conman ("with such a man, it is hard straight away to believe in the sincerity of his intentions," but put his name forward for repatriation anyway).[37]

Gladyshev did not in the end repatriate, although whether this was because he changed his mind or because the Soviets (uncharacteristically) turned him down is not clear.[38] Grigory Salnikov, born 1919, a Jew from Soviet Ukraine passing as Russian, actually did repatriate. His travels before coming to Australia in 1948 took

33. GARF: 9526/6s/888, ll. 74–5, 81, 84, 132, 180, 187 (Knagis).
34. GARF 9526/6s/890, ll. 28, 69, 71, 73, 99.
35. See Nilsson chapter in this volume.
36. For more on adventurers, see Sheila Fitzpatrick, "The Prodigal's Return: Voluntary Repatriation from Displaced Persons Camps in Europe to the Soviet Union, 1949–50," *Cahiers du monde russe* 62, no. 4 (2021): 529–51.
37. GARF 9526/6s/890, ll. 61, 69, 71–2. Gladyshev/Granin is not listed among arriving repatriates in the GARF files, so probably he changed his mind. NAA files register neither the arrival nor naturalization of anyone with either of those names, suggesting that he used yet another name on entry to Australia.
38. GARF: 9526/6/889, ll. 421–3 (interview), 424; GARF: 9526/6s/890, l. 71 (report).

him to Poland, Hungary, France, Algeria, and Morocco; and after spending six months in Australia he went on (according to his account) to England, the Canary Islands, and West Africa before repatriating from London. On his return to the Soviet Union, he told Soviet officials about Russians in migrant camps near Perth and Melbourne, naming two that he thought worked for American intelligence and offered a detailed description of a film showing at the University of Melbourne organized by the Australia-Soviet society for cultural relations. Otherwise he volunteered little other than that he had worked on repairs on the railways (officials noted that he "had forgotten a lot, or perhaps more precisely did not want to show his knowledge for some kind of personal reason").[39]

An adventurer in a slightly different register was Elena Nesterovskaia, who told Gordeev that she was a Russian born in Kronstadt who grew up in Soviet Ukraine and was taken to Germany during the war as a forced laborer. (As a DP she had claimed to be Polish, but changed this to "stateless, previously Ukrainian" in a 1948 statement to the Australians.)[40] She claimed she had been taken to Germany during the war as an Ostarbeiter. In Germany after the war, she managed to get some university education and married a fellow DP, the Russo-Polish Yugoslav-born Mstislav Chlopoff, with whom she came to Australia in August 1948. They both seem to have hated Australia and refused to abide by the terms of their contracts, for which her husband was deported back to Germany, expecting—or so he later said—his wife to follow with their possessions. Elena, however, told Australian authorities that they were divorced and that she had married again, this time allegedly an Australian. Whether this was so or not, she soon came up with another plan, namely to repatriate (without either husband) to the Soviet Union. The Soviets accepted her, despite the oddness of her story, although she had trouble getting her exit visa from the Australians because of her lack of an official document of divorce, and she duly departed on the *Oceania*, reaching St. Petersburg on Christmas Day, 1952.[41]

Repatriation of "China" Russians

Whereas for the Soviet DPs coming from Europe, "repatriation" had a fearsome ring because of its associations with forced repatriation just after the war and the kidnapping of war criminals by Smersh[42] in subsequent years, the "China" Russians were more likely to think of it in more benign terms, as one of the available options

---

39. GARF: 9526/6/669, ll. 112–14: repatriation interview in Leningrad, October 2–3, 1949. For more on him, see Fitzpatrick, "Prodigal's Return."

40. NAA: A11855, 737, Helena Nesterovskaja.

41. GARF 9526/6s/888, ll. 206–14; GARF 9526/6s/890, ll. 73, 75, 79; Bad Arolsen, ITS file #6501 (thanks to Jayne Persian for this); NAA A11855, 737: Helena Nesterovskaja.

42. A Soviet counter-intelligence agency operating in the years 1943–6 whose tasks included tracking down Soviet war criminals.

in the late 1940s and 1950s if departure from China became inevitable. There was a sinister history of repatriation from China too, notably mass arrests during the Great Purges of a large number of Harbin Russians repatriating in 1935-7. But at the end of the war, when many Harbiners used Soviet passports as identity papers and had generally good relations with the briefly occupying Red Army, there were actually more Russians wanting to repatriate (from Shanghai and other coastal areas as well as Manchuria) than the Soviets were able to process. This meant that large-scale return migration from China had to wait until 1954, when repatriation became one of the means of recruiting labor for Khrushchev's Virgin Lands scheme in Kazakhstan. The numbers involved were considerable, and among the "China" Russians who came to Australia in the 1950s, most seem to have had friends or family who decided to repatriate rather than emigrate, while some admitted to having given it serious thought themselves.

Young Yury Skorniakov's family broke up when his father took his elder brother to the Soviet Union to work in the Virgin Lands, while his mother took Yury to Australia.[43] A young married couple, Natalia and Sviatoslav Prokopovich, decided to go to Australia (where Sviatoslav's elder sister had already gone) rather than the Virgin Lands only after long hesitation.[44] The Masloffs from Shanghai made the same decision, though other family members went to the Soviet Union.[45] Ludmila Lastrebova, working in Dairen when the Red Army arrived in 1945, fell in love with a Soviet officer and wanted to marry him (and presumably return with him to the Soviet Union), but was thwarted when the Soviet consulate refused to approve the officer's marriage with an emigrant, so she ended up going to Australia.[46] In the musical Abaza family from Harbin, two sisters went to Australia and their brother to the Soviet Union, where he graduated from the conservatorium.[47] Another musician, pianist Larisa Ramenskaia, was working in a choir in Harbin in the immediate postwar years: she was one of six members of the choir who went to Australia (she already had a brother in Sydney), while the rest returned to the Soviet Union and pursued careers in opera and operetta.[48] The Churkin family, who came from Urumchi, became separated in 1942, most of them ending up in the Soviet Union but one son coming to Australia.[49] Another Urumchi family, the Treskins, similarly separated, with one brother going to the Virgin Lands and another brother and sister going to Australia.

43. *Avstraliada* 19 (1999): 30-1.
44. *Avstraliada*, Supplement 2 (2000): 57-9. "Avtobiograficheskii ocherk N. N. Prokopovich (ur. Oparina)."
45. Antonia Finnane, *Far from Where? Jewish Journeys from Shanghai to Australia* (Melbourne: Melbourne University Press, 1999), 64-5, 218-19.
46. *Avstraliada* 29 (2001): 50-1. Lidiia Iastrebova, "Ludmila Panskaia."
47. *Avstraliada* 45 (2005): 30-1. E. B. and V. B.Abaza, "A.B.Abaza."
48. *Avstraliada* 46 (January 2006): 33-7.
49. *Avstraliada* 67 (April 2011): 2-11.

Once in Australia, it was harder for Russians to repatriate than it had been in China, but people sometimes thought of it or even did it. Lydia Hitrova (Khitrova), a member of the left-wing Russian Social Club in Sydney, did not like Australia and wanted to repatriate in the late 1950s, according to an ASIO report, but her mother was still in Harbin and she wanted to get her to Australia first so that they could repatriate together. In the event, she married another Russian migrant and stayed in Australia.[50] Another Russian Social Club habitué, Erik Levitsky from Shanghai, was reported by ASIO to be planning to return to the USSR because of his son's nervous breakdown in 1956—though in the end he stayed in Sydney, and died there at over a hundred years old. But the Koshevsky family—artist father Nikolai, mother Aleksandra, and teenage daughter Natasha—actually did repatriate three years after their arrival from China in 1951. This was basically because Natasha—beautiful, headstrong, and indulged—who, fresh from her Soviet school in Harbin, had become a Soviet patriot (although, born in China, she had never set foot in the country) and, more unusual in repatriates, a convinced socialist. The parents, to be sure, might not have acceded to her wishes had an exhibition of Nikolai's paintings at the David Jones Gallery not been panned by Australian critics. After their return, Nikolai Koshevsky found work in a provincial art school (a bit of a comedown from the days when his painting *Samurai and Bogatyr* had been bought for the Emperor's Palace in Tokyo during the Japanese occupation of China), while Natasha made her way to cosmopolitan Leningrad, where she was disappointed with Soviet socialism but nevertheless found a place in the cultural elite.[51]

A trickle of departures from the China and European DP contingents continued over subsequent decades. Lydia Savva's eldest son Evgeny, who had partially grown up in the Soviet Union, briefly repatriated in the 1950s before coming to Australia on his sister's invitation in 1961. She decided to go back to the Soviet Union at the age of eighteen after seven years in Australia, subsequently marrying in the USSR and making her home there.[52] Nikolai Apollonov, who came to Australia aged about twenty with his mother and brother in 1957, felt he didn't fit in (his long hair

---

50. NAA 6122, 2801 (thanks to Ebony Nilsson for this information).

51. On the shipboard denunciations, see *Sun*, September 21, 1951, 3; *Sydney Morning Herald*, September 22, 1951, 4; *Mail*, September 22, 1951, 4; *Advocate*, September 22, 1951, 1; *Brisbane Telegraph*, September 22, 1951, 2, supplemented by emails from Anastasia Fokina (Natasha's daughter, living in St. Petersburg, Russia; December 24, 2018 and March 15, 2019) and Evgeny Koshevsky (Natasha's grandson, September 4, 2018). Reviews of Nikolai's exhibition in *Sun* (Sydney), January 28, 1953, 13, and *Sydney Morning Herald*, January 28, 1953, 2. Repatriation: NAA A6980 S250276: L. Guest, "Nicolai Koschevsky, wife and daughter. Soviet Citizens—Return to Soviet Territory," December 22, 1954; interview by Sheila Fitzpatrick with Anastasia and Anna Fokina in St. Petersburg, Russia, June 9, 2019.

52. *Avstraliada* 69 (2011): 27–30. 50 let v Avstralii, mnogo eto ili malo? Lidiia Savva rasskazyvaet o svoei zhizni.

was criticized) and moved on to the Soviet Union in 1962. Fifteen years later, however, on his mother's urging, he returned to Australia.[53]

Agents and Informers

Fear and rumors about Soviet spies were rife within the postwar Russian community, as in other Baltic and East European ethnic groups with a large DP migrant contingent, and this fear was surely justified.[54] ASIO was also apprehensive about Soviet agents and informers among DP migrants, but whether it actually uncovered any is not known. (If it had, and turned them into double agents, their files would not yet have been declassified.) Another of ASIO's worries concerned repatriation. "Repatriates could form part of a plan for [Soviet] espionage," warned Colonel Spry, Director of ASIO, in 1952. "It is possible that the U.S.S.R. is developing a pool of persons experienced in Western life and conditions with experience of the various languages, for subsequent use at a later stage."[55] Given the shortage of shipping berths in the postwar period and the close monitoring of international departures by the Australian authorities, it was also likely that, if the Soviets had had an agent not accredited as a diplomat or journalist that it wished to return to base, they would have used the cover of a repatriating DP.

ASIO interviewed the departing repatriates without apparently identifying any of them as belonging to this category. But in fact there was one man, not a DP but repatriated as if he were one, who might fit the bill, judging by material in the Soviet archives. Nikolai Yalynycheff, born in 1925, was a Russian sailor who escaped from a Soviet ship in Alexandria. The Egyptian authorities arrested him, but the intervention of Vladimir Temnomerov, a Russian émigré official in IRO saved him and got him a visa and landing permit for Australia, for which he departed in February 1950.[56] Temnomeroff's efforts to get Yalynycheff classified as a "mass resettlement" DP migrant under IRO auspices had been unsuccessful. But when, after a few years in Australia, he applied to depart for the Soviet Union, he was processed as a repatriating DP. An ASIO interviewer found nothing untoward in Yalynycheff's pre-departure interview, merely recording a bit of gossip on the Russian community he had passed on.[57] The anomalies are in the Soviet handling

---

53. *Istoriia russkikh v Avstralii* (Sydney: Avstraliada, 2013), vol. 4, 162–3.

54. See, for example, the Soviet report of infiltration of a German DP camp in V. N. Khaustov et al., *Lubianka: Stalin I NKVD-NKGB-GUKR "Smersh," 1939-mart 1946* (Moscow: Materik, 2006), 550–52, and, for a fictionalized autobiographical account, V. I. Borin, *The Uprooted Survive: A Tale of Two Continents* (London: Heinemann, 1959).

55. NAA, A6980 S250323, ASIO Director Col. Spry to Department of Immigration, October 29, 1952.

56. *ITS archives*, Bad Arolsen, Archive number 6501 (Jayne Persian).

57. NAA A6122 2739.

of his case, details of which were of course unknown to ASIO at the time. Gordeev organized Yalynycheff's departure, along with other repatriates, but his reports back to Moscow contain none of the preliminary conversations and biographical details that normally preceded a decision to repatriate; and when Yalynycheff arrived back in the Soviet Union, his name, unlike that of his DP companions, was not in the repatriation agency's files of arrivals, suggesting that his case was special and handled by a state agency other than repatriation, presumably intelligence.[58]

The Russian diaspora was constantly alert for signs of Soviet penetration; mutual accusations of spying for the Soviets were a perennial staple of internal quarrels, both among émigré political groups and in the Orthodox Church. In Europe, anti-Soviet organizations like NTS and the Vlasovites (Soviet POWs who had joined the German-dominated anti-Soviet forces led by former Soviet general Andrei Vlasov) had a wartime history of collaboration with the Nazis, and Reinhard Gehlen's military intelligence operation quickly became enmeshed with Western intelligence agencies after the war, particularly the CIA. But they were equally notable for their susceptibility to penetration by Soviet intelligence, and complicated patterns of double agency abounded. In postwar Germany, there were "multiple known instances of Soviet penetration" of the anti-Soviet organization NTS—even the head of NTS operations, Georgy Okolovich, who worked closely with the American CIA, came under suspicion[59]—and the same was true of the Vlasovites.[60]

Both NTS and the Vlasovites had organizations in Australia whose members were almost all postwar arrivals from the European DP camps; and NTS's influence was particularly strong because the main Russian-language newspaper, *Unification* (*Edinenie*), was edited by an NTS activist, Oleg Perekrestov.[61] The sensational assassination attempts, defections, and Soviet kidnappings that formed part of the dramatic backdrop of émigré life in Germany were closely watched in Australia, not just by Russian migrants but in the Australian press. Aleksandr Trushnovich, who was kidnapped and killed in 1954, was a friend and former colleague of several leaders of the Melbourne Russian community, and the event was given top billing in the newspapers, trumping even the Royal Commission on espionage sparked by Petrov's defection that was going on at the same time.[62] Despite endemic alarm about Soviet penetration of the Russian émigré community in Australia, and a high degree of vicarious involvement in the European dramas,

---

58. GARF files containing Gordeev's interviews with prospective repatriates were where he should have shown up.

59. Benjamin Tromly, *Cold War Exiles and the CIA* (Oxford: Oxford University Press, 2019), 173, 178, 180 (quotation).

60. Tromly, *Cold War Exiles*, 59–65.

61. For a detailed discussion of NTS and other anti-Soviet organizations in Australia, see Fitzpatrick, *White Russians, Red Peril*, 189–98.

62. *Edinenie* 19 (May 7, 1954): 1: K. C. Halafoff, "Dr Alexander Trushnovich." A meeting of indignation about the Trushnovich kidnapping was held in Adelaide (*Edinenie* 22 [1954]).

no similar scandalous betrayals, unmaskings, murders, or kidnappings appear to have occurred in Russian anti-Soviet political organizations here.

Petrov's brief as a Soviet intelligence (MVD) agent had included making contact with the anti-Communist Russian migrant community, but in fact he was a lazy and unsuccessful agent and appears not even to have tried to carry out this assignment, contenting himself with frequenting the left-wing Russian Social Club and making a few contacts in the Canberra journalist-political world and the Communist Party. His only agent—not recruited by him, but reactivated on Moscow instructions from earlier recruitment in Riga in the early 1940s—was a Latvian DP who reported to him for a few years on the Latvian, but not the Russian, immigrant community in Australia.[63] Gordeev and Pavlov were officers of the competing Soviet intelligence network, the GRU, working under diplomatic cover, but they had been seconded to the civilian Repatriatian Agency, and their task in Australia seems to have been purely repatriation.[64]

There *were* some Soviet spies in the Russian Orthodox Church, outwardly a bastion of anti-Communism, as was confirmed decades later. But they had been recruited in Europe in the 1940s, and Petrov and other undercover personnel in Australia appear to have known nothing about them. The church in postwar Australia, staffed mainly by DP priests from Europe, recognized the jurisdiction of the strongly anti-Communist and anti-Soviet Russian Orthodox Church Abroad (ROCA), a competitor with the Soviet-sponsored Moscow Patriarchate for the allegiance of Russian Orthodox communities throughout the world. In the 1940s, when ROCA was based in Europe, it ordained many of the priests who, as DPs themselves, served in the DP camps and later came out to Australia and set up parishes, first in the migrant camps and then outside them. In the 1950s and 1960s, the Orthodox Church in Australia was riven by divisions, often between DP priests and parishioners from Europe and priests and parishioners from China whose parishes had, for a few years after World War II, come under the jurisdiction of the Moscow Patriarchate. The priests from China were less vehemently anti-Communist than the European ones, and the earlier-arriving Europeans often suspected them of Soviet sympathies.[65] In fact, however, the two spies in Australia's postwar Russian Orthodox Church unmasked after the fall of the Soviet Union were not from China but from Europe.

---

63. Wilhelm Agrell, *Mrs Petrov's Shoe* (London: I. B. Tauris, 2019), 112–13. The agent was Andrei Fridenbergs (Friedenbergs), who appears to have collaborated successively with the Soviet occupiers of Latvia and the German. He had tried to shed the Soviet intelligence connection, disappearing without informing his handlers that he was migrating to Australia, but they found him again when he wrote to his sister in Latvia. See Robert Manne, *The Petrov Affair* (Sydney: Pergamon, 1987), 211–13.

64. See Fitzpatrick, *White Russians, Red Peril*, 212. Petrov confirmed this in his testimony to the Royal Commission on Espionage.

65. See Michael Alex Protopopov, "The Russian Orthodox Presence in Australia," Ph.D. dissertation, Australian Catholic University, 2005, 242–8.

Father Igor Susemihl, brought up in a Russian émigré family in Berlin and drafted into the German Army during the war, was ordained as a priest by ROCA in Europe in 1947 and arrived in Australia two years later as a resettled DP. It is not clear exactly how he was recruited as a Soviet spy, but it was evidently before the war in Berlin. There were always "sinister rumours" about him in the DP camps (though he was certainly not alone in that, and such rumors were often false). In his Australian parish, he ran into trouble, partly as the result of embroilment in a parishioner's divorce, and briefly went over to the Greek Orthodox Church. Then, in the mid-1950s, he left Australia and, it seems, his wife.[66] In 1960, he showed up in Germany, having received an ecclesiastical divorce (qualifying him, under Orthodox rules, for high church office), and been ordained by the Moscow Patriarchate. As Bishop Irenaeus, he served as auxiliary bishop of Munich and West Germany in 1966 and then became Metropolitan of Austria in 1975. It was in this period that his main activity as a Soviet agent is documented. In his Berlin childhood, Susemihl's mother and stepfather had taken in the child of an impoverished White émigré, George Trofimoff, who showed up in postwar Germany as a colonel in the US Army, specializing in military intelligence. He was short of money, and Bishop Irenaeus provided money and recruited him as a Soviet spy. This was discovered in the early 1990s, when KGB man Vasili Mitrokhin defected. Irenaeus and Trofimoff were briefly arrested by the German authorities in 1994, but released without charge. While Trofimoff was later convicted of treason and espionage in Florida, Irenaeus/Susemihl remained Metropolitan of Austria until his death in 1995.[67]

The other Soviet spy, Vladimir Jankowski, grew up in a Russian émigré family in Lithuania, where he was recruited as a spy during the Soviet occupation in the early 1940s. Working as a journalist and traveling widely in Europe during the war, he became active in the Russian émigré community as well as forming connections with the Nazi Directorate of Russian Émigré Affairs. After the war, Jankowski was ordained by ROCA and served as a priest in a Bayreuth DP camp; some fellow DPs suspected him there of informing on Vlasovites to the Soviets. Jankowski came to Australia as a DP in 1949, serving as a priest in the Bonegilla migrant camp before moving to a parish in Adelaide, but after trouble in his parish he was removed from his office and in the mid-1950s left Australia. The US was his first destination, but spy accusations resurfaced, and in 1956 he moved on to Moscow.

---

66. Protopopov, "Russian Orthodox Presence," 96, 166–7, 191, 416–17; Michael Protopopov, *Preosviashchenneishii Feodor (Rafal'skii): Arkhiepiskop Sidneiskii i Avstraliisko-Novozelandskii 1895-1955 i ego epokha* (Melbourne: University of Melbourne Press, 2000), 283–7, 306–13; G. I. Kanevskaia, *"My eshche mechtaem o Rossii . . ." Istoriia russkoi diaspory v Avstralii* (Vladivostok: Izd. Dal'nevostochnogo Universiteta, 2010), 126–7. His wife Tatiana (but not Igor) applied for Australian naturalization in 1955: NAA, A446, 1955/42023.

67. "Irenaeus (Susemihl)," https://en.wikipedia.org/wiki/Irenaeus_(Susemihl)Wikipedia, Irenaeus; Protopopov, "Russian Orthodox Presence," 386; Protopopov, *Preosviashchenneishii Feodor*, 174–5; Kanevskaia, *"My eshche,"* 124.

Jankowski's identity as an undercover agent, with details of his early career, were published in an archive-based post-Soviet history of Soviet foreign intelligence operations.[68]

* * *

The Soviets were unreconciled to the "theft" of their DP citizens, and did their best to recover them, even after resettlement in Australia. While rumors were rife in the émigré community of kidnapping by the Soviets and forced return, no concrete evidence of such incidents in Australia has been found. To be sure, there were undercover repatriation agents attempting to persuade migrants to return, but judging by Gordeev's reports to Moscow, they did this by way of repeated earnest conversations rather than any kind of violence or coercion, and were very seldom successful. Their contacts, like Petrov's, were mainly with the left-leaning Russians and other former Soviet citizens in the Russian-speaking Russian Social Club, not with the anti-Communists who were more representative of the migrant community as a whole. The rumors of Soviet spies planted in the Orthodox Church and other institutions were not, however, unfounded, although the two known cases had been recruited in Europe, either before or during the war, and spent less than a decade in Australia before departing again—perhaps for new pastures that were more fertile from the standpoint of their Soviet masters. Australia was not a major Soviet object of interest, and the spies planted in the Russian community almost certainly reported largely on that community, not on broader matters. For ordinary Russians in Australia, contact with friends and relatives in the Soviet Union remained difficult throughout the Cold War, although somewhat easier after Stalin's death in 1953. The rift between the diaspora and the mother country was ended only after the collapse of the USSR in 1991, followed in the 2000s by the reconciliation of the Russian Church Abroad with the Moscow Patriarchate and Putin's conspicuous embrace of the diaspora.

68. Protopopov, "Russian Orthodox Presence," 174–5; *Istoriia rossiiskoi vneshnei razvedki* (Moscow: Inostrannaia literature, 1999), vol. 3, 282–7.

Chapter 6

UNDERSTANDING BRITISH RETURN MIGRATION: THE AUSTRALIAN DEPARTMENT OF IMMIGRATION, BRITISH YOUTH CULTURES, AND THE FAILED PROMOTIONAL TOUR OF AUSTRALIA IN 1960

Rachel Stevens

Numerically, the peopling of the Australian continent has been dominated by the arrival of British settlers. Even in 2022 and after decades of nationality-blind immigration policies, the largest group of overseas-born people in Australia identify as "English."[1] Of the 7.6 million migrants living in Australia, just under one million were born in England.[2] Yet, these figures conceal an equally significant trend: the departure of British migrants from Australia. This "returnee problem," as it was termed in mid-century, has been a subject of sustained inquiry, notably through the work of Alistair Thomson, James Hammerton, and Reg Appleyard.[3] This chapter is distinct, as it focuses exclusively on the experiences of British youth, a uniquely

---

1. Australian Bureau of Statistics (ABS), "Australia's Population by Country of Birth," Census 2021, released April 26, 2022, https://www.abs.gov.au/statistics/people/population/australias-population-country-birth/latest-release.

2. ABS, "Migration, Australia. Statistics on Australia's international migration, internal migration and the population by country of birth," released April 22, 2021, https://www.abs.gov.au/statistics/people/population/migration-australia/latest-release; Australian government, Department of Home Affairs, "Australia's migration program—country rankings, 2019–20," https://www.homeaffairs.gov.au/research-and-stats/files/country-position-2019-20.PDF.

3. A. James Hammerton and Alistair Thomson *Ten Pound Poms: Australia's Invisible Migrants* (Manchester: Manchester University Press, 2005); Reg Appleyard, with Alison Ray and Allan Segal, *The Ten Pound Immigrants* (London: Boxtree Limited, 1988); Alan Richardson, *British Immigrants and Australia: A Psycho-Social Inquiry* (Canberra: ANU Press, 1974); Parliament of Australia, *Immigration Advisory Council Committee on Social Patterns: Final Report, Inquiry into the Departure of Settlers from Australia* (Canberra: Government Printer of Australia, 1974).

energized and aspirational generation in a distinctly prosperous and culturally adventurous mid-twentieth-century Britain. To do so, this chapter uses the 1959 student essay competition and subsequent tour of Australia in 1960 for the four winners as a case study to examine young people's expectations of Australia and Australians, their life goals, and their attitudes towards migration. Although never migrants, the documented experiences of these teenagers during their tour of Australia help explain why so many young British settlers left Australia in the 1950s and 1960s. In doing so, this chapter presents a cultural history of British repatriation in a field often reliant on statistics, government reports, and retrospective memoirs or interviews. It applies a generational approach to understanding British return migration during the turbulent 1950s and 1960s, in which youth, an oft ignored historical category, is front and center of the analysis. This chapter concludes that British return migration, especially among young people, can be explained by a vast cultural gap and chronic misunderstanding between Australian immigration officials and the British youth they sought to recruit.

The 1950s was a challenging decade for the Australian Department of Immigration. Australian government officials fretted about two connected trends: first, the sharp decline of British and Irish immigration to Australia since 1951–2, and second, the persistent level of British departures from Australia. Figure 6.1 illustrates British and Irish settler arrivals by financial year. Historical statistics do not distinguish between Irish, Welsh, Scottish, or English migrants, reflecting the attitudes of the era that people from the British Isles were one nationality. Data unequivocally shows that from 1952–3, numbers declined sharply, and after a slight rise in 1954–5, arrivals languished at levels approximately two-thirds of the

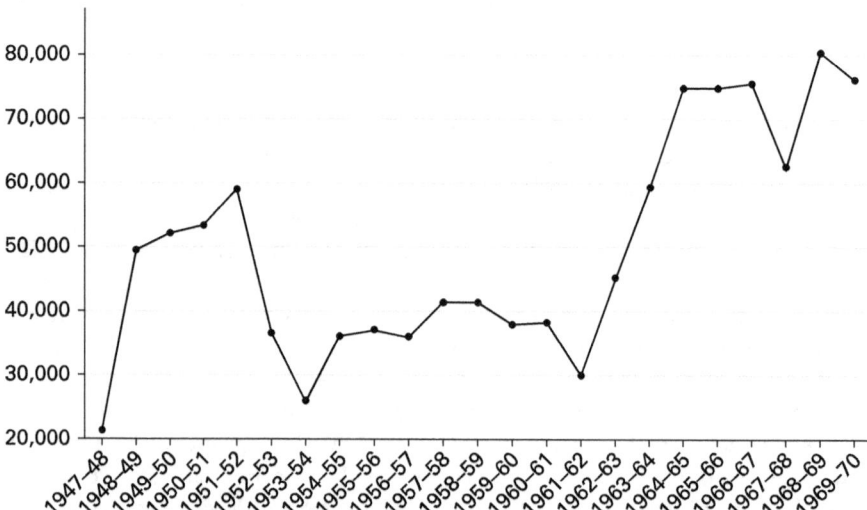

Figure 6.1 Settler arrivals from the UK and Ireland, 1947–8 to 1969–70. Source: Department of Home Affairs, *Historical Migration Statistics*, https://data.gov.au/data/dataset/historical-migration-statistics.

immediate postwar years (1947–51) for the decade. British (and Irish) arrivals to Australia only presents a partial picture of emigration trends.

Table 6.1 focuses on emigration from the UK by sea, the most common form of long-distance travel from 1947 to 1960. This table illuminates two trends: the overall decline of departures, regardless of destination; and that Canada, more than any other country, was Australia's main competitor for British migrants. In 1956 and 1957, Canada received *more* British migrants than Australia. Both countries offered British migrants, especially the working class, escape from overcrowded cities, ample employment opportunities, and a relatively high quality of life. The main difference was climate, which the Australian Department of Immigration emphasized in its publicity materials, as we will see.

A declining pool of incoming British migrants was only one side of the coin. The other side was departures, and again, the data was alarming for Australian officials (see Justine Greenwood's chapter in this volume). At the time, it was widely accepted that approximately 25 percent of British settlers returned to their homeland, although social scientists reported higher rates. Reg Appleyard, who was commissioned by the Australian government in 1957 to investigate the returnee problem, estimated that 29 percent of British migrants returned, but of this figure, between one-third and one-half remigrated to Australia soon after. Notwithstanding the remigration of British returnees, a return rate of over one in four for British migrants was higher than the general return rate of 6 percent in 1959.[4]

Table 6.1 Emigration of Commonwealth citizens from the United Kingdom by sea (in 000s)

Country	1947–54	1955	1956	1957	1958	1959	1960	Total	%
Commonwealth									
Australia	328	36	32.2	35.1	37.4	38.8	39.2	546.7	29.7
Canada	236.4	26.4	41.5	59.4	16	11.8	10.9	402.4	21.9
South Africa	99.8	5	4.8	5.5	5.3	4.4	2.8	127.6	6.9
New Zealand	82.5	10.2	11.5	10.2	10.8	8.8	6.5	140.5	7.6
South Asia	43.8	3.3	3.8	3.2	3.5	3.4	3.3	64.3	3.5
Other countries	201.8	20.2	20.5	23.2	20.8	18.6	16.7	321.8	17.5
Sub-total	992.3	101.1	114.3	136.6	93.8	85.8	79.4	1603.3	87.1
Foreign									
USA	124.9	12.8	13.9	15.2	9.7	8.3	7.8	192.6	10.5
Other countries	33	2.6	1.6	1.8	1.5	1.5	1.5	43.5	2.4
Sub-total	157.9	15.4	15.5	17	11.2	9.8	9.3	236.1	12.9
Grand total	1150.2	116.5	129.8	153.6	105	95.6	88.7	1839.4	100

Source: Commonwealth Department of Immigration, *Quarterly Statistical Bulletin* 38 (April 1961): 23.

4. Parliament of Australia, *The Departure of Settlers from Australia: Final Report of the Committee of Social Patterns of the Immigration Advisory Council* (Canberra: Commonwealth Government Printer, 1968), 5. Alistair Thomson, "'I live on my memories': British Return Migrants and the Possession of the Past," *Oral History* 31 (2003): 57.

Until 1959, government statistics did not distinguish between former settlers (of any nationality) departing and Australian residents departing. This changed in 1959 and, for the first time, data became available that documented who was departing. Table 6.2 demonstrates that British settlers were nearly three times more likely to return than the Dutch, the second highest nationality of returnees. Return migrants (of all nationalities) were also skilled and educated migrants, and, as shown in Figure 6.2, were young. Especially for males, from childhood through to early adulthood, rates of return rose exponentially before a sharp, then gradual, decline in old age. In short, departing migrants were precisely the type of individuals the Australian government sought to recruit for permanent settlement.

The question of why British settlers returned defies simple answers. Reg Appleyard demarcated two distinct time periods of British postwar emigration, which partially explains the decision to return. The first period, between 1947 and 1952, was characterized by what James Hammerton labeled "migrations of austerity."[5] Suffering from postwar shortages and squalid urban conditions, these emigrants initially oversubscribed to the reactivated Assisted Passage Scheme. An estimated 400,000 Britons registered for the scheme in November 1947, with only a fraction accommodated in a time of shipping shortages.[6] For the selected migrants, most of whom had personal nominators to provide accommodation on arrival, return rates were low, as Australia offered abundance and opportunities *relative* to the privations of Britain.

Table 6.2 Permanent departures of former settlers by nationality and occupation, 1961

Nationality	Former settlers departing	Occupation	Former settlers departing
United Kingdom	1884	Craftsmen and production	1596
Dutch	690	Professional and technical	600
German	551	Clerical	580
Australian	402	Labourers	441
New Zealand	320	Service, sport and recreation	306
Italian	197	Sales	239
American	163	Administrative, executive, managerial	191
Ireland	131	Transport and communication	190
Austrian	130	Farmers, fishermen, hunters, timbergetters	139
Canada	67	Miners, quarrymen	42

Source: Commonwealth Bureau of Census and Statistics, *Australian Demographic Review* 143, "Oversea arrivals and departures," 4.

5. A. James Hammerton, "Postwar British emigrants and the 'transnational moment': exemplars of a 'mobility of modernity,'" in Ann Curthoys and Marilyn Lake (eds.), *Connected Worlds: History in Transnational Perspective* (Canberra: ANU Press, 2005), 125–36 (126).

6. Appleyard, *The Ten Pound Immigrants*, 144–7.

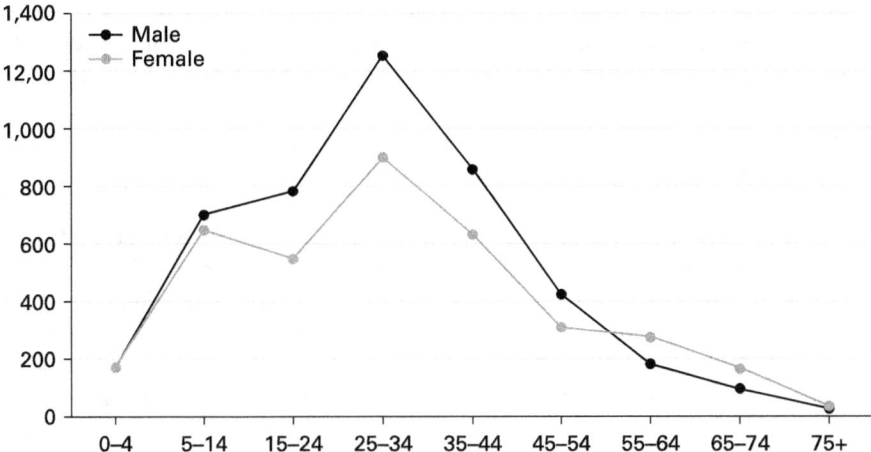

Figure 6.2 Former settlers departing by age and gender, 1961. Source: Bureau of Census and Statistics, *Australian Demographic Review* 5.

The second period, from 1953 to 1970, was a time for "migrations of prosperity."[7] By the mid-1950s, economic conditions in the UK were improving and rationing was over, changes that impacted the socio-economic characteristics of British migrants. Rather than belonging to the working class, the British migrants from the mid-1950s were increasingly middle class, had tertiary qualifications, and were cosmopolitan in their outlook.[8] In 1958, Britons could secure an assisted passage with greater ease than the postwar years, which engendered a casual "take a look and see if we like it" mentality, notwithstanding the two-year residency requirement.[9] Furthermore, during the 1950s British migrants could enter without a personal nominator to provide accommodation. The Australian government provided accommodation, albeit through the much-maligned migrant hostels. Collectively, these reasons dovetailed to make return to Britain an appealing and increasingly affordable option for British migrants.

These macro explanations are useful but obscure individual motivations for repatriation. Alistair Thomson and James Hammerton exhaustively examined

7. Hammerton, "Postwar British emigrants and the 'transnational moment,'" 7.

8. A. James Hammerton, "Growing up in 'White Bread' England in the Sixties I might as well have come from Mars," *History Australia* 7, no. 2 (2010): 32.4. For an example of an upwardly mobile, tertiary educated couple migrating to Australia, returning to Britain, traveling and finally settling in Australia, see Anisa Puri, "Youth Migration to Post-War Australia (1946–73): A Social, Cultural and Oral History," Ph.D. dissertation, Monash University, 2021, 95.

9. Migrants who left within two years were required to repay the cost of transit to the Australian government. Appleyard, *The Ten Pound Immigrants*, 96.

personal narratives in various fora, including diaries, journals, audio letters, letters, memoirs, anthologies, autobiographical novels, oral history interviews, and surveys. Unlike mid-twentieth-century social scientists who examined these questions at a moment in time, either singularly or longitudinally, Thomson and Hammerton framed their research as life histories, thereby understanding migration as an ongoing experience rather than a static state with a beginning and endpoint. The life history approach enables researchers to uncover deep-seated and complex motivations for return, factors that may only become evident after lengthy reflection and distance, emotionally, spatially, or temporally.[10]

Table 6.3 lists the main reasons for the return of survey respondents, grouped by theme. The thematic groupings allow us to disentangle variables beyond the control of the Australian Department of Immigration, such as family or economic pressures, from factors that could be influenced by government actions, for example by managing expectations of life in Australia. The most cited reason for return was homesickness. Ostensibly an affective state of longing for one's place of

Table 6.3 Factors influencing return migration (in percentages)

Family	Care responsibilities	32
	Reunite with family	28
	Trapped on return to Britain	24
	Marital breakdown/tensions	18
	Pregnancy/birth of children	16
External	Employment problems	28
	Ill-health	24
	Financial difficulties	15
Emotional	Homesickness	52
	Return for love/marriage	13
	Wanted to grow old and die in Britain	7
	Loneliness	5
Australia	Environment and wildlife	14
	Society and way of life	12
	Australian character	10
	Never belonged/too British	9
	Hated Australia	6

Source: Derived in part from Hammerton and Thomson, *Ten Pound Poms*, 277.

---

10. Alistair Thomson, "'My wayward heart': homesickness, longing and the return of British postwar immigrants from Australia," in Marjory Harper (ed.), *Emigrant Homecomings: The Return Movement of Emigrants, 1600–2000* (Manchester: Manchester University Press, 2012), 105–30; Alistair Thomson, "Voices we never hear: The unsettling story of Postwar 'Ten Pound Poms' who returned to Britain," *Oral History Association of Australia* 24 (2002): 52–9; Alistair Thomson, "'Good Migration': Place, Meaning and Identity in Audio Letters from Australia, 1963–1965," in Wilfred Prest and Graham Tulloch (eds.), *Scatterlings of Empire* (Perth: Curtin University Press, 2001), 105–16.

origin, Thomson argues that homesickness "was about problems with life in Australia as much, if not more than, about life missed in Britain."[11] British returnees offered many grievances about Australian life, not least of which was widespread anti-British attitudes within the host society. British migrant David Bailey recalled in an oral history interview that he was called a "Pommie bastard" by a "little kid" on his second day in Australia. Bailey believed Australians were "all sort of brainwashed from birth to dislike Poms," "beating them and putting them down and trying to belittle them all the time."[12] Some Australians dismissed the vitriol as harmless baiting. In his own oral history interview, Appleyard described the verbal abuse as "take[ing] the mickey out of them."[13] Bailey rejected this interpretation: "You get sick of the bloody Pommie jokes, you know, and that 'term of endearment' thing, you know. It is, sometimes it is, but ninety percent, it's not."[14] Anti-British bias was not exclusively an Australian experience; rather, it was common in Canada and New Zealand, too.[15]

The Australian High Commission in London, Australia House, pitched migration to Australia as a journey to another part of the British Empire. In doing so, immigration officials exaggerated the significance of superficial similarities between Australia and Britain, concealing differences in the natural environment and society. For some return migrants, the heat was intolerable and they never adjusted to the vibrant insect life. As we will see, the Australian Department of Immigration emphasized the Australian climate as a drawcard during the schoolchildren's promotional tour—possibly to elicit favorable comparisons with Canada. It was inconceivable to the officials that British migrants may prefer a milder climate that facilitated indoor activities. Poorly insulated homes with tin roofs only exacerbated the sweltering conditions for migrants, providing further evidence that Australia was a primitive frontier that lacked the comforts of modernity.[16]

At an Immigration Planning Council meeting in Melbourne on May 4, 1959, the ministerial appointed members of leading industrialists, economists, and trade unionists considered the proposed immigration program for 1959–60.[17] The

11. Thomson, "'My wayward heart'," 128.

12. David Bailey interviewed by Jim Hammerton in the Ten Pound Poms collection, June 7, 1998, National Library of Australia (NLA).

13. Reginald Appleyard interviewed by Nikki Henningham, Academy of the Social Sciences in Australia collection, November 8, 2005, NLA.

14. Bailey interview.

15. A. James Hammerton, *Migrants of the British Diaspora Since the 1960s: Stories from Modern Nomads* (Manchester: Manchester University Press, 2017), 35.

16. Hammerton and Thomson, *Ten Pound Poms*, 282.

17. The Immigration Planning Council, established in November 1949, was concerned with planning of the large-scale postwar immigration program. Members were appointed by the Immigration Minister based on "outstanding services to industry or other sectors of the community." John B. Chifley, "Prime Minister's Statement of Policy, General Elections, 1949," November 14, 1949, 35.

council was concerned about declining British migration, the rising costs of advertising in the UK, and the increasing preference of Britons to migrate to countries geographically close, namely, Canada. Amid these challenges, the council agreed on a solution: "Vigorous, sustained and imaginative publicity campaigns ... will be required in intensified form in 1959/60 to attract migrants of the right type in the numbers required to maintain the level necessary to achieve the Government's immigration aims."[18] In this statement, there is implicit acknowledgment that some British migrants would return, thus necessitating additional British arrivals "in the right numbers" to achieve government objectives. Specifically, the council recommended that the "keynote" of immigration publicity for 1959–60 must be "to 'sell' the attractions and opportunities of Australia for migrants." This aggressive publicity campaign would utilize new media (television) and target two key audiences: prospective British migrants in Britain and Australians considering personally nominating a British migrant.[19]

For the British market, the Department of Immigration initiated a publicity campaign to promote what it deemed to be "modern Australia," a country with bountiful work and an enviable lifestyle to match. Eschewing a typical, overt advertising campaign, the department instead opted for an indirect approach, enlisting British school students aged eleven to sixteen in an essay contest on Australia for which the winners would receive a free trip across Australia as their prize. Through the essay contest, students compiled information on life in Australia and presented their insights to classmates, parents, and the wider community via newspaper coverage of the contest.[20] Australia House in London received thousands of entries, ultimately selecting four students (two boys and two girls) as winners.

The Essay Topic: "My Journey through Australia"

Australia House and the Australian Immigration Department organized informational materials on Australia to assist students prepare their essays. The Immigration Department collaborated with two large British companies, J. Lyons & Co. Ltd. and Educational Productions Ltd., to produce and distribute information packs across Britain. Department figures indicate that J. Lyons & Co. Ltd. alone

---

18. Commonwealth Immigration Planning Council—Agenda, Notes and Minutes of 30th and 31st meetings held during 1959. NAA: A10875, 1959/101.

19. Commonwealth Immigration Planning Council—Agenda, Notes and Minutes of 30th and 31st meetings held during 1959, 102.

20. "Publicity Co-ordination in London," in Discussions with Sir Eric Harrison during visit to Australia—1959. NAA: A1209, 1959/157. Examples of local press coverage include the *Evening Express* (Aberdeen), December 7, 1959, 8; *Liverpool Echo and Evening Express*, December 31, 1959, 9; and *Coventry Evening Telegraph*, November 16, 1959, 8.

spent £150,000 on publicity of the school contest, including distributing 50 million picture cards across all public, grammar, secondary modern, and technical schools throughout Britain. Educational Productions distributed study kits and literature on Australia, also at great company expense.[21] Meanwhile, the Australian government spent only £500. In addition to outsourcing production and publicity expenses to private companies, the Australian government used this advertising stunt to garner free media coverage on television and radio and in print. Consequently, the Australian government co-opted foreign and Australian journalists to promote Australian attractions and work opportunities to the world. Not only was the advertising free, but by nature of the "human interest" aspect to these stories, media coverage of the essay contest commanded "a higher readership that cannot be bought for money."[22]

The school essay contest itself has a long history. For example, the Commonwealth essay contest began in 1883 and since 1913 has run every year with the exception of the war years of 1939 and 1940. These essays provide a window into the minds of children and youth and their understandings of imperialism and nationalism as it was experienced at the time.[23] The social attitudes of young people can also be gleaned through the student essays. For instance, Laura Tisdall has analyzed thousands of student essays in terms of how they imagined their adult lives in the 1960s and 1970s, thereby revealing adolescent attitudes towards marriage, parenthood, and sexuality.[24] Thus, the essays themselves are a valuable source for historical inquiry, offering historians access to the inner life of young people, a cohort that does not typically archive substantial quantities of autobiographical material. As Benita Blessing commented, "childhood, lost forever to 'grown-ups', proves almost as elusive for adults in its historical context." But the remnants of school assignments, whether essay contests, homework, or tests, do present an entry point into the "black box" of education, the classroom, that is not reliant on memory or retrospective oral history interviews.[25]

Unfortunately, it has been impossible to locate the submitted essays. However, the four winning entries were summarized in newspaper accounts and by the winners themselves in a television interview. For instance, *Good Neighbour*, the national newspaper of the state-funded pro-immigration society, the Good

21. "Free trip to Australia," *Biz* (Fairfield, NSW), March 18, 1959, 7.

22. Commonwealth Immigration Planning Council—Agenda, Notes and Minutes of 32nd and 33rd meetings held during 1960. NAA: A10875,1960/33.

23. Line E. Gissel, "From links of iron to slender rope: Essays in the Empire and Commonwealth Essay Competition," *Round Table* 96, no. 388 (2007): 37–9.

24. Laura Tisdall, "'What a Difference it was to be a Woman and not a Teenager': Adolescent Girls' Conceptions of Adulthood in 1960s and 1970s Britain," *Gender & History* 34 (2022): 495–513.

25. Benita Blessing, "Methodological Considerations: Using Student Essays as Historical Sources. The Example of Postwar Germany," *Paedagogica Historica* 43 (2007): 757–8.

Neighbour Council, described at length the essay by Ann Wills, aged fifteen, of Totteridge, London. The *Good Neighbour* noted that Ann's essay was "so convincing that it is difficult to realise that she has never been to Australia."[26] Her entry comprised 310 pages and included more than 200 photographs of birds and animals, as well as images of industry (mines, ships, planes, and the Snowy Mountains Hydro Electrical Scheme). In her television interview, Ann acknowledged that she sourced her information from Australia House in London.[27] The *Good Neighbour* also provided extensive column inches to the youngest of the winning group, Shirley Godfrey, aged eleven, of Nottingham. Shirley presented a fictional narrative of her mother and her joining Shirley's father on a business trip from Perth to the Great Barrier Reef through all the states. Similar to Ann, Shirley described the flora and fauna with a particular focus on the kookaburra:

> I heard a rattling noise and I turned around to see, up in a high tree, a bird which looked like a kingfisher. It was shaking itself violently and its great beak was rattling loudly. Uncle Bill told me that it was a kookaburra, often called the "Laughing Jackass". I was soon to see why it was called the "Laughing Jackass" for about a minute later there was a chuckling noise which soon changed to loud laughing. Then I heard a great many more birds joining in the song and soon even I was laughing to hear all the strange noises made by these birds.[28]

In reports of the winning essays by the two grammar school boys—John Bailey, aged fifteen, of Upton Heath (near Chester), and David Clark, also aged fifteen, of Aberdeen—the *Good Neighbour* adopted gendered language and content. For example, the *Good Neighbour* described the work of John as a "hard, business-like" essay that "one might expect from a young man of 15." In his essay, John provided a celebratory account of Britain's voyages of discovery and colonization, before turning to a summary of Australia's expanding primary industries, especially the mining of raw materials. The article included a direct quotation from the essay:

> While the heavy industries of Australia are firmly based upon reserves of coal and iron ore, many other minerals are becoming more and more important to the nation's economy. Intensive exploration of this vast land and the exploitation of the minerals has given the stimulus for an agricultural nation to gain increasing prosperity from industry. Therefore, on my trip I would like to study the most important and interesting mines.[29]

---

26. "Notes on Top Essays: Fine detail points to careful study," *Good Neighbour*, January 1, 1960, 2.
27. People [Series 1960]—British Teen Essay Contest Winners—Segment [ABC television interview]. NAA: C475,1995/429.
28. "Notes on Top Essays: Fine detail points to careful study."
29. "Notes on Top Essays: Fine detail points to careful study."

Like Ann, John sought information about Australia independent of the study kits provided by Educational Productions Ltd. In his television interview, John recalled sourcing information from his personal library, a clear indicator of his middle-class, grammar boy roots.[30] In a similar vein to its report on John Bailey, the *Good Neighbour* described David Clark's essay as a "factual," "clean-cut," and "well-balanced" account of European settlement and the Australian economy. Like John, David described European exploration, colonization, and the growth of primary and secondary industries. His discussion of wheat is a case in point:

> Wheat occupies seven out of every 10 acres of cultivated land in Australia, where it is second to wool in importance. Australia is the third largest wheat exporting country in the world.[31]

Although the sample of essays summarized here is small, there is evidence of a clear gender divide in the focus of the narratives. Boys offered "factual," "business-like" accounts of Australia's colonial history and contemporary economy; girls conversely focused on the natural environment, drawing attention to native wildlife and natural beauty. Irrespective of gender, however, all the winning entries demonstrated a commitment to the British Empire, the conquest of indigenous lands, and economic orientation towards the exploitation and export of natural resources.

This essay contest aimed to correct false impressions of Australia, particularly to an increasingly affluent and selective British public. The Immigration Department wanted to demonstrate to British schoolchildren that Australia was "not just a place of kangaroos and cricketers."[32] Although schoolchildren were the primary audience, they were not the sole market for this publicity. By structuring the essay contest as a nine-month-long event, the Immigration Department was assured of ongoing media attention in Britain and Australia, with a widespread readership. The department also expected the children to act as conduits, relaying information about Australia to parents, family members, and teachers—adults who had the capacity to make decisions about migration to Australia. In this sense, the schoolchildren inadvertently became ambassadors for Australia, disseminating information provided by the Australian government to those in their social circle.

The essay contest attracted 5,000 entries, resulting in twelve finalists who traveled to Australia House, London, for a "luxury weekend" on November 14 and 15, 1959 and met with the Australian High Commissioner to the UK, Sir Eric Harrison. These finalists all received a record player, donated by a tea firm, which was presented to each of the finalists at ceremonies in their local schools.[33] In other

---

30. John Bailey was a pupil at Chester City Grammar School. "Chester Boy for Australia. Prize in Essay Competition," *Liverpool Echo and Evening Express*, December 31, 1959, 9.

31. Extract from David Clark essay in "Notes on Top Essays: Fine detail points to careful study," 2.

32. "Chester Boy for Australia. Prize in Essay Competition," 9.

33. "David's 6 to 1 chance," *Evening Express*, December 7 1959, 4.

words, the finalists received public recognition and bestowed a degree of status and prestige among peers and teachers, especially in the academically selective grammar schools. The decision of the Immigration Department to employ a competitive element to this publicity campaign was effective from a marketing standpoint but was arguably problematic from the perspective of students.

Social theorist Tobias Werron has described competition as "an institutionalized modern imaginary" at the core of capitalist society.[34] Beginning in the mid- to late eighteenth century, Adam Smith's theory of classical economic liberalism argued that competition in the market was valuable, as it helped producers meet consumer needs. By the nineteenth century, competition entered the popular lexicon to describe a range of activities, including political, artistic, and scientific rivalries.[35] In the mid-nineteenth century, modern sports competitions flourished in the UK and US, which in turn triggered public debates over the virtues of competition as an end rather than a medium to benefit society overall. By the twentieth century, competition became a feature of the classroom. But rather than viewing this development as intrinsically beneficial to help students achieve their potential, we should be mindful of its potential social impacts. For example, when educators introduce a competitive aspect to student assignments, they pressure children to compare themselves with their peers and rank their position accordingly. Moreover, competing students in an essay contest invariably consider their audience (the judges), who typically remain anonymous. The student becomes sensitized to the needs and interests of the anonymous (adult) judge by imagining the content they wish to read, a pedagogical phenomenon known as the "washback effect."[36] In the context of this essay contest, therefore, competition served to inculcate young minds with the values and ideals of the Australian Immigration Department, such as the relationship between empire and migration, and ideas about productive work and virtuous leisure activities. The inducement of a prize, and the public recognition that came with it, also acted to discipline and motivate the student at the time of writing the essay. As we will see in the next section, by the time the winning students arrived in Australia, they were free of such behavioral expectations and revealed their true feelings about Australia.

---

34. Tobias Werron, "Why do we believe in competition? A historical-sociological view of competition as an institutionalized modern imaginary," *Distinktion: Journal of Social Theory* 16 (2015): 186–210.

35. Stephan Pühringer, Georg Wolfmayr, Carina Altreiter, Claudius Gräbner, and Ana Rogojanu, "Theorizing competition: an interdisciplinary approach to the genesis of a contested concept," *ICAE Working Paper Series* 117 (October 2020): 3–27.

36. For the classic study on the "washback effect," see J. Charles Alderson and Dianne Wall, "Does Washback Exist?" *Applied Linguistics* 14 (June 1993): 115–29.

The Tour of Australia

The four winners were chosen by Immigration Minister Sir Alec Downer and there is no evidence on what basis they were selected. Most likely, the "luxury weekend" in London attended by the twelve finalists was used by immigration officials to determine the media savviness of the contestants. Furthermore, the winners were all attractive, white, middle class, and articulate, thereby ensuring their abilities to perform to the Australian public and journalists. The prize of a tour around Australia covered every state and more than 10,000 miles. The winners were accompanied by a young, female chaperone, Miss Josephine Shaw of Yorkshire, a trained British teacher but someone who had no prior connection with the students. Additionally, the students were accompanied by three immigration publicity officials and two staff from Education Productions Ltd., who were tasked with creating a film of the tour. During the trip, the students engaged in so-called typical Australian activities, including "boiling a billy" in the outback, getting "sand in their food at beach picnics," and learning to surf.[37] They also met with dignitaries, including the Immigration Minister and Prime Minister Sir Robert Menzies, Australian schoolchildren, and British migrant children. Educational empire tours were nothing new, however. They reached their zenith during interwar years as a tool for instilling imperial knowledge among privileged students (mostly boys) and teachers, thereby shoring up support for a fading empire among the next generation of leaders. The 1960 tour was distinct, as it deviated from precedent by being initiated by a Commonwealth government in pursuit of its own goals (migration), rather than those of the empire.[38]

This tour was based on the long-held assumption in the Australian government that the "migrant follows the tourist."[39] The itinerary was devised to appeal to the emerging "lifestyle emigrant" of the 1960s whose attitude towards migration was shaped by a sense of adventure, consumption of transnational experiences, and an

---

37. Press Statement by the Minister for Immigration, "Four UK Children to Fly to Australia. Essay Contest Winners," 2 in United Kingdom—essay competition [details of visit by competition winners, Ann Wills, Shirley Godfrey, David Clark and John Bailey—sponsored by the Department of Immigration; J Lyons and Company Ltd; and Educational Productions Ltd]. NAA: P3, T1959/2204.

38. Benjamin Bryce, "Citizens of Empire: Education and Teacher Exchanges to Canada and the Commonwealth, 1910–1940," *Journal of Imperial and Commonwealth History* 45 (2017): 607–29; Sarah Winfield, "Travelling the Empire: The 'School Empire Tours' and their significance for conceptual understandings (1927–1939)," *History of Education Review* 40 (2011): 81–95; Marjory Harper, "'Personal contact is worth a ton of textbooks': educational tours of the empire, 1926–39," *Journal of Imperial and Commonwealth History* 32 (2004): 48–76.

39. For other examples, see Justine Greenwood, "The Migrant Follows the Tourist: Australian Immigration Publicity After the Second World War," *History Australia* 11 (2014): 74–96.

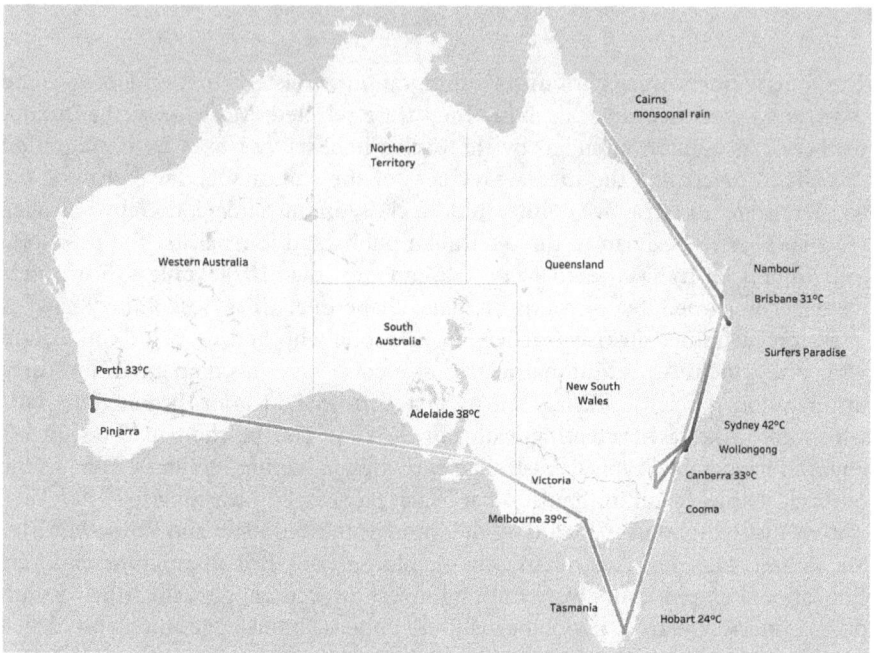

Figure 6.3 Itinerary of tour of Australia, with maximum temperatures in capital cities. Map created by author.

eye for expatriate moneymaking.[40] To showcase exotic locations and an active, outdoorsy lifestyle, immigration officials deliberately allocated a number of days to Queensland. The state was selected because the Immigration Department expected the "publicity to be particularly fruitful," specifically the imagery "of the tropics [contrasting] sharply with the English winter."[41] Outside of Queensland, the tour included visits to national attractions, including the Barossa Valley, Healesville animal sanctuary, and yachting in Sydney Harbour. These highlights were mixed with less appealing stops, such as numerous factory tours (General Motors Holden near Melbourne; paper mills and the Cadbury chocolate factory near Hobart; the British Motor Corporation in Sydney; the BHP site at Port Kembla; and a pineapple cannery in Nambour). The economic focus continued with visits to primary industry sites, such as apple orchards, sheep graziers, and national building projects such as the Snowy Mountain Hydro Scheme.

40. A. James Hammerton, "Life Stories, Family Relations and the 'Lens of Migration': Postwar British Emigration and the New Mobility," in Desley Deacon, Penny Russell, and Angela Woollacott (eds.), *Transnational Ties: Australian Lives in the World* (Canberra: ANU Press, 2008), 136.

41. Internal memo, "Essay Competition—Publicity Arrangements," undated, in United Kingdom—essay competition. NAA: P3, T1959/2204.

Far from a lazy summer holiday, the winning students were drafted into working on thirty-two of the thirty-four days of the tour. Each day was filled with staged activities, meet-and-greets, interviews with local media outlets, and travel. A grueling journey, the teenagers enjoyed very little free time to themselves, allocated just two full free days, two free afternoons, and one free morning. Immigration officials had assumed that the winning students would blindly promote migration to Australia, citing plentiful (low-skilled) work opportunities and unfamiliar leisure activities as drawcards. What actually happened was that the exhausted teenagers resented the constant media attention and the incessant demands to endorse Australia as a desirable migrant destination. When asked by an ABC TV journalist if they themselves would migrate to Australia, the two boys bluntly said "no." David Clark continued, elaborating that "I can see little in this country to attract my friends in Scotland."[42]

The way the tour had been planned almost guaranteed that the publicity campaign would fail to achieve departmental aims, for three reasons. First, the timing of the trip was poorly considered. All four students lived in towns that averaged maximum daily temperatures in January between 4C and 5C. On arrival in Perth on January 11, 1960, local newspapers reported warm temperatures from the start (24 C and 29C) before heating up to 33C on January 13. The teenagers were not given any time to acclimate nor adjust to the new time zone. The British visitors seemed blinded by the sunshine, making a request "several times" for sunglasses.[43] Temperatures continued to rise as the students traveled through Adelaide (38C on January 16) and Melbourne 38C on January 17; 39 C on January 18). The teenagers found the weather so hot in Adelaide that they "coaxed" their chaperone for "romps" in the sea to cool down despite their busy schedule.[44] In Sydney, the students had the misfortune of arriving during Sydney's worst heatwave on record at that time, which claimed the lives of twenty-two people. On January 27 and 28, temperatures reached 42C; on January 29, the maximum temperature reached 39C before a cool change arrived, although humidity remained high at 87 percent on January 30.[45] Given the extreme weather—either heatwaves in Sydney or tropical storms in Queensland—the students encountered the severity of Australia's climate. Far from being enamored with the sunny beach days, the teenagers were left feeling the brutality of the Australian summer. Even though the students were instructed on how to apply sunscreen while at a beach on the Gold Coast, they still experienced sunburn. John Bailey described his very burnt legs as

42. People [Series 1960]—British Teen Essay Contest Winners. NAA: C475, 1995/429.

43. Michael Edmonds, Publicity Officer—Melbourne, letter to Tom Mellor, January 26, 1960, in NAA: P3, T1959/2204.

44. Department of Immigration, "Essay Contest Winners," summary of activities, January 21, 1960, in UK School Essay Contest—Itinerary for winners. NAA: D400, SA1959/11663.

45. Press coverage of heatwave from *Sydney Morning Herald*, January 29 and 30, 1960, cover.

painfully "red raw."⁴⁶ The contrast in the skin complexions of the two boys and a local man in Figure 6.4 is a visual reminder that the young Brits were ill suited to Australian conditions.

If the students struggled with the Australian temperatures on the mainland, their time in Tasmania offered a welcome respite from the heat, while they were also comforted by familiar landscapes. On January 22, 1960, Ann Wills wrote to Tom Mellor, the Chief Migration Officer in the Department of Immigration in Hobart, saying how much she and her compatriots enjoyed their time in Tasmania. She wrote, "I am sure we shall all remember Tasmania for its close resemblance to our home country, linking us with our home so many miles around the world."⁴⁷ Their chaperone, Jo Shaw, similarly wrote a thankyou letter to Tom Mellor, conveying that she and the students "think Tasmania is a wonderful place ... an island of friendliness and sunshine." She wrote that "when we say Hobart was hot, people are almost incredulous." During their stay, Hobart experienced maximum temperatures of 24 C, a far cry from what they would encounter in Sydney the following week and certainly mild by Australian summer standards. Although Australian immigration officials thought tropical Queensland would be most appealing to the travelers, it was in fact Tasmania, and its evocations of home, that was most pleasing to the Brits.⁴⁸

Another problem for the Immigration Department was that it had made assumptions about the class background of the students and their aspirations for the future. In their essay applications, Ann Wills expressed a desire to become a veterinary surgeon, while John Bailey noted that he wanted to pursue a career as a geologist or mineralogist. Both John and David Clark attended academically selective grammar schools. Furthermore, the fact that three of the winners were fifteen and still in school reflects their solidly middle-class status. Indeed, between 1939 and 1970, 70 percent of young British people were in full-time work.⁴⁹ Thus, Ann Wills, David Clark, and John Bailey were presumably on the top rungs of the socio-economic ladder by virtue of the fact they had the luxury to continue their education. Despite the explicit ambitions of the students to pursue professional careers, the tour focused on primary industries and manufacturing. The chasm between the life ambitions of the teenagers and the itinerary that focused on manual labor is represented in Figure 6.5. In the photograph, farmer Doug Hyles explains the intricacies of wool extraction from one of his sheep. The three students watch on, politely feigning interest in the condition of the ewe's coat. From the archives, we know that the Immigration Department was aware of the economic situation in the UK: at an August 1959 Immigration Planning Council meeting, members discussed the "sound condition" of the British economy, with

46. People [Series 1960]—British Teen Essay Contest Winners. NAA: C475,1995/429.
47. Ann Wills, letter to Tom Mellor, January 22, 1960 in NAA: P3, T1959/2204.
48. Jo Shaw, letter to Tom Mellor, January 22, 1960 in NAA: P3, T1959/2204.
49. Selina Todd and Hilary Young, "Baby-Boomers to 'Beanstalkers,'" *Cultural and Social History* 9 (2012): 454.

Figure 6.4 David (left) and John are sprayed with a special chemical that prevents sunburn at Surfers Paradise on Queensland's Gold Coast. Image courtesy of the National Archives of Australia, NAA: A1211, 1/1960/34/39.

Figure 6.5 Mr. Doug Hyles, of Uriarra, thirty miles from Canberra, shows the wool of one of the 12,000 sheep on his 7,000-acre property. Image courtesy of the National Archives of Australia, NAA: A12111, 1/1960/34/18.

unemployment standing at just 2.1 percent.[50] Yet the council failed to understand fully how a strong postwar economy would impact society in general and youth cultures in particular.

Youth as a distinct category warrants historical analysis, as it presents an entry into the space beyond work, the family, and school environments.[51] In examining youth attitudes, we can access emerging ideas about consumption, the development of identity, and cultural and political interests.[52] As Jon Garland et al., explain, youth is not just a chronological category defining the period between childhood and adulthood. It is a "metaphorical device to embody both the aspirations and anxieties of a particular historical time."[53] In the case of postwar British youth, this "breakthrough generation" enjoyed expanding media, significant wage increases proportionate to British adults, and access to more cultural and educational institutions than previously.[54] All four students were born after 1945, and therefore had no experience of wartime privations. They grew up in a time of increasing affluence. British teenagers were no longer essential breadwinners for their families, and this created greater freedom for leisure activities. Notably, youth prosperity was a distinctly British experience not shared with their European counterparts. In the context of economic stability and prosperity, young people and their parents raised their social and economic expectations of what was possible in their lives, ushering in a period of ambition and aspirational desires.[55] It should come as no surprise, then, given British young people's penchant for consumerism and expectation of affluence, that on departure the four students had 50kg of excess luggage, including 4.5kg of cake, costing the Australian government an additional £231.17.6 in freight costs.[56]

Another issue was that the set activities for the students were vastly at odds with the expectations of middle-class British youth of the time. Back in Britain, urban youth enjoyed an array of leisure pursuits, from dance clubs, coffee bars, emerging subcultures ("teddy boys," mods, rockers), and the rise of popular music. British

---

50. Commonwealth Immigration Planning Council—Agenda, Notes and Minutes of 30th & 31st meetings held during 1959, 11.

51. For a detailed analysis of the intersection between youth histories and migrant histories, see Puri, "Youth Migration to Post-War Australia," ch. 5.

52. Catherine Ellis, "The Younger Generation: The Labour Party and the 1959 Youth Commission," *Journal of British Studies* 41 (April 2002): 202.

53. Jon Garland, Keith Gildart, Anna Gough-Yates, Paul Hodkinson, Bill Osgerby, Lucy Robinson, John Street, Pete Webb, and Matthew Worley, "Youth Culture, Popular Music and the End of 'Consensus' in Post-War Britain," *Contemporary British History* 26 (2012): 266.

54. Lynn Abrams, "Liberating the female self: epiphanies, conflict and coherence in the life stories of post-war British women," *Social History* 39 (2014): 15.

55. Todd and Young, "Baby-Boomers to 'Beanstalkers'," 452–7.

56. Correspondence between F. Kelly, F. Robson, Commonwealth Migration Officer—Sydney, and Department Secretary, Tasman Hayes, February 22, 1960, in Immigration—United Kingdom School Essay Contest [Box 120]. NAA: C3939, N1960/75006.

youth culture became "sites of symbolic resistance" to conventional social structures. Thanks to increased affluence, young people embarked on an "expressive revolution" in which they could define and assert their identities with hairstyles, clothing and record purchases.[57] As one "mod," Janet Coolen, described it in an interview, "everything was swinging in London ... I was a mod and I had my hair sort of like Cilla Black [beehive bob] and I wore big boots and denim jacket with fur at the top."[58] In contrast to her stylish, fashion-forward look, Australian girls "were still wearing sticking out dresses with petticoats, real sort of fifties ... everybody had a hat on ... they had gloves ... They were way behind. I thought I had stepped back in time when I came [to Australia]."[59] What we have, then, is a period in British society of empowered youth self-expression, cultural vibrancy, and experimentation, characteristics that were notably absent in Australia until the late 1960s at the earliest. During the tour, no cultural activities were arranged, either of a high-brow or popular variety, which most likely would have been of interest to the erudite students. Instead, activities were outdoorsy, physically demanding, and often in rural or picturesque locations. Some of the activities undertaken by the quartet included horse riding near Canberra, surfing on the Gold Coast, yachting in Sydney Harbour, and surf-skiing on the Great Barrier Reef. Some of these activities were challenging to the uninitiated. The students were given surfing lessons, a sport notoriously difficult to learn. John Bailey complained in an ABC television interview that he had been "dumped a few times in the surf," a literal and metaphorical reference to his inability to embody a rugged Australian masculinity.[60]

Arguably, cultural activities were not overlooked by organizers; rather, they did not exist in the manner expected by the young Brits. British migrants routinely expressed shock at the absence of "sophisticated urbanity" in Australian cities. Unlike the vibrant cities of the UK, youthful migrants found themselves in Australian cities with nothing to do. Expressions such as "social and material backwardness," "wasteland," "primitive," and "unsophisticated" dot the interviews by Hammerton and Thomson.[61] British migrants were most disappointed with the Australian pub. In Britain, the pub is arguably the most egalitarian space, one that fosters social interaction, conviviality, and fellowship. In contrast, Australian pubs at the time were gender-segregated and promoted male binge drinking before the early 6 pm closing time. Rather than promoting warmth and goodwill, Australian pubs engendered division and alcohol-induced violence. Even if large Australian cities did have

57. Lynn Abrams, "Heroes of Their Own Life Stories: Narrating the Female Self in the Feminist Age," *Cultural & Social History* 16 (2019): 206–7; Garland et al., "Youth Culture," 268.

58. Janet Coolen interviewed by Justin Madden in the Hostel Stories Project, October 11, 2012. Held at State Library of South Australia.

59. Coolen interview.

60. People [Series 1960]—British Teen Essay Contest Winners. NAA: C475, 1995/429.

61. Hammerton, "Growing up in 'White Bread' England," 32.2–4.

cultural activities, they were not woven into everyday life, let alone into conversations at the pub. A strand of anti-intellectualism pervaded Australian society, too, leading to the well-known Australian creative exodus to London in the 1960s.[62] Teenage migrant Mary Rose Lavery lamented that her generous but unimaginative Australian friends had no books in their home, made inane conversation, and used the radio to follow the football scores.[63] But as Anisa Puri observes, the long-established discourse about an absence of culture in Australia has deep roots in settler colonialism and has been employed as an argument to rationalize European conquest.[64]

Australian superficiality also made an impression on the essay contest winners. Just before boarding a plane at Sydney Airport for London, David Clark dropped the positive veneer that the students had been forced to maintain for thirty-four days. He told the press that "Australians talked a lot about the sun and the surf. This is all rather shallow."[65] David lamented that he "was sick of the sound of the word 'migrant', tired of being asked ... whether he would like to come back here to live."[66] In a television interview, John Bailey similarly rejected any press attempt to cajole him into advocating migration to Australia, commenting, "I don't think I could live here for the rest of my life."[67] It is evident in these damning appraisals that the teenagers were exhausted, even resentful, of the whirlwind trip around Australia that was supposed to be a prize rather than a five-week promotional tour. In another newspaper, David commented, "you can't enjoy yourself in the sun and the surf all the time."[68] Here, David's reference to time is pertinent. From the late 1950s, British cities were catering to the tastes and desires of young people: venues and organizers created new spaces outside the home for youth to socialize without adult supervision; city councils granted licenses for late-night venues to operate into the early hours of the morning. Consequently, youth culture increasingly became enmeshed with the night-time economy. In the coffee bars, beat clubs, church halls, and pubs, young British people formed group identities based around their social network.[69] In contrast, the sleepy cities of Australia lacked urban spaces that facilitated youthful self-expression, entertainment, and social mixing.

62. Simon Pierse, "Australian artists in London: The early 1960s," in Carl Bridge, Robert Crawford, and David Dunstan (eds.), *Australians in Britain: The Twentieth-Century Experience* (Melbourne: Monash University Press, 2009), 178–93.

63. Hammerton and Thomson, *Ten Pound Poms*, 140.

64. Puri, "Youth Migration to Post-War Australia," 158–9.

65. Letter to the Editor, Norman Carr, Strathfield, "A message for David," *Daily Telegraph*, February 17, 1960, 2.

66. This quote and above quote from "Boyish Critic," *Sun-Herald*, February 21, 1960, 42, in Immigration—United Kingdom School Essay Contest [Box 120], 5. NAA: C3939, N1960/75006.

67. People [Series 1960]—British Teen Essay Contest Winners. NAA: C475, 1995/429.

68. NAA: C3939, N1960/75006.

69. Sarah Kenny, "Unspectacular Youth? Evening Leisure Space and Youth Culture in Sheffield, c.1960–c.1989," Ph.D. dissertation, University of Sheffield, 2017, 67–102.

Conclusion

Scholars have explained British return migration in large part by the increasing ease of travel in the mid-twentieth century, family pressures, and homesickness. Yet these factors prioritize (older) adult recollections at the expense of how British youth encountered Australia and Australians at a time of unsynchronized social and cultural change between metropole and periphery. This chapter has used youth as a prism to explore cultural changes underway in late 1950s and early 1960s Britain. Unlike young people in prior generations, this cohort was distinctively self-empowered, ambitious, adventurous, and willing to resist conventional social and economic structures. As living conditions improved in mid-century Britain, so too did the desires and expectations of an affluent and vibrant British youth who expected more from a migrant destination than ever before.

The 1960 promotional tour of Australia illustrates the gap between Australian immigration officials and middle-class, educated British youth. Australian immigration officials chose to showcase Australia's extreme weather and its abundant low-skilled employment opportunities, and to promote physically active rather than cerebral leisure pursuits. The quartet, however, were underwhelmed by the "shallow" preoccupations of Australians. Through archival documents, press reports, and interviews, these students recorded how Australia appeared to them, in all their adolescent petulance. Unlike the constructed personal narratives created by migrants for their families, the four teenagers provided spontaneous reflections. They were not migrants and therefore were not emotionally invested in creating a grand narrative of migration that justified their decisions for family consumption. Despite pressure from the Australian government to advocate unequivocally migration to Australia, remarkably these teenagers resisted, maintaining their independence. In doing so, Ann, Shirley, John, and David provide us with an unfiltered, historically specific account of why many young, skilled British migrants departed Australia in the mid-twentieth century.

Chapter 7

"UND ICH DREH' MICH NOCHMAL UM" (HILDEGAARD KNEFF): GEORGE DREYFUS, GERMANY, AND THE REVOLVING DOOR OF RETURN

Kay Dreyfus, with Jonathan Dreyfus

At ten years of age I was torn away from Germany, but in my cultural soul have always remained there.[1]

There are many ways to think about that aspect of the migration experience which involves return (to the original homeland) and departure (from the country of destination). George Dreyfus is a German-born Australian Jew whose life can be viewed as a revolving door of departures and returns, of going and not going, staying and not staying. It is not a duality that causes him grief. His many trips to Germany have enriched and validated his identity as a musician and, paradoxically, as an Australian. Australia, which has given him a safe haven, nurtured and frustrated his career and allowed him to see his family expand into a third generation, also confronts him with cultural values against which he defines his Germanness. Musical activities provide a practical link to the Germany of today, but the Germany he inhabits in daily consciousness is the lost homeland of his childhood and exile, the Germany of the Weimar Republic, the Third Reich and World War II. It is not a homeland that he wishes to return to, and yet he finds comfort in its familiar terrain, in stories that unfold in the same way every time but never lose their fascination. In several of his compositional projects he has transformed his view of the German past into contemporary creative statements, through settings of German texts and topics. This chapter tells George's story, drawing on words and themes from his four autobiographical books and from informal conversations and interviews that have taken place over several decades.

---

1. George Dreyfus, "How come a nice Jewish boy from Camberwell writes not one but two operas for Germany," in George Dreyfus, *Being George—and Liking It! Reflections on the Life and Work of George Dreyfus on his 70th Birthday* (Richmond, Victoria: Allans Publishing, 1998), 53, originally published in George's essay "Schmooz Downunder: Australian/Jewish Writing," *Westerly* 41, no. 4 (Summer 1996): 97–101.

The "Minefield of Belonging": The Dreyfus Family in Germany and Australia, 1925–51

An early catastrophe for me, I was 23 at the time, was the premature death of my father, Alfred. A second degree victim of Nazi persecution, he was able to save his life, but could not survive the separation from his German cultural environment. After the war he wanted to return . . . but his reluctant family made it impossible, and inwardly the fear of being unwanted in Germany, his mother Paula's suicide in 1942—the year of the great deportations—all these conflicts were too great for him. He just died and I retained a deeply buried guilt feeling, I retained a wound. Perhaps I should have gone back with him. It is all somewhat unclear, but certainly mirrored in my own relationship with Germany, which is equally unclear. One moment here, one moment there, always backwards and forwards, just like the waves of the ocean.[2]

In her chapter on the Dreyfus family, historian Hedwig Brüchert writes that it was certainly no coincidence that George's parents met. Their fathers were respected merchants in Elberfeld and, moreover, both were descended through their grandparents from well-established Mainz men's clothing companies, the Brettheimers and the Dreyfuses. The families undoubtedly had social and business relations with one another.[3] This may seem like a somewhat unusual observation to make about a twentieth-century marriage. To understand it, we need to remember that throughout the nineteenth century and lasting into the imperial period (1871–1918), most middle-class Jewish marriages continued to be arranged, either by marriage brokers or, more often, with the aid of parents and relatives.[4] Almost in the manner of aristocratic marriages, these alliances between textile, clothing, and fashion merchant families consolidated business and social standing and influence. Arranged or not, the families would have been well pleased by this union.

The Dreyfuses were secular, highly assimilated, German-speaking, cultivated, middle-class, urban Jews. Not fabulously wealthy, but comfortably affluent and integrated. Consider George's description of his grandfather, Wilhelm Dreyfus:

---

2. Dreyfus, *Being George*, 52–3. In 1948 Alfred had had an offer from his former business partner, then a successful businessman in England. He wanted Alfred to join him there. But his wife Hilde did not want to go, and neither did either of his sons. George Dreyfus, *The Last Frivolous Book* (Sydney: Hale & Iremonger, 1984), 31.

3. Hedwig Brüchert, "Familie Dreyfus," in Renate Knigge-Tesche und Hedwig Brüchert, hrsg., *Der Neue Jüdische Friedhof in Mainz: Biographische Skizzen zu Familien und Personen, die hier ihre Ruhestätte haben* (Mainz: Sonderheft der Mainzer Geschichtsblätter, 2013), 66–7.

4. Sharon Gillerman, "Germany: 1750–1945," *The Shalvi/Hyman Encyclopedia of Jewish Women*, Jewish Women's Archive, https://jwa.org/encyclopedia/article/germany-1750-1945.

Dieser Grossvater hatte den ur-deutschen Vornamen Wilhelm und war—wie Photos zeigen—ein ausgesprochen stattlicher Mensch mit Monokel ... Er soll, wie mein Vater mir erzählte, zu jeder Wagner-Aufführung nach Köln gefahren sein und sogar jedes Wagner-Libretto auswendig gekonnt haben.[5]

Alfred and Hilde were married in 1925 and the births of their two sons followed promptly: Richard in 1926, George in 1928. The family enjoyed a comfortable lifestyle in a nice house at Platzhofstr in Wuppertal. George has written (in German) about his father at this time:

By the way, I only saw my father very rarely in Wuppertal. He went to the business early in the morning and when he came home for lunch at noon, you weren't allowed to say "pieps". He was very strict, especially when it came to spanking; presumably because he himself was brought up very strictly in this way. Otherwise he was a very lively, daring and entertaining—if not always lovable—man, who always liked to have people around him; he was also an enthusiastic Skat and piano player who improvised mainly dance music and early jazz on the piano.[6]

Alfred accompanied Schubert Lieder beautifully. He also played tennis well enough to be chosen to compete at the Jewish Olympic games in Tel Aviv in 1935.[7] Not untypically, no one has much to say about what Hilde was doing or how she filled her days. A Kindermädchen helped with the children.

All this changed with the coming of the Third Reich.

In August 1935, Alfred moved his family to Berlin, believing they would be safer in a large city.[8] There was also the matter of the children's schooling. In 1933, 75 percent of all Jewish students attended general public schools in Germany. On April 25, 1933, the German government issued a "Law against Overcrowding in Schools and Universities" which dramatically limited the number of Jewish

---

5. "This grandfather had the ultra-German first name Wilhelm and was—as the photos show—an extremely stately person with a monocle ... As my father told me, he would have gone to every Wagner performance in Cologne and even knew every Wagner libretto by heart." George Dreyfus interviewed by Manfred Brusten, "*Mr New Music* in Australien," in Dreyfus, *Being George*, 71.

6. Brusten, "*Mr New Music* in Australien," 72 (transl.).

7. Dreyfus, *Being George*, 53, 73.

8. Manfred Brusten explains as follows: This general move of Jews to the larger cities was finally also the subject of a Nazi strategy paper by the Berlin Gestapo "on the treatment of Jews in the Reich capital city." The reason given is "that the Jews in the provinces, as a result of the strict supervision that is possible there, see increasingly limited opportunities for existence and therefore strive to go into hiding in a big city like Berlin" ("*Mr New Music* in Australien," 95, n. 8; transl.).

students attending public schools.⁹ From Wuppertal, the nearest Jewish school was in Cologne; too far for two small boys to travel every day.

Alfred—not an especially religious man—began to feel more Jewish in Berlin. He started attending synagogue with Hilde and they went to concerts with the Jüdische Kulturbund, where they heard only Jewish music played by only Jewish musicians. "Mendelssohn, not Beethoven," wrote George. "My father started working in the office of the Zionist Federation on a voluntary basis, helping other Jews, in Berlin, helping Jews to emigrate from Germany."[10] Richard and George attended Jewish schools, first the Theodor Herzl Schule, then, when that school was closed, the Leonore Goldschmidt School in the Grunewald.[11]

Kristallnacht, November 1938, was the tipping point towards emigration for the Dreyfus family, as for many other German Jews.[12] Alfred was warned that the pogrom was coming. For three days, George relates, Alfred rode around on trains, constantly on the move.[13] Others were not so lucky. Some 30,000 Jewish males were arrested and despatched to concentration camps like Buchenwald, Dachau or Sachsenhausen.

Alfred secured places for George and Richard on a Kindertransport leaving for Australia at the beginning of June 1939. He and Hilde left seven weeks later, around 1 August: first to London, then to Palestine.[14] They were on the boat in the Adriatic when war was declared. From Palestine they flew via Karachi and Bombay to Darwin and on to Sydney, arriving two months after they had left Germany, on October 4, 1939.[15] Their destination was not so much a matter of choice as an absence of choice, a matter of what was possible.

The family was finally reunited at the beginning of 1940, living in a small apartment in Charnwood Road, St. Kilda, where George shared a room with his

9. https://www.ushmm.org/learn/timeline-of-events/1933-1938/law-limits-jews-in-public-schools.
10. Dreyfus, *The Last Frivolous Book*, 11.
11. Dreyfus, *The Last Frivolous Book*, 11.
12. https://encyclopedia.ushmm.org/content/en/article/kristallnacht.
13. Dreyfus, *Being George*, 74.
14. "Emigrants to Palestine were permitted to transfer a relatively large proportion of their assets to Palestine," an arrangement made possible by the 1933 Ha-avara agreement between the Reich Economics Ministry and Jewish organizations. See Frank Bajohr, "Aryanization and Restitution in Germany," in Martin Dean, Constantin Goschler, and Philipp Ther, (eds.), *Robbery and Restitution: The Conflict over Jewish Property in Europe* (New York and Oxford: Berghahn Books, 2008), 35. Papers in George's collection relating to the Australian Taxation Office's investigation of his father's financial affairs after Alfred's death show that a sum of 30,000 RM was transferred to Palestine by Hilde's parents and that the Dreyfuses collected this money before their departure for Australia. Wilhelm Hegglin Hornbach (Steuerberater, Wiesbaden), Statutory Declaration, September 1, 1952; Fritz Sternberg, letter to Richard Dreyfus, December 23, 1953.
15. Dreyfus, *Being George*, 76. See also National Archives of Australia (NAA): A12508, 21/940; Item ID 7128169.

brother. As the children's lives took shape through their schooling, things were not so simple for Alfred. After the attack on Pearl Harbor, he was drafted (not unwillingly) into an Australian Army labor corps; Hilde worked as a nurse.[16] On his release in 1943, Alfred bought a carpet cleaning business in which Hilde also worked, the boys helping out at the weekends. Alfred (together with his dependants) was naturalized on September 27, 1946.[17]

George has not written much about what his mother was feeling in those early days. "She adjusted much better," he writes, "her main problem was my father's unhappiness."[18] Alfred found his life in Australia very depressing and wanted his old life back. The family was not doing badly; they had moved to a comfortable house in Waverley Road, Melbourne, where Hilde would live until shortly before her death. But Alfred was not flourishing, not getting rich like other refugee émigrés. "It was a bitter experience for my father, whose whole tradition was that money is the sign of a successful life." Alfred got some mileage out of stories about how he charmed the rich ladies of Toorak while he cleaned their carpets—he was a charmer, says George. But, as George puts it so eloquently, "Carpet cleaning was a pretty yukky business."[19]

Alfred yearned to return to Germany, believing that he would recover everything he had lost to the Nazis: the business he had been forced to sell and the four houses his family once owned. His greatest wish was to have coffee again at the Kaiser-Wilhelm-Ring in Cologne.[20] As is often the case with émigré dreams about the lost homeland, there was a gap between the dream and the present reality. Did Alfred know how Cologne was damaged during the war? Would that have helped him become reconciled to his life in Australia? George writes, "He just went to the doctor all the time and took pills. It was very sad."[21] At night, he cried.

By 1951 the boys were grown. Richard was working in London. George, though still living at home, was employed as a bassoon player at His Majesty's Theatre. Alfred and Hilde made plans to return to Europe. Tickets were purchased and Alfred had high hopes that the restitution process then underway would come through for them. Then suddenly Alfred was dead. George remembers his mother coming into his bedroom one morning to tell him that she thought his father had

---

16. Alfred's service records are at NAA: A13860, V377455; Item ID 31547901.
17. NAA: A715, 9/2911; Item ID 31672733.
18. Dreyfus, *The Last Frivolous Book*, 19.
19. Dreyfus, *The Last Frivolous Book*, 19, 31; 25, 23. Frank Bajohr has written that many German Jews associated economic and professional success with the desire for recognition and social integration. He discusses how feelings of self-esteem and identity, "moored on material wealth," were shattered by Aryanization—intensified, in Alfred's case, by forced emigration and reduced social circumstances. Dean, Goschler, and Ther, *Robbery and Restitution*, 44.
20. Dreyfus, *Being George*, 77.
21. Dreyfus, *The Last Frivolous Book*, 25.

died. He also recalls her remarking that she had slept well for the first time in ages; the crying had stopped. George does not know the official cause of Alfred's death but thinks his father died of his unsolvable problems, of unresolved internal conflicts, of a broken heart. George has written, that he himself did not want to die of such unsolvable problems. "I did not want to grapple with this 'minefield of belonging' so directly." Nor did he want to grapple with the problem of whether to have anything to do with Germany at all.[22]

Living Duality: The Revolving Door of Return

Not for George the attitude of some German-Jewish refugee survivors who would not take restitution money ("blood money"), who refused to speak German, go back to Germany, drive a German car, take an interest in German affairs or even, in extreme cases, disembark during stopovers in Frankfurt airport.[23]

George has, at various times through his autobiographical writings, addressed this somewhat thorny issue of his willingness to return to Germany regularly, take German money whenever it is offered, drive a Mercedes, and play a German bassoon (a Heckel). "Soll ich etwa auf einem schlechteren Fagott spielen, nur weil es nicht aus Deutschland kommt?! Ein so schlechter Fagottist wie ich, der muß zumindest auf einem guten Fagott spielen."[24] Expanding on this theme, as he told Manfred Brusten in an interview in February 1993, "Für mich ist Deutschland dagegen ein äußerst interessantes Land; und wenn ich etwas interessant finde, dann muß ich dort auch hin."[25]

We might attribute this difference in attitude in part to the young age at which George was forced to leave Germany, to the fact that he did not experience the Holocaust as directly as some older survivor friends may have done, or perhaps to his own father's somewhat remarkable desire to remigrate. George takes a remarkably intense interest in the Holocaust and in the fates of his relatives, as well as composers and musicians (Jewish or otherwise) under the Third Reich or in exile. These themes paradoxically fuel and sustain his connection to German language and history, but as George himself notes, "I have no feeling [for the fact] that people or their relatives in the past may have 'done things.'"

---

22. Dreyfus, *Being George*, 53.
23. Dreyfus, *Being George*, 53.
24. "Should I play a bad bassoon just because it doesn't come from Germany?! A bassoonist as bad as me should at least play a good bassoon." Dreyfus, *Being George*, 88.
25. "For me, however, Germany is an extremely interesting country and if I find something interesting, then I have to go there too." Brusten, "*Mr New Music* in Australien," 89.

The First Trip, 1955: Wiedergutmachung *and the Proper Length of a Musical Note*

When one is twenty years old, one tends to want to go abroad. It's because we have the feeling that Australia is nothing, that orchestras are bad and that there's no compositional scene; it's part of Australia being a country on the periphery of the arts and one always wanting to go to the centre. So I wanted to leave Australia too.[26]

Though we may not recognize this description so readily now, it is a potent view of the 1950s. George's decision to return to Germany in 1955 and then to study bassoon in Vienna was in this way not very noteworthy. It was a time when many young adult Australians chose to go abroad in search of something—education, opportunity—that they felt they could not find at home. More unusually, it was also informed by his lifelong idealization of German musical culture—"Where else would I go to but Germany to learn to play the bassoon?"—and directly facilitated by the circumstances of his initial expulsion.

From the early 1950s monetary reparation was made available by the German federal government to German-Jewish victims of the Holocaust.[27] The first indemnification law, the Federal Supplementary Law, was passed by the German Bundestag on July 29, 1953 and went into force on October 1 of the same year.[28] The law outlined categories of damage eligible for compensation to individuals and included a category of "harm to career and economic advancement." Within that category, victims could also claim assistance to make up their missed education. George makes it sound easy:

> You just had to prove that you'd been living in Germany until you were virtually thrown out and that, if the Nazis hadn't come, you would have had a certain career. It's hard to predict what sort of career I would have had if history hadn't taken the turn that it did, so I made a submission saying I had come from a musical household and would have been a musician in any case, perhaps a conductor, but now I was a bassoon player in the Melbourne Symphony Orchestra and needed to improve my technique by going to Vienna, to study under Professor Öhlberger.[29]

---

26. Dreyfus, *The Last Frivolous Book*, 37.

27. For an overview history of German reparations, see Ariel Colonomos and Andrea Armstrong, "German Reparations to the Jews after World War II," in Pablo de Greiff (ed.), *The Handbook of Reparations*, Oxford scholarship online, 2006.

28. Colonomos and Armstrong, "German Reparations to the Jews after World War II," 402, 404.

29. Dreyfus, *The Last Frivolous Book*, 37.

This contrasts sharply with the complex effort of securing restitution for material assets, property and real estate owned by the Dreyfus and Ransenberg families, set in train by Hilde and Richard in 1951. Their case, mediated by a London-based German-Jewish lawyer and requiring extensive documentation, was significantly complicated by Alfred's death. By the end of this process, which lasted for over a decade, neither Richard nor Hilde wanted much more to do with Germany.

George, on the other hand, was granted a monthly stipendium linked by legislation to the cost of living, and he departed for Germany in early 1955, intending to return permanently. Though his personal circumstances brought him back to Australia in 1956, the development of George's ongoing cultural and social presence within Germany itself, which has endured to this day, begins here.

Before going to Vienna, George spent four months (mid-May to mid-September 1955) playing in an orchestra in Bad Hersfeld.[30] The orchestra played light music three times a day in the rotunda: early morning, midday, and early evening. George did not know the music, the others did. They played requests: "If the Klofrau [woman who cleans the toilets] asks for something, we play it." There was no audition. George remembers the Musikdirektor Hans Petsch, a former SA member, who had still been parading around in his uniform at the end of the war talking about *Durchhalten* ("never surrender").[31] George recalls going to a local cinema to see a film about the July 20, 1944 assassination attempt on Hitler.[32] Looking around the theater, he noticed that Petsch was the only other person there. "He found the idea of employing a German Jewish boy from Wuppertal via Australia too delicious." No one talked about the immediate past.

Perhaps this time in Bad Hersfeld also gave George an idea of what life might be like for a musician who was not quite good enough for the top orchestras. Set alongside his burgeoning ambitions as a composer, we find doubt creeping in about the idea of remaining in Germany. "Very much like my father I did not want to sit alone in a room in Cologne or Berlin and fear no-one would take any notice of me."[33]

Nonetheless, George's future attitudes towards music-making were indelibly shaped by his experience in Vienna:

---

30. The *Dienstvertrag* (Service Contract) outlining the terms of George's Bad Hersfeld employment, including his salary, is in George's private collection, together with other documents relating to his restitution claim.

31. For a discussion of why Germany kept fighting, a topic of great interest to George, see Ian Kershaw *The End: Hitler's Germany 1944–45* (London: Allen Lane, 2012).

32. Two films on this topic were released almost simultaneously in Germany in the summer of 1955: Falk Harnack's *Der 20. Juli* and G. W. Pabst's *Es geschah am 20. Juli*. George might have seen either one. Sixty-six years later, in 2021, George composed a choral piece with a German text reflecting on the significance of the events of July 20, "Andenken zum 20. Juli." "You see," he said wonderingly, "I was already interested in 1955."

33. Dreyfus, *Being George*, 53.

> Vienna was marvellous: three lessons a week with the greatest bassoon teacher in Europe! It was a big class; you turned up at two and went home at about half-past five. The aim was ... that you would not only learn from your mistakes, but from the mistakes of everybody else. It was also a social activity: you chatted to other players, but you actually *lived* the bassoon.[34]

The method of teaching was structured and traditional, consolidated over generations of players whose families had formed dynasties of orchestral musicians not unlike the aristocrats they had entertained.

Perhaps the most enduring lesson that he brought back from Vienna and one that was to shape his attitude to music-making in Australia, not always to his benefit, was his commitment to the Viennese sound style. George believes that "There is actually a style of playing the Central European classics which is, in their vision, the correct one." George shares that conviction:

> Style is about the length of notes, about letting a phrase rise and fall; it's about when to play short or long notes at the end of a phrase, about black and white, about contrasts ... It's about gaps: if the sound is continuous in a phrase, the ear becomes immune ... where the gaps should be, I learnt from Professor Öhlberger in Vienna.[35]

According to George, this idea of style is connected to the German language (all those glottal stops), a linkage he intuitively understood. But Australia does not offer many advantages to an advocate of this approach to musical style. One author has argued recently that flatness, a dominant feature of the natural landscape in Australia, has also entered musical life and the accents of speech,[36] an observation with which George would concur. Flatness and the elongation of melodic shape do not lend themselves to a realization of the basic principle of Viennese style.

The Second Trip, 1966: Anpassen, Zelig, and would the Real George Dreyfus Please Stand Up?

George returned to Australia with a pregnant wife in April 1956. He did not go to Germany again until September 1966, when a UNESCO Creative Arts Fellowship gave him the opportunity to study in Cologne with the then iconic German modernist composer, Karlheinz Stockhausen. By then George's focus had shifted from attempting to be a professional bassoon player—he was dismissed from the

---

34. Dreyfus, *The Last Frivolous Book*, 39.
35. For this and the previous quotation, see Dreyfus, *The Last Frivolous Book*, 40.
36. See, for example, B. W. Higman, "Musical Flatness," in *Flatness* (Chicago: University of Chicago Press/Reaktion Books, 2017), 202–3. For George's views, see "Entwicklungen," in Dreyfus, *Being George*, 102f.

Melbourne Symphony Orchestra in 1964 for "dumb insolence," attributable at least in part to his overt contempt for Australian orchestral standards—to surviving as a freelance composer. Together with a small group of "young Turks" of roughly his generation, he rebelled against the English-derived conservatism of the previous generation of Australian composers, and positioned himself, in both his composing and his related entrepreneurial concert-giving activities, as "Mr New Music." He taught himself how to be a modern composer from scores, LPs, and German music magazines.

> But I never really got to work with him [Stockhausen], except for five afternoon sessions in which he drooled on unmercifully, often in French for the French composers who could understand neither German nor English, delivering himself of his *Weltanschauung*. But I moved around grandly, meeting lots of composers . . . and I went to concerts and the opera, all over Germany.[37]

Between September 28, 1966 and March 19, 1967, George went to the opera and (less often) the ballet some eighty-three times—new operas as well as standard repertoire pieces—in addition to attending new music concerts and masterclasses, something every day, often in a different city. These were the days of the Eurail pass, when one felt if one was not on a train one was wasting money. Much as George loves the German opera scene, and always checks the German theaters' *Spielplan* list of upcoming opera performances as a first step on arriving, it was never a question of relocating. As he writes, "if I had returned with my father in 1948 or 1951 I would have been burnt out by the sheer effort of simply keeping up with the ever changing German cultural trends . . ."[38]

Back in Australia in March 1967, a Creative Arts Fellowship at the ANU temporarily relieved George of the financial pressures that necessarily bedevil a freelance composer in a country with a relatively small music industry. But as the 1960s morphed into the 1970s and George came to rely ever more heavily on income generated by film composing, another philosophical shift took place, the German word for which is *Anpassen*:

> [I]t is best understood in terms of a tailor making a client a personally fitted suit, rather than offering him one from the rack.[39] *Anpassen* is what I did after I left the orchestra and had to live off my wits as a film composer. I had to write the "just right" music to go with a film, so that the word would get around that George had a knack for writing "just right" music and then I would get more work . . .[40]

---

37. Dreyfus, *The Last Frivolous Book*, 71.
38. Dreyfus, *Being George*, 55.
39. The clothing metaphor is highly appropriate since many of George's ancestors worked as clothing manufacturers and retailers.
40. George Dreyfus, "*Anpassen*: Is there a Jewish Attitude to Music?," in Dreyfus, *Being George*, 42, originally published in *Generation* 5, no. 4 (Sivan 5756/June 1996): 45–7.

George claims this ability to adapt as particularly Jewish: "Attempting to fit into the world around you, once given permission to do so, is a common Jewish characteristic." His interest in "Exil-musik," the lives and works of German-Jewish composers in exile, has provided him with favorite examples of successful (Kurt Weill and Erich Korngold) and unsuccessful (Melbourne-based Felix Werder) German-Jewish composer adaptation, "those who did it and those who didn't." Although he admits that these composers, being older, already had major careers when they were forced into exile, while he, as a child, "really only had my subconsciously inherited tradition," he is quite comfortable in their company.[41]

Spurred by the examples of Weil and Korngold who, in his view, had succeeded both as composers of commercial music and *Hochkunst*, George embraced *Anpassen* with enthusiasm. If the decade of the '60s, say 1964 to 1974, was broadly characterized by George's rather aggressive identification with a style of international modernism represented by the music of Pierre Boulez, Karlheinz Stockhausen, and the icons of the German music magazines, the decade of the 1970s was shaped by an equally strenuous embrace of what has been described as his own brand of "gumnut nationalism."[42] Starting with the *Theme from Rush* (1974), with its hotly-contested appropriation of Australian folk-song melodies, George wrote music for an abundance of Australian films, television series, and nationalistic theater pieces, some of which—like the aforementioned *Theme from Rush*—achieved a degree of public recognition and popularity unusual for a classical music composer.

From the earliest years of his career, George had organized concerts in which he played his own wind chamber music alongside the music of other composers in recognizably conventional settings and formats and he continued to do this, in Australia and, later, in Germany for several decades. From the 1970s, however, he arranged his film and television music for a variety of instrumental groups and took it into an assortment of venues at home and abroad—school classrooms, community and amateur music-making situations of all kinds—often devising a novel performance situation. He took on Australia's notoriously conservative brass band movement, with limited success but enormous joyfulness. He began to acquire a reputation for self-promotion that appeared to be increasingly at odds with his deep-seated, passionate, and engaged commitment to his Central European heritage of musical correctness.

---

41. Dreyfus, *Being George*, 43. George is particularly fond of pointing to Felix Werder as an example of unsuccessful *Anpassen*. "Felix ... turned out to be a fabulous role model: of what not to do, to become a music critic, to write the wrong music for the wrong place." "It's not my first work!," in George Dreyfus, *Don't Ever Let Them Get You* (North Fitzroy: Black Pepper Publishing, 2009), 5. Or again, "Australia is no place for Felix's linear counterpoint" (Dreyfus, *Being George*, 44).

42. John Whiteoak, "Brass Banding Meets George Dreyfus," in Dreyfus, *Don't Ever Let Them Get You*, 111.

> Those who have encountered George Dreyfus in self-promotional mode—a not uncommon occurrence—and know a little about early Australian music history will probably agree that at these times George Dreyfus *is* a brass band.[43]

Inspired perhaps by his association with the anarchic, iconoclastic, and irreverent theatrical presentations (and personalities) at Melbourne's Pram Factory, George ventured into more colorful modes of self-promotion.

> To be a creative member of this theatre group you had to be *kulturpolitisch korrekt, genau so wie in den schönen Zeiten des tausendjährigen Reiches*, you had to be anti-British, anti-German, anti-American, it was anti-Vietnam war time—and above all, anti-Hollywood, which meant anti-commercial.[44]

In his so-called one-man show (though he always needed a keyboard player) *George Dreyfus—Live!* (1977), he presented himself as composer, performer, and larrikin entertainer, telling a few jokes, playing a few short pieces, singing, even, at the end of one song, doing a little dance twirl. Indulging an instinct for satire alongside his by now well-established disregard for hierarchy, George took the text of an adverse critique of his *Symphony No 1* and turned it into the lyrics of an impertinent cabaret-style song that involved much throat-clearing, in tribute to the then current obsession with the Watergate informant known as Deep Throat.[45] "Of course, that wasn't the right behaviour for a Bruckner-type composer," George blithely admits, "not fitting to the traditional image. But then Australia doesn't have a tradition about anything; anything goes and we can take risks."[46]

Australia may not have traditions about anything, but Germany certainly does. Music is not just another art form in Germany. Historically, music has enjoyed a role of unique significance and power in the German imagination of nationhood and collective identity, one that has persisted through the vicissitudes of modern German history and is reflected in the multitude of orchestras, opera houses, and conservatoriums.[47] Germans take their classical music very seriously. So when George took a German-language version of the second incarnation of his one-man show, *Surviving*, on tour in Nordrhein Westfalen and Hessen in the second half of the 1990s, his German audiences did not know what to make of it.

43. Whiteoak, "Brass Banding Meets George Dreyfus," 97.

44. "culture-politically correct, just like in the beautiful times of the thousand-year Reich." George Dreyfus, "*Rathenau*: Ist die Oper eine australische Tragödie?" in Dreyfus, *Being George*, 18.

45. Text and music of Deep Throat can be found in Dreyfus, *The Last Frivolous Book*, 116–17; a recording of George's performance from his CD *George Dreyfus – Live!* may be found at https://music.youtube.com/watch?v=IEEgiJtO2RA&list=RDAMVMIEEgiJtO2RA.

46. Dreyfus, *The Last Frivolous Book*, 114.

47. See Celia Applegate and Pamela Potter, "Germans as the 'People of Music': Genealogy of an Identity," in Celia Applegate and Pamela Potter (eds.), *Music and German National Identity* (Chicago and London: University of Chicago Press, 2002), 1–35.

It was firstly a matter of the content, which synthesized George's interest in composers who had survived the Third Reich within Germany with elements of his own story of survival as a composer, compressed to the point of incomprehensibility for non-Australian listeners. Then there was the presentation, in which George talked as much as he played the music. Then there was tone. Here was someone speaking German like a native, but expressing sentiments that were both deeply idiosyncratic and clearly foreign (read Australian) in an ironic, self-deprecating, anti-authoritarian vein that is fundamentally anathema to German sensibilities. With few points of reference for such a presentation, the audience responses ranged from baffled to hostile. This, perhaps more than anything else George ever did musically in Germany, was a measure of how far he had traveled from the ideals of the musical homeland that had sustained him since Vienna (short notes notwithstanding).[48] This, more than anything, showed the extent to which the fact that his formal education in Germany stopped when he was ten had inhibited the process of becoming German.

Not Just German, but Jewish

It's only in recent years that I've become interested in my Jewishness.[49]

George's relationship to the Holocaust is complex and multilayered and yet it is his absorbing interest in the event that forced him to leave, above all other connections, perhaps, that has anchored him to the physical reality of Germany as a country—its landscape, geography, and historical markers—and given purpose to his many returns.

> In any case, you cannot get to know Germany from Australia; especially not when it comes to the Holocaust. I have no inhibitions in this regard because it interests me; and I am also interested in how my grandparents and others from my family perished in the "Third Reich".[50]

Three of his grandparents and numerous members of his extended family were murdered, but as is so often the case, the German past was not something that was spoken about in George's birth family.

---

48. The text of *Surviving* may be found in Dreyfus, *Don't Ever Let Them Get You*, 22f.
49. Dreyfus, *The Last Frivolous Book*, 14.
50. "Deutschland kann man jedenfalls nicht von Australien aus kennenlernen; vor allem dann nicht, wenn es um den Holocaust geht ... Ich habe in dieser Hinsicht keine Hemmungen, weil es mich interessiert; und mich interessiert auch, wie meine Großeltern und andere aus meiner Familie im 'Dritten Reich' umgekommen sind." Dreyfus, *Being George*, 89.

Although we were deeply affected by the Holocaust, we practically never talked about the Holocaust in our own families ... Back then, people rarely talked about the Holocaust anyway. That actually only changed a few years ago after the film "Holocaust" was shown on television [in 1979].[51]

Nor was it the first thing that brought him to his interest in the Holocaust.

Because of my own personal history, I have always been fascinated by how people who happen to be Jewish have responded to historic necessity.[52]

In the beginning, however—I have to admit this—I wasn't too interested in the Holocaust myself. All of that actually came to me later through music and began with a book by Fred Prieberg about music in the Nazi state and with reports about the life of artists in the Third Reich and how this continued afterwards.[53]

A seminal moment in George's search for information about his family occurred in March 1983 when he visited the Wiesbaden Jüdische Gemeinde in Friedrichstraße and looked through a series of photographs documenting the deportation of the city's Jewish residents. The images had been enlarged for the purpose of an exhibition—George did not have the details[54]—and in one of the photographs George saw his grandfather's face:

There he was, in the yard of the Wiesbaden Railway Station, with that determined look on his face that I remember so well! He was facing a security guard, a *Sicherheitsdienstmann*, who had his back to the camera, and there was no mistaking the familiar features seen over the guard's shoulder.[55]

---

51. "Obwohl wir vom Holocaust sehr betroffen waren, haben wir dennoch in unserer eigenen Familie praktisch nie über den Holocaust geredet ... Man hat damals sowieso nur selten über den Holocaust geredet. Das änderte sich eigentlich erst vor wenigen Jahren, nachdem im Fernsehen der Film 'Holocaust' gelaufen war." Dreyfus, *Being George*, 87.

52. George Dreyfus, "Gustav & Me," in Dreyfus, *Being George*, 6, originally published in *Generation* 3, no. 2 (Tishrei 5753/September 1992): 52–6.

53. "Anfangs habe ich mich allerdings—das muß ich schon zugeben—auch selbst nicht allzu sehr für den Holocaust interessiert. Das kam bei mir eigentlich alles erst später über die Musik und begann mit einem Buch von Fred Prieberg über 'Musik im NS-Staat' und mit Berichten über das Leben von Künstlern im 'Dritten Reich' und wie diese hinterher weitergemacht haben" (Dreyfus, *Being George*, 87). Fred K. Prieberg, *Musik im NS-Stadt* (Freiburg: Fischer-Taschenbuch-Verlag, 1982).

54. The exhibition was mounted in the Wiesbaden City Hall in November 1980 as the city's annual Kristallnacht commemoration for that year. It was created out of a co-operation between the city of Wiesbaden, the Wiesbaden Jüdische Gemeinde, the German–Israeli Society, and the Society for Christian–Jewish Cooperation.

55. Dreyfus, *The Last Frivolous Book*, 17.

George's response to this discovery was entirely characteristic. He "raced down the street to the shop of the photographer who had made the enlargements," Foto Rudolph, which claimed copyright in the images, and purchased a set of eighteen prints. Then he looked for someone who could tell him more about the photographs and someone who could confirm his identification of his grandfather. Equally, he looked for someone who could explain to him why his grandmother was not there.

In seeking to know and understand the fates of these people, George has visited concentration camps at Ravensbrück, Theresienstadt, Buchenwald, Auschwitz, and elsewhere, along with cemeteries and sites of commemoration in Wiesbaden and Wuppertal, where memorial Stolpersteine are laid outside his grandparents' former homes. He has built up a network of German contacts and scholars who are dedicated to documenting the lives of the Jewish communities of their cities, a very distinctive locally-focused branch of Holocaust history.

George's awareness developed with the unfolding and changing historiography of Holocaust studies and his library reflects his dedication to creating a collection of books and homegrown narratives that consolidates his personal connection to these events. Within Germany, however, as Holocaust survivors age and die, George has reclaimed the exotic status he enjoyed as a young man among his colleagues in the 1950s. In interviews and spoken commentaries in which he speaks as an exile and survivor, German audiences are at once bemused by his Australian particularity as they are intrigued by his stories of a musician's life "Down Under." It is a form of belonging that does not require his continuous presence, but ensures acceptance when he returns, especially in those cities where he is known and has connections.

Anpassen *Fractures: Defiance and the Folly of Opera*

When I'm in Europe I go to the opera every night ...
There was never any scene for which I wrote the music.[56]

George is very well aware of the folly of writing operas for a market that does not really exist in Australia. And yet opera, that quintessential European artform, has remained a lifelong fascination for him. For George, opera is a "marvellous thing" ...

> [I]t has everything going together: it has music, dancing, sets and it also has the "word". That the "word" in opera is incomprehensible doesn't matter. Opera has always been the *Gesamtkunstwerk*, the total work of art, incorporating everything.[57]

---

56. Dreyfus, *The Last Frivolous Book*, 89.
57. Dreyfus, *The Last Frivolous Book*, 32.

An early enthusiasm for Wagner was nurtured in his family's émigré environment by his parents' acquaintance with the Viennese painter Robert Hofmann.[58] Hofmann had been deported to Australia in 1940 on the *Dunera*. He became a "house friend" of George's parents on his release from internment and lived in Australia until he departed for the US in 1956, leaving his collection of Wagner vocal scores with George. As a teenager, George went hunting in second-hand record shops for 78 RPM recordings that he could afford. Early purchases included excerpts from *Tristan* (the whole opera on twenty recordings) and an early LP of *Parsifal*, the first complete Wagner opera he owned.[59] Hardly a typical Australian adolescence.

His eighteen-month apprenticeship with J. C. Williamson's 1948–9 Italian Opera Company cemented both George's knowledge of and passion for opera:

> In the time I toured with them, we played *Madame Butterfly* seventy-five times! Before they finally went back to Italy, we were playing *Butterfly* three times a week. Melbourne just wanted to see that opera. It was a craze, like *Star Wars*. I still think it's a marvellous piece.[60]

This operatic passion would become a major challenge to *Anpassen* and set him on a collision course with the Australian operatic establishment.

> [George] makes no bones about the fact that in his heart of hearts he has always felt more connected to his lost and partly recovered European cultural milieu, and in opera, to "*Gesamtkunstwerk*", the total work of art incorporating everything.[61]

Casanova (1960), George's first operatic venture as a composer, was a failure. He never finished it. But George has always been sanguine about failure in opera— other people's failures, at any rate. "To fail in opera is no disgrace," says George.[62] He collects scores of what he calls "orphan operas," operas performed at most a few times for a short while (if ever) and then never again. He assembles data about operatic failures, American, Australian, and German, noting ruefully (but gleefully), "These composers and their operas are ... *völlig verschollen* [completely lost]."[63]

---

58. https://www.dunerastories.monash.edu/dunera-stories/85-dunera-stories-with-gallery/229-the-tales-of-hofmann-a-life-across-three-continents.html.
59. Dreyfus, *The Last Frivolous Book*, 27.
60. Dreyfus, *The Last Frivolous Book*, 31.
61. Whiteoak, "Brass Banding Meets George Dreyfus," 125–6.
62. Dreyfus, *The Last Frivolous Book*, 56.
63. Dreyfus, *Being George*, 12. As sources, George cites Julius Matfield, *A Handbook of American Operatic Premieres 1731–1962* (n.p.p.: ISI, 1963); Elizabeth Wood, "Australian Opera, 1842–1970: A History of Australian Opera with Descriptive Catalogues," Ph.D. dissertation, University of Adelaide, 1979; Prieberg, , *Musik im NS-Stadt*, 300–7.

George has written two operas for Australia, neither of which has been performed by the national opera company or state-based companies, despite the fact that the second of these, *The Gilt-Edged Kid*, was actually commissioned by the Australian Opera in 1970. George does not see the non-performance of *The Gilt-Edged Kid* as a failure but as a betrayal, an injustice of historical magnitude.[64] He does not shrink from comparing his treatment by the Australian Opera to that meted out by the French Army to his father's namesake Alfred Dreyfus (he of Devil's Island fame), nor from conflating the responses of the opera administration with those of the perpetrators at Hadamar.[65] For four decades he has mounted a Zola-esque David and Goliath battle for justice for *The Gilt-Edged Kid*—largely unsuccessfully except for the media attention that some of his more outrageous protest stunts have attracted.[66] "The wrong decision I made was to write a piece for an industry that doesn't exist here."[67]

It is in the field of opera, however, that we may find George's supremely defiant creative departures.

> I finally solved my personal problem with opera in Australia by creating two huge (naturally) operas for the German market with my very own monumentally inspired genius, my court-German, *ich bin sein Hof-Jude*, Volker Elis Pilgrim.[68]

In 1991, George was awarded the Australia Council's Don Banks Music Award, allowing him once more to commit to full-time opera composition. He already had a subject in mind and a prospective librettist. Volker Elis Pilgrim was a highly individual and successful German author with very un-Australian views about the God-given privileged status of creative artists. Pilgrim was living in Australia at the time, having become an Australian citizen in 1989. Between 1989 and 1995, the two convened in George's music-room in Camberwell and through regular hour-long discussions ("in German, *natürlich!*")[69] created two full-length operas for the German stage. Surely a spectacular example of *innerer Aufbruch* [inner departure].

Unlike his "Australian" operas, George's subject-choices for these two operas were entirely informed by his German-Jewish heritage, with a strong overlay of what was increasingly coming to dominate his worldview, a view born of displacement, his father's untimely death, and his own dualities, "not knowing where one wants to be":

---

64. *Garni Sands* was staged by Roger Covell with his University of NSW Opera Company in Sydney (four performances) and Melbourne (two performances) in 1972.

65. George Dreyfus, *Brush Off! Saving* The Gilt-Edged Kid *from Oblivion* (Melbourne: Three Feet Publishing, 2011), 51, 52.

66. For George's retelling of this modern Dreyfus case, see Dreyfus, *Brush Off!*.

67. Dreyfus, *The Last Frivolous Book*, 89.

68. Dreyfus, *Being George*, 46.

69. Dreyfus, *Being George*, 12.

> Into all [my] traumas of fatherdeath, of hiding from oneself what one really wants, of not knowing where one wants to be, my two opera protagonists fitted perfectly; Rathenau with his trauma of wanting to remain Jewish, but at the same time wishing to fit snugly into German society, showing off his money of which he had more than enough, and Marx, with his trauma of rejecting his Jewishness, hated by German society, railing against money and always needing more.[70]

Both operas were performed in Germany: *Rathenau* in Kassel in 1993; *Die Marx Sisters* in Bielefeld in 1996. Both attracted significant attention from the German press.[71] George's assessment of the success of the operas is typically rueful:

> I think back to the simultaneous fifty-fifty *Triumph und Zeriss* (triumph and shredding) of my opera *Rathenau* in Kassel 1993, I think back to the total, except for the prestigious *Süddeutsche Zeitung*, totalem *Zeriss* of my opera *Die Marx Sisters*, in Bielefeld 1996.[72]

Australia has shown no interest in either opera, despite the best efforts of the German publisher and the fact that, according to George, "*Rathenau* is the first opera written by two Australian citizens, resident and creating in this country, which has ever been staged in an overseas opera house." "You always think," ruminates George, "that you're the one who's not going to fall off the train. You think, 'Mine will be different; mine will be so good that it will break through.' But, it doesn't." "Composers, however, have been programmed to wait for the recognition of their genius until they are dead," writes George, "Anyone for a pistol?"[73]

Summing Up

> [W]hen I can I go back to the source of my music, back to Vienna, back to Germany.[74]

---

70. Dreyfus, *Being George*, 54. The choice of subject for Rathenau was George's. As for *Die Marx Sisters*, Pilgrim had already written a book about Marx's wife and daughters: *Adieu Marx. Gewalt und Ausbeutung im Hause des Wortführers* (*Violence and Exploitation in the House of the Spokesman*) (Reinbek bei Hamburg: Rowohlt, 1990). Revised as *Jenny, Helene, Marianne: Die drei Frauen von Karl Marx* (Hamburg: Osburg, 2018).

71. George includes a listing of thirty-eight reviews of *Rathenau* and forty-eight of *Die Marx Sisters* in "Surviving," in Dreyfus, *Don't Ever Let Them Get You*, 27–30.

72. George Dreyfus, "Border Crossings or The Worst News Is . . .," in Dreyfus, *Don't Ever Let Them Get You*, 57–58.

73. Quotations in this paragraph are (in order) from Dreyfus, *Being George*, 12; Dreyfus, *The Last Frivolous Book*, 89; and Dreyfus, *Being George*, 23.

74. Dreyfus, *The Last Frivolous Book*, 134.

The geography of George Dreyfus's life has certainly been shaped by many border crossings, by returns and departures and re-returns:

> I have always crossed borders, sometimes willingly, sometimes unwillingly, crossing from Germany to England and then to Australia in 1939, crossing from Australia to Italy and then back to Germany in 1954 [sic: 1955], and countless times thereafter[75]

The first line of the lyrics for Hildegaard Kneff's poignantly evocative song "Und ich dreh' mich nochmal um" echoes the ambivalence of yearning for what has been lost, of all those turnings about, though yearning is not all that defines the complexities of George's relationship with Germany.[76]

As a musician and a composer George committed to the highest ideals of Central European classical music, the heritage of his German homeland. But his ambition "to keep himself alive in Australia solely by writing music" has also entailed many creative departures: "I had to split myself, I had to do anything that came along. From Schoenbergian high art to popularist realism."[77] For George, then, "departure" was more than a physical activity but a state of mind, a creative position. He applies the metaphor of border crossing to his creative outputs too:

> [M]y symphonies cross with my suites of film music ... my operas cross with my Pram Factory-inspired musicals ... my high-art and ideologically committed *Didjeridu Sextet* crosses with the light hearted ditties of the *Galgenlieder*.[78]

It was not a compromise that came without cost:

> [T]he serious music people only like my popular music ... The popular music people only like my serious music.[79]

> Man sollte Australien nicht zu leicht unterschätzen, ein Riesenland mit Riesenflächen ohne Berge, mit Riesenhitze ohne Regen, mit riesen innerere Stärke, was ein Künstler mit einer fremden, mitgebrachten Kultur schwerlich überwinden kann.[80]

---

75. Dreyfus, *Don't Ever Let Them Get You*, 54.
76. The lyrics of the Kneff song may be found at https://www.hildegardknef.de/Texte/undichdrehmichnochmalum.htm.
77. Dreyfus, *Don't Ever Let Them Get You*, 55.
78. Dreyfus, *Don't Ever Let Them Get You*, 55.
79. Dreyfus, *Don't Ever Let Them Get You*, 56.
80. "Australia should not be underestimated too easily, a huge country with huge areas without mountains, with huge heat without rain, with huge inner strength, which an artist with a foreign culture he has brought with him can hardly overcome." George Dreyfus, "*Entwicklungen*," in Dreyfus, *Being George*, 102.

Successful migration usually involves adaptation, and at one level George has succeeded in accommodating the challenges of Australian cultural life through his much-vaunted capacity for *Anpassen*.

Like *Till Eulenspiegel*, George likes to dart about a bit, avoiding seriousness and any discussion of his feelings. There are those who have characterized George as someone wearing a mask of extroverted adaptability that has provided "the sometimes impenetrable barrier disguising the private inner search for the deeper cultural meanings of his heritage."[81] He likes to compare himself to Zelig, that chameleon-like character from a 1983 film by Woody Allen, a person "who wants to fit in with every group he comes in contact with" and takes on the characteristics of the strong personalities around him.[82] But, as is so often the case with people who speak two languages, we may detect signs of cross-cultural interference. George's dedication to amateur and community music-making is very real but his European training has made him a hard task-master and his approach is not always appreciated by Australian musicians. On one memorable occasion, an entire choir walked out of a rehearsal in protest. On the other hand, his acquired self-deprecating Australian larrikinism and apparent lack of seriousness often disconcert his German audiences.

It is well-established in the migration literature that involuntary migration often makes adjustment in the new homeland more difficult. In George's case, his departure from Germany is connected to the Holocaust, an event that attracts and repels him in equal measure, drawing him back to Germany but ensuring that he is happy to leave, fueling his intellectual life, feeding his creativity, defining his worldview. George is a man who lives comfortably with duality:

> I am entitled to point to my further uniqueness as a half German-Australian composer of half German-Australian music.[83]

---

81. Andrew McCredie, "Introduction," in Dreyfus, *Being George*, xviii. See also P. G. Downs, "George Dreyfus's First Symphony," *Meanjin Quarterly* 27, no. 4 (December 1968): 486–8.
82. Dreyfus, *Being George*, 7, 8.
83. Dreyfus, *Being George*, 15.

Chapter 8

GREEK DEPARTURES: SHIPS, STOWAWAYS, AND THE POLITICS OF RETURNS

Joy Damousi

In January 1960, the Greek liner *Patris* sailed into Sydney Harbor from Greece for the first time. Its arrival in Australia took place without much attention and fuss as it glided into the harbor. But its unheralded entry into Sydney marked the arrival of the Chandris Lines of ships, which for the next decade or so would make departures and arrivals possible for thousands of migrants traveling to and from Australia. The Chandris Lines dated from the turn of the twentieth century when, in 1911, John Chandris began a tramp steam operator business. In the 1950s his sons, Dimitrios and Antonios, established the D&A Chandris line and in 1959 began to compete with the Italian liners which previously had had a monopoly of the Europe to Australia emigration route.[1]

After this rather inauspicious entry, the *Patris* became a regular and familiar feature of the fanfare of arrivals and departures of immigrants in Australia, carrying Greek and British migrants to Australia and back. The *Patris* made a total of ninety-one voyages to Australia between 1959 and 1975, traveling regularly via the Suez Canal, stopping at ports such as Aden, Port Said, and Colombo. In 1967, when the Suez Canal was closed due to the Six-Day War, the *Patris* detoured around Africa, stopping at Cape Town and Durban, on the way to Australia, a route it would follow for the next five years. Another notable Chandris Line ship was the *Ellinis*, which became well known for transporting British migrants from Southampton to Australia between 1963 and 1977, completing fifty voyages over that time.[2]

Departures and arrivals to and from Australia would have been impossible for thousands of migrants without the Chandris Lines ships. Yet little scholarly attention has been given to the history of these liners and how the movement of

---

1. Peter Plowman, *Australian Migrant Ships, 1946–1977* (Dural: Rosenberg Publishing, 2006).
2. Plowman, *Australian Migrant Ships*. Museums Victoria, RHMS Ellinis, Chandris Shipping Line, 1933–1987.

immigrants was shaped and determined by them. In the history of immigrant ship voyages, the steam ships of the nineteenth century and early twentieth centuries have been a focus of research, but the boom in immigrant shipping in the immediate postwar period awaits further exploration. Towards this end, this chapter argues that any consideration of the relationship between departures and arrivals demands a scrutiny of the logistics, routes, and finance of immigrant ships combined with a much fuller understanding of the experience of traveling as an immigrant on an ocean liner. In doing so, I seek to contribute to three historiographies: the immigrant experience in the postwar period; the histories of oceans; and the place of the immigrant voyage in shaping our understanding of departures, arrivals, and the intersections between the two. The aim is to capture experiences of departures and arrivals that have yet to be documented or examined.

This chapter first focuses on aspects of migrant departures and arrivals which have not yet drawn the attention of historians. This examination aims to present a varied picture of how we might write a different history of migrant "departures" and "arrivals." It examines these variations by identifying first, stowaway immigrants who used these ocean liners to depart and arrive at different ports, for a host of reasons, some of which I have been able to identify and others not. Many of these were dramatic entries and exits and were invariably reported in the press with drama and color. I pay specific attention to the Greek stowaway migrants who were apprehended on the Greek liners *Patris* and *Ellinis*. The second aspect of this study considers an unwritten chapter in the history of the *Patris* which involved the prevention of its departure from Australian ports in 1970–1 by Australian seamen, the Seaman's Union and the Waterside Workers' Federation in protest against political prisoners being held and tortured in Greece under the military junta. If we are to consider the factors that enhanced and made possible the departures and arrivals of migrants, the forces that prevented these or worked against them are also worthy of our attention. In this instance, this involves a protest against the political situation in Greece which was then ruled by a right-wing military dictatorship. Those traveling to Greece at this time from Australia during the rule of the generals were also urged by left-wing activists not to leave Australia. Departures to Greece at this time were seen by these protestors as offering tacit support to an undemocratic, oppressive, and authoritarian regime. Returning immigrants were asked to reconsider their plans, as their return could be seen as a political, anti-democratic act.

Beyond this focus, this chapter also considers the wider backdrop of questions scholars and government officials asked of departing migrants, especially of British migrants in contrast to Greek immigrants. This points to an overemphasis on British migrants, the overwhelmingly favored group in Australian immigration policy throughout the twentieth century. A comparative study suggests the argument—explored by several contributors to this volume—that the concern about and focus on departures mainly related to British migrants and why they chose to leave more than on others—and how they might be persuaded to return.

A History of Migrants Departing and Arriving at Sea

The arrival and departure of migrants to Australia on the seas has a long and well-documented history. Since the 1850s, sailing ships, then iron-hulled steamers from 1852 brought free settlers to Australia and returned them. By the 1880s, steam ships began to make a profit and to carry immigrants. The perilous conditions at this time are well documented and historians have shown what passengers endured, as the route involved encountering icebergs, wild oceans, passing to the south of the Cape of Good Hope, seeking the "Roaring Forties"—the winds that blew from west to east between 40 and 50 degrees south. When the Suez Canal was opened in 1869, it provided ships traveling from Europe with an alternative route. By the turn of the century, with steamships traveling via the Suez Canal, reducing the travel times by thirty-five to forty days, the trip was more comfortable, offering the migrant traveler a greater variety of activities on the ships themselves. By the early twentieth century, several main shipping lines dominated the route from Britain to Australia, including the Aberdeen Line, the Blue Funnel Line, the Orient Line, the P&O Line, the P&O Branch Line, and the White Star Line. From the 1920s and 1930s, steamships provided recreation in the form of concerts, sporting games, and other activities.[3]

With the outbreak of World War II, Australian ports were closed to immigration. But after the war a new era began with the Australian government's postwar immigration program. The first group to arrive in large numbers were the displaced persons (DPs), 170,000 of whom arrived between 1947 and 1953. The second wave arrived in the 1950s and 1960s, mainly migrants from the "less desirable" countries of Southern Europe, including Italy, Greece, Croatia, and Turkey.[4] As postwar migration began to flourish and prosper, the competition for this clientele intensified. The most common route during the 1940s and 1950s was through the Suez Canal. The stopovers were in Egypt, Yemen, and Colombo in Sri Lanka, and then across the Indian Ocean to Fremantle in Western Australia. Another route was round the Cape of Good Hope in Africa, via Lisbon to Cape Town and then across to the Indian Ocean to Fremantle, and then on to Melbourne and Sydney.[5]

Memories and Mementos

The journey on the ship became an important part of migrant memories and it forms a crucial part of the emotional history of migration. Mementos, scrap books,

---

3. https://museumsvictoria.com.au/immigrationmuseum/resources/journeys-to-australia/#1940s-60s.

4. James Jupp, *From White Australia to Woomera: The Story of Australian Immigration* (Cambridge: Cambridge University Press, 2002), 10–19.

5. https://museumsvictoria.com.au/immigrationmuseum/resources/journeys-to-australia/#1940s-60s.

and photographs were collected by migrants on the liners that took them to Australia. Many have recorded their memories of their experience on the ship. The *Fairsea*, which operated from 1949 to 1969, was an aircraft carrier and cruise ship during the war which was refurbished after the war as a migrant ship. It made eighty-one voyages from 1949 to 1959 transporting in particular assisted immigrants from Britain. Doreen Hakowski, who migrated from England in 1956, remembered her trip fondly:

> The *Fairsea*—our home for five weeks, was the best part of my early life. I had been born in an air-raid shelter in London, so only knew destruction around me. My trip was very exciting. We had lovely meals, dances, entertainment, deck games, swimming and many other pastimes. We stopped off in Aden and rode a camel through the streets. I can't even remember feeling sad at leaving my home country, England.[6]

Others recall traveling on older, less glamorous ships. The *Castel Felice*, which traveled operated between 1952 and 1970, was rebuilt from a British India steamship. Although refurbished, with air conditioning, a swimming pool, and large public rooms, it was cramped, as Wolfgang Kahran, who migrated from Germany on it in 1960, recalled:

> As far as we were concerned, the *Castel Felice* was already in the scrap yard. The crew tried their best, but the ship was unsteady. We were eight men in a double cabin—four tiered bunks! There were no luxuries for us.[7]

These too could be perilous journeys. In July 1964, the crew of the *Ellinis* rescued a twenty-seven-year-old Greek-Australian man after he fell overboard. The passenger, George Gerovassilis, fell in the sea in the early morning, 400 miles east of Aden, traveling to Southampton. He had swum after falling and was unharmed, although according to reports, he "had fallen into waters infested by sharks."[8] Some departed on these ships but never arrived. In 1974, two men died of "natural causes" before they disembarked.[9] The press at the time reported adventure, peril, and novelty in the departures of the ocean liners that brought migrants to and from Australia. For this generation of migrants, travel by sea could provide novelty and adventure and it forms part of a longer history of migrant arrival and departure. There is more work to be done on these aspects of the immigrant experience of traveling on ships, charting their experiences and how these

---

6. https://museumsvictoria.com.au/immigrationmuseum/resources/journeys-to-australia/#1940s-60s.
7. https://museumsvictoria.com.au/immigrationmuseum/resources/journeys-to-australia/#1940s-60s.
8. *Canberra Times*, July 7, 1964, 4.
9. *Canberra Times*, June 25, 1974, 7.

memories shaped their understanding of their identities and departures and arrivals.

The focus of this chapter is on one of the largest ethnic groups to arrive in Australia: those from Greece. An entirely unexplored dimension to this story is that of immigrant stowaways as a form of departure, and in particular the experience of Greeks stowaways. Greeks arrived legally and departed in large numbers to and from Australia during the postwar period, constituting one of the largest immigrant groups in Australia, especially in the years 1945–72. Over this period, a total of 214,304 Greek immigrants arrived. They were attracted to Australia because of the demand for labor after the war, but the numbers increased after Commonwealth assistance was provided in 1952. Australia became a desired destination. Between 1946 and 1952, there were only 8,962 permanent settlers from Greece. By mid-1956 this had expanded to an intake of 29,344, of which 16,833 arrived on assisted passages. In 1961 the census showed this figure had trebled to 77,333, reaching its peak of 160,000 in 1971. Almost half of this number (47%) of Greeks resided in Melbourne.[10]

Greek Departures 1945–75

In her 1984 study of Greek migration, Gillian Bottomley observed how the emphasis by scholars had been on those who arrived in Australia in unprecedented numbers, their assimilation, and the experience of Greeks settling in Australia. After almost forty years since Bottomley's short study, this remains the case. Bottomley argued that most studies were of immigration because this was where more research resources were available, focusing on the problems and related issues of migration. She challenged the assumption that migrants leave home as permanent migrants, as this denied the link back to the homeland. Any understanding of migration, she noted, needed to be broad ranging, and had to consider political, economic, and social forces[11] In her own research, which began in 1969, Bottomley wrote that the flow of Greek migration had reversed since the early 1970s. "Since 1972 more people have been returning than arriving" from Greece, she observed.[12] In her discussion, Bottomley stressed the need to maintain an "international perspective on migration," which was vital in considering the

---

10. Joy Damousi, *Memory and Migration in the Shadow of War: Australia's Greek Immigrants after World War II and the Greek Civil War* (Cambridge: Cambridge University Press, 2015), 73–4.

11. Gillian Bottomley, "The Export of People: Emigration from and Return Migration to Greece" (Wollongong: Centre for Multicultural Studies, University of Wollongong, Occasional Paper 1, 1984), 1. https://ro.uow.edu.au/cgi/viewcontent.cgi?article=1001&context=cmsocpapers.

12. Bottomley, "The Export of People," 1.

flow and ebb of migrations.[13] She noted that much of the material available about Greeks returning over this period was from German sources, where research had identified returning Greeks from Germany in the 1970s and 1980s.[14] In the Australian case, Bottomley wrote that the return was high, but that accurate figures were difficult to find. She drew on the work of Theodore Lianos, whose studies of the in- and outflow of Greek migrants remained key for the period 1945–75.[15] As Bottomley noted, Lianos estimated that between 1968 and 1972, 39 percent of returned migrants came from Australia. Drawing on Australian figures, between 1947 and 1968, the ratio of settler loss/settler arrival of people born in Greece or Cyprus was 27 percent—that is, 220,494 arrived and 59,634 left in that period.[16] Bottomley identified similar issues with Greeks returning from Germany. Many in Australia had established small businesses such as restaurants, cafes, hotels, and so on. Several of them had connections, both social and economic, in Greece and Australia, and spent time in each place, a practice Bottomley characterized as a form of "alternating migration."[17]

Bottomley was interested in the experience of Greeks who had returned to Greece. She noted how social life was intense in Greece, especially in the summer months, and this was an attraction for those returning. She discussed two associations that had been established in Athens to assist Greeks departing for home. The Greek-Australian Association organized social activities in Athens, including an annual ball where debutantes were presented, as they had done at the balls of the Greek Orthodox Community of New South Wales. Bottomley noted this was an old British tradition which shows a "colonial custom [moving] from Britain to Australia and back to Greece!"[18] She also described how others had established a connection with Australia. One hotelier ran the Hotel Sydney in Rhodes, featuring an interior that could be found in a south-western suburb of Sydney. She continued, "Its proprietor, who lived in Sydney for 15 years, welcomes a number of Australian tourists each year and benefits from the extensive information network that operates among Greeks in Australia."[19] Bottomley observed that in many of the cases she studied, the departures from Australia did not mean severing ties with Australia completely. Here is her explanation:

> Migration to Australia took place over a long period of time and through a system of chain migration that enabled networks to be constructed and maintained at both ends of the migration process. As a result, those who return

---

13. Bottomley, "The Export of People," 2.
14. Bottomley, "The Export of People," 6–7.
15. See Theodore P. Lianos, "Flows of Greek Out-Migration and Return Migration," *International Migration* 13, no. 3 (July 1975): 119–33.
16. Lianos, "Flows of Greek Out-Migration and Return Migration," 8.
17. Lianos, "Flows of Greek Out-Migration and Return Migration," 8.
18. Lianos, "Flows of Greek Out-Migration and Return Migration," 9.
19. Lianos, "Flows of Greek Out-Migration and Return Migration," 18.

have usually come back to kin and friends in Greece, but also retained contact with kin and friends in Australia ... this can lead to a kind of alternating migration. Some of the families I have interviewed, with business and kinship ties in both countries, spend several years in one and then the other. Others, especially older emigrants, have offspring in Australia and move backwards and forwards if they can afford it.[20]

This feature of alternating migration was not distinctive to the Greek community, but it remained a feature of Greek "departures," while not available to all— Bottomley in fact noting that "it is available to relatively few":

> The industrial workers who form the bulk of Australia's Greek population simply cannot opt to spend part of their lives part in Greece and part in Australia. Nevertheless, people have been revisiting Greece more frequently in the last few years, memories have been refreshed and ties with those who remain in Greece have been strengthened.[21]

Bottomley did not return to this work on departures. In her extensive research into Greek communities in Australia, she explored rather its cultural forms: the second generation and many other aspects of cultural life—but not departures.[22] Return migration of Greeks has also been considered in other contexts, such as the American and Italian cases, but this remains fragmentary research.[23]

Greek Immigrant Stowaways on the Patris and Ellinis

It is impossible to say how easy it was for immigrants to become a stowaway on a liner. Judging from several cases I have been able to identify to date, it appears that it was not that difficult, especially on Greek liners. Stowing away seemed a remarkably regular occurrence, especially from within the Greek community. The reasons for people doing so are much less clear. In June 1965, the *Canberra Times*

---

20. Lianos, "Flows of Greek Out-Migration and Return Migration," 10
21. Lianos, "Flows of Greek Out-Migration and Return Migration," 15.
22. See Gillian Bottomley, *After the Odyssey: A Study of Greek Australians* (Brisbane: University of Queensland Press, 1979); Gillian Bottomley, *From Another Place: Migration and the Politics of Culture* (Cambridge: Cambridge University Press, 1992).
23. Anastasia Christou, *Narratives of Place, Culture and Identity: Second-Generation Greek-Americans Return Home* (Amsterdam: Amsterdam University Press, 2006); Andrea Pelliccia, "Ancestral Return Migration and Second-Generation Greeks in Italy," *Journal of Modern Greek Studies* 35, no. 1 (May 2017): 129–54; Eftihia Voutira, "Ethnic Greeks from the former Soviet Union as 'Privileged Return Migrants,'" *Espace populations sociétés* 3 (2004): 533–44; Klaus Unger, "Greek emigration to and return from West Germany," *Ekistics* 48, no. 290 (September–October 1981): 369–74.

reported how a seventeen-year-old Greek girl, Nitsa Paniotakes, a hairdresser from Athens, was a stowaway who arrived in Melbourne's Station Pier on the liner *Ellinis*. Paniotakes was permitted to land pending a decision by the Department of Immigration on whether she could remain.[24] It soon transpired that she had stowed away because she was "pining for her parents, who had migrated." Remarkably, it was seven days after she arrived that it was discovered that she was a stowaway, but Paniotakes was allowed to remain in Australia for three months while her case was being assessed and processed.[25] Other stowaways had more dubious, or perhaps sinister, intentions. In 1964, a Greek man, Eleftherios Tsakalias, a deserter from the Greek navy, had "jumped ship" from the *Patris* to "swim ashore in quest for a bride." Both the Criminal Investigations Branch and Water Police were unable to trace him; he was known to be a good swimmer.[26] Another Greek stowaway found on the *Patris*, Stefanos Velonias, aged twenty-four, had stowed away in the liner when it left Sydney for Hong Kong. Australian police were on his trail, as someone who could assist them with their inquiries into the shooting of Mr. and Mrs. Harry Velonias, presumably his parents.[27] In 1963, two stowaway Greek men, Athansios Roupas and Dimitrios Kospectas, were found on the *Patris*. In dramatic scenes, Roupas "smashed open his cell door and made a bid for freedom...pushed aside crew members as he made his dash along a companionway. He tried to reach the large, milling crowds of Greeks meeting the liner, but was overpowered."[28] It is unclear what Roupas was running from or to in his "escape for freedom."

In other cases, there appeared to be explicit motives for choosing a stowaway departure. In November 1966, Theofannas Golfinopolous stowed away aboard the *Patris* with his son, Peter. Margaret Golfinopolous, Peter's mother and Theofannas' wife, had chased her son "halfway around the world" to retrieve him and return with him to Melbourne. Theofannas, a taxi driver, had told his wife that he was taking their son to the zoo for the day. By ten o'clock that evening he had stowed away and was on his way to Colombo. Margaret flew to Colombo and arrived two days before the *Patris*. She successfully obtained a court order for Peter's return and was reunited with him in Aden, while her husband continued on to Greece. This drama unfolded when Margaret Golfinopolous gained some idea that her husband had such intentions when a neighbor delivered a letter which had been placed by mistake in the neighbor's letterbox. The letter was written in Greek by Mr. Golfinopolous's father in Greece, indicating that Theofannas was planning to take Peter to Greece. Mrs. Golfinopolous had been told that her husband "had completed formalities which would recognise the child as his own in Greece."[29]

24. *Canberra Times*, June 18, 1965, 11.
25. *Canberra Times*, June 19, 1965, 8.
26. *Canberra Times*, October 2, 1964, 3.
27. *Canberra Times*, February 18, 1965, 3.
28. *Canberra Times*, September 25, 1963, 18.
29. *Canberra Times*, November 2, 1966, 3; October 28, 1966, 1.

This episode, which was widely reported in the Australian press, points to stories of departures on immigrant ships that give a different perspective on how we might understand "departures." Another factor to consider is how departing could be perceived and understood as a political act at the time of the right-wing rule of the Greek military.

Departing Australia at the Time of the Military Junta in Greece

In 1967, a group of right-wing colonels in the Greek army seized power in a coup, resulting in a military junta ruling Greece from 1967 to 1974. The erosion of democratic structures and institutions began immediately, with political freedoms and civil liberties suppressed. Political parties were disbanded, Communist and political prisoners were rounded up, tortured, and exiled, while the freedom of the press disappeared. Military courts were established. The international protest movement began immediately, with Amnesty International highlighting the practice of torture against civilians and political activists. Other European nations swiftly protested. Denmark, Norway, Sweden, and the Netherlands approached the European Commission of Human Rights to accuse Greece of violating most of the human rights protected by the European Convention of Human Rights.[30] In Australia, protests condemned the regime and its oppression, with left-wing organizations organizing rallies and public meetings opposing the coup. The Committee for the Restoration of Democracy in Greece was formed in 1967, seeking to mobilize Greeks in Australia to voice their opposition as well as engage Australian politicians and trade unionists.[31] One of the campaigns launched at this time by left-wing activists was to discourage Australian and Greeks from traveling to Greece— either as tourists or as immigrants returning home. Greece was seen as an idyllic destination for Australians in the 1960s and 1970s: a place of beauty and tranquility encapsulated by the highly publicized life of Australian writers George Johnston and Charmain Clift on the Greek Islands. But this contrasted with the harsh reality of living in Greece under military rule. To return was to condone an oppressive regime.[32] The *Patris* became the target of protests by the trade union movement, which staunchly opposed the right-wing regime and expressed solidarity with the trade unionists who had been arrested and tortured.

In October 1970, members of the Sydney branch of the Waterside Workers' Federation refused to provide tugs for the *Patris*. Waterside worker George Gotsis explained to passengers and crew that the actions of the union "were ... directed ... against the Greek regime and its backers."[33] The restoration of democracy,

---

30. Alexandros Nafpliotis, *Britain and the Greek Colonels: Accommodating the Junta in the Cold War* (London: I.B. Tauris, 2012).
31. Damousi, *Memory and Migration in the Shadow of War*, 123–35.
32. Damousi, *Memory and Migration in the Shadow of War*, 124.
33. *Tribune*, October 7, 1970, 4.

Gotsis argued, "would open the way to a better life in all ways for the people of Greece." Members of the Waterside Workers' Federation "declared solidarity with the democratic Greek people; demanded the release of all jailed trade union leaders and other detained democrats; called for announcement of a date for general elections in Greece to restore democratic government and asked the Federal Government and the ACTU [Australian Council of Trade Unions] to use their influence for this."[34] Members of the Seamen's Union and a dozen waterside workers then met with the captain of the *Patris*, Iionnis Tourvas, to warn him that "there was rising feeling among the Australian workers against the Greek junta and its jailings, and that further action against Greek ships could be expected." What Tourvas made of the deputation is unknown, but his patience as well as his astute intuition won the workers over. The captain was "all courtesy, providing Foster's lager [beer] for the deputation while the discussion proceeded," promising pass on the workers' resolution to Chandris headquarters and to the government—both of which seemed unlikely.[35] *Patris* sailed the following day. The *Ellinis* experienced similar delays, with its captain promising to "secure a reply" from the government; "on that basis" the trade unionists agreed to allow the *Ellinis* to sail the same evening.[36]

A similar stoppage had occurred in June 1970, with protests launched by the seamen and waterfront workers. Again, on the *Patris*, seamen refused "to provide services for the liner," and waterside workers "held up the movement of luggage and stores." Furthermore, "wharf crane-drivers delayed the lowering of gangways until passengers and crew were told what the stoppage was about."[37] In this instance, the captain "was at first arrogant, ordering the ship's band to continue playing to drown out the loudspeaker of the protestors." But the workers said they would continue the boycott and impose a similar one on another ship, the *Australis*. The captain succumbed to their demands, saying he would pass on the demands of the unions to the government. It was recorded that the response by the passengers was "good," with "a number applauding."[38] Members of the crew, however, were not so positive, many of them expressing hostility and frustration over the delay. Another ship, the *Captain Luis*, also became embroiled in a further campaign in Adelaide in July 1970. Seamen in South Australia banned the ship "until the military junta in Greece releases Nikos Kaloudis, a former official of the Greek Seaman's Union." There were discussions about whether to ban the *Patris*, but this would seriously inconvenience the 1,400 passengers on board.[39] At this time the Seaman's Union had joined an international movement calling for all political

---

34. *Tribune*, October 7, 1970, 4.
35. *Tribune*, October 7, 1970, 4.
36. *Tribune*, October 7, 1970, 4.
37. *Tribune*, June 3, 1970, 3.
38. *Tribune*, June 3, 1970, 3.
39. *Tribune*, July 15, 1970, 3.

prisoners to be released,[40] an issue that further delayed the travel of the *Patris* and *Ellinis*. Greek and Australian authorities, it was alleged, had attempted to obstruct the travel plans of opponents of the junta moving to and from Greece.[41] In 1971, the issue continued to be debated in the press, especially whether the *Patris* and more generally the Chandris family could be held responsible for the political situation. In a letter to the *Age*, J. N. Zigouras argued that while the Chandris family did not run the Greek government, the family "was one of the first to publicly support the military junta ... In fact it is the darling of the Greek junta."[42] Zigouras acknowledged that the whole affair was an inconvenience to those passengers stranded on the liner, but surely, he argued, this was "trifling ... compared to the murders, bashings, tortures and imprisonments the military junta has inflicted."[43] The debate about halting the *Patris* continued, with the Greek consulate condemning the action and accusing Zigouras of fabrication regarding political prisoners and trade unionists enduring torture.[44]

The eventual fall of the junta in 1974 saw a mass return of left-wing intellectuals from all over the world to assist in the building of a new democratic Greece.[45]

* * *

What draws together these two disparate examples of Greek stowaways on the *Patris* and the *Ellinis*, and the boycott of the the *Patris* by the Australian trade union movement during the regime of the colonels? By exploring the myriad ways in which we understand the departures and arrivals of migrants, we can identify how these experiences were manifest in ways which have yet to be documented. The stowaway phenomenon of Greek migrants coming to and from Australia provides a new chapter in how departures and arrivals might be understood. In halting the departure and arrival of the *Patris*, the political context is shown to be inescapable when considering international departures and arrivals. In both examples, the *Patris* is the key actor in the unfolding drama of migration. Positioning migrant ships in this way—as central agents—directs our attention to tales of departure and arrival that remain elusive. But it can also illuminate the complexity and diverse way in which migrant ships shaped and determined coming and going, and the multiple ways in which those movements were enacted.

40. *Tribune*, July 15, 1970, 3.

41. *Tribune*, July 8, 1970, 6.

42. Clipping, the *Age*, January 11, 1971, Box 2, Folder 3/10, Defence of Democracy in Greece, Box 1, Folder 3/1/2, Committee for the Restoration for the Democracy in Greece, 102/15, University Archives, Melbourne.

43. Clipping, the *Age*, January 11, 1971, Box 2, Folder 3/10, Defence of Democracy in Greece, Box 1, Folder 3/1/2, Committee for the Restoration for the Democracy in Greece, 102/15, University Archives, Melbourne.

44. Damousi, *Memory and Migration in the Shadow of War*, 132.

45. Katherine L. Pendakis, "On the value of failing and keeping a distance: narrating returns to post-dictatorship Greece," *Identities* 25, no. 6 (2017): 687–704.

These forms of departure were in contrast to those of other ethnic groups, whose departure took place against the backdrop of several issues relating to migrant movement. This aspect of the history of departures of Greek migrants concerned Australian government policymakers less than did that of other migrant groups, such as the more favored British migrants. This latter group was the focus of much attention while others, like the Greeks, did not attract this level of scrutiny in relation to departures. But a comparitive examination of Greek and British departures also highlights the differences in legal and illegal departures as well as capturing the wide variety of types of departure. It also addresses the question of why migrants leave and the issues that are at the heart of many reports and investigations into the movement of British migrants.

In a rare consideration of migrant groups other than the British, a survey conducted by the Good Neighbour Council of New South Wales in January 1967 identified reasons for the departure of non-British groups. In what was labeled the "returnee migrant problem," 160 migrants were interviewed to "ascertain why some migrants leave Australia and return to their country of origin."[46] In addition, the council interviewed a range of those who were actively involved in working with migrants, such as the editors of non-English-language newspapers, officials of the World Council of Churches, and those involved in the law, child welfare, and the banking sector. According to the World Council of Churches official interviewed, Greek migrants departed for a range of reasons. These included family and personal reasons; the setting up of businesses with the capital they had accumulated; homesickness; ill health and a "lack of trust in Australian doctors"; expecting too much too soon; the climate; the family structure (a "lack of parental control in Australia"); and military conscription.[47] A non-English-language newspaper editor noted that another reason for return migration was the better social security system in Greece, where medical, hospital, and sickness benefits were paid by the employer and covered the whole family. Another strong theme was found to be nostalgia, although once married with children, this nostalgia was less pronounced. For young people, the difficulty in bringing out their parents to Australia, or a lack of success in doing so, is cited as a reason to return, preferable to living "in exile."[48] Further reasons cited for return migration were the lack of

---

46. "Returnee Migrant Problem," Commonwealth Immigration Advisory Council Supplementary Committee Meetings Held During 1967, Series number A2170, Control symbol 1967B, National Archives of Australia.

47. "Returnee Migrant Problem," Commonwealth Immigration Advisory Council Supplementary Committee Meetings Held During 1967," Series number A2170, Control symbol 1967B, 13, National Archives of Australia.

48. "Returnee Migrant Problem," Commonwealth Immigration Advisory Council Supplementary Committee Meetings Held During 1967, Series number A2170, Control symbol 1967B, 10, National Archives of Australia.

housing and prohibitive housing prices.[49] Good Neighbour branch members were of the view that these were key issues. Cultural reasons were also mentioned:

> Friendship is the most important thing in life—we have never offered friendship. The Australians are hosts but no Australians act as hosts to migrants. All migrants experience prejudice of some sort.[50]

This report made three recommendations relation to communication: that all official publications should be reviewed and revised frequently; that official publications should not paint a glossy picture; and that for two years all migrants should receive free legal advice regarding the purchase of land and housing.[51] In summary, the report observed that the "reasons why migrants return to their homeland differs vastly between British and non-British migrants." For the non-British, it was lack of social security for themselves and their family, as well as cultural issues, while for the British it was the cost of housing.[52]

The Question of Departures from Australia, Post-1945

The wider question of departures exercised the Australian authorities as the number of migrants leaving Australian began to rise. The main focus of concern was the much-coveted British migrants, whose return to Britain became such a source of anxiety that in 1967 a report was dedicated to exploring the reasons for these departures. The Committee of Social Patterns of the Immigration Advisory Council included three social scientists who made significant contributions to the analysis of why departures were occurring at this time: the demographers Professor Reginald Appleyard, Dr. Charles Price and psychologist Dr. Alan Richardson.

In his 1962 study, Appleyard had focused on British migrants returning between November 1958 and June 1959.[53] His view was that the migration program "could

---

49. "Returnee Migrant Problem," Commonwealth Immigration Advisory Council Supplementary Committee Meetings Held During 1967, Series number A2170, Control symbol 1967B, 10, National Archives of Australia.

50. "Returnee Migrant Problem," Commonwealth Immigration Advisory Council Supplementary Committee Meetings Held During 1967, Series number A2170, Control symbol 1967B, 13, National Archives of Australia.

51. "Returnee Migrant Problem," Commonwealth Immigration Advisory Council Supplementary Committee Meetings Held During 1967, Series number A2170, Control symbol 1967B, 15, National Archives of Australia.

52. "Returnee Migrant Problem," Commonwealth Immigration Advisory Council Supplementary Committee Meetings Held During 1967, Series number A2170, Control symbol 1967B, 9, National Archives of Australia.

53. R. T. Appleyard, "The Return Movement of United Kingdom Migrants from Australia," *Population Studies* 15, no. 3 (March 1962): 214–25.

be measured by the proportion of immigrants who settle permanently in Australia."⁵⁴ Appleyard traveled on the boat the *Fair Sea* to conduct his research, describing the responses to the question of what led migrants to make the decision to leave as "long and often introspective." In this report, homesickness and family relations figured centrally as reasons for return.⁵⁵ By the early 1970s, Richardson was challenging this view, arguing that the reasons why migrants chose not to stay were more complex and did not necessarily reflect discontent with Australia.

Appleyard captured the fluidity of decision-making and the challenge of categorizing those who chose to leave. He gave the example of a migrant to Australia from the UK who might indicate that they had intended to remain "permanently," so they would be registered as a "long-term or permanent arrival from the UK." If they changed their mind, they would be counted as a "temporary departure" because they had not resided in Australia for longer than six months. They might then change their mind again after being in the UK for six months, which would further complicate the record.⁵⁶ Transport also had a significant impact on departure statistics, as these were skewed by how and where they were collected. The Board of Trade statistics covered those who traveled by long sea routes, and "thus exclude persons who travel to Australia via ports in Continental Europe and the Mediterranean Sea and all persons who travel by air." The Australian statistics which were all-encompassing showed that these gaps were not serious. There were, too, passport implications relating to returning migrants. Appleyard noted that documents of identity were issued for most of the government-assisted emigrants, replacing a passport, but these documents of identity for a one-way voyage only. If the holder of this document sought to return, they would need a UK passport for the return voyage, either by birth or naturalization. The same person could obtain an Australian-issued passport by registering as an Australian citizen with the Australian Department of Immigration.⁵⁷

Similar studies were undertaken in other countries, such as Canada. In his paper to the Canadian Association of Sociology and Anthropology in June 1967, the sociologist Anthony Richmond identified the three categories of returned British migrant from Canada to Britain of those who entered Canada between 1956 and 1965. The three categories were quasi-migrants who originally planned to return to Britain; permanent expatriates who originally intended to settle in Canada but would remain in Britain; and finally, those migrants who moved backwards and forwards between two or more countries without settling in one. In

---

54. Appleyard, "The Return Movement of United Kingdom Migrants from Australia," 214.

55. R. Appleyard, "Determinants of Return Migration—A Socio-Economic Study of United Kingdom Migrants Who Returned from Australia," *Economic Record* (September 1962): 362.

56. Appleyard, "Determinants of Return Migration," 216.

57. Appleyard, "Determinants of Return Migration," 217.

comparison to the Australian data, neither homesickness nor dissatisfaction with life in Canada were identified as a major reasons for return migration, but limited employment opportunity was a factor in this area.[58]

In his 1974 publication, Richardson examined the psycho-social aspects of British migration. In this study he examined the reasons for people's departure and made two observations. The first was that permanent settlement is relative to time, place, and circumstances. Richardson argued that it became increasingly easy both financially and socially to reverse the decision to settle permanently. He believed that prior to World War II, job uncertainty meant that once a family had moved for employment reasons, they were less likely to the leave. Since 1947 and by the 1960s, the demand for highly skilled labor had increased, while, significantly, the means of transport now allowed for quicker movement than before. The relaying of information also created a situation where decisions could be made quickly. "During the same period," noted Richardson, "faster and cheaper modes of transport made it possible for larger and larger sections of these societies to travel from one place to another in search of better job opportunities and other ways of life," while more detailed information was accessible concerning jobs and the nature of local communities. Richardson argued that the question of permanent settlement did not become a consideration until arrival. Even if the decision was made to stay, changing circumstances could also see that decision changed.[59]

The second observation that Richardson made in his 1974 study was that a decision to return to a country of origin was rarely accompanied by any ill-feeling towards Australia. He argued that the assumption that returnees must have disliked Australia was as erroneous as the view that emigrants must all have been profoundly discontented with Britain to come to Australia in the first place. In his examination of the category he calls "permanent returners," it was the failure to satisfy material expectations in Australia that was the key motive for returning. Richardson noted issues ranging from working very long hours to make a living to having no ties or roots and experiencing homesickness. Feeling "unsettled and insecure" was much less prominent among those who he categorized as "potential re-emigrants." In assessing the motives of the latter group, Richardson identified factors which had not been prevalent before arriving in Australia, such as the declining health or death of a parent or relative in Britain.[60]

---

58. Anthony H. Richmond, "The Thousand Dollar Cure: A Study of Return Migration from Canada to Britain," paper presented at the meetings of the Canadian Association of Sociology and Anthropology, Ottawa, June, 10–11, 1967, 7, 10, in Commonwealth Immigration Advisory Council—Agenda, notes, information items and minutes of fifty-sixth and fifty-seventh meetings and committee meetings held during 1967, Series number A2170, Control symbol 1967A, NAA.

59. Alan Richardson, *British Immigrants and Australia: A Psycho-social Inquiry* (Canberra: Australian National University, 1974), 118.

60. Richardson, *British Immigrants and Australia*, 123–4.

Richardson also considered the profile of the emigrant. He observed that a single person was in a better position to move as they were unhindered by obligations and ties, resulting in people in that category outnumbering those who were married in return statistics for the period 1959–66 (30 percent compared to 14 percent respectively).[61] Richardson found that the key factor for married people leaving was money and resources: the ability to leave was dependent on having the financial means to do so. Concluded his 1966 shipboard study of returned migrants to the UK, he observed that it "appears that those who leave Australia come from the better off section of the British immigrant population."[62] Richardson also highlighted the fact that a sponsored migrant might feel less likely to leave because of a sense of obligation to their sponsor.[63] Another observation was that only 55 percent of potential re-emigrants had lived in a hostel at some time compared to a figure of 73 percent for permanent returners.[64]

We have no comparative information in the same period for other migrants, least of all Greek migrants, except for ad hoc information that might have been collected by small organizations across a limited sample of respondents.

* * *

The question of departures traverses both legal and illegal dimensions and cuts to the heart of the choices migrants make in deciding to leave after deciding to migrate in the first place. The chapter opens several themes relating to departures: the vessels and ships which facilitated departures in the first place; the specific experience of Greeks in their multiple departures and all its variety; and a focus on the reasons why migrants chose to leave as documented by scholars and government officials. These reasons did not encompass all the factors related to leaving, but do highlight the greater emphasis on British migrants in analysis of return migration.

A further consideration examined in this chapter points to the illegal as well legal aspects of departure and the political aspects of departing, which presents a fertile field for future research. By embedding departures, and not just arrivals, within migration history, the overall story of migration is seen to be a dynamic enterprise, one that is in constant flux. As demonstrated above, departures can highlight different practices in this enterprise, such as stowaways and the politics of departures, to broaden out our understanding of the subject beyond an exclusive focus on a return to the original homeland.

---

61. Richardson, *British Immigrants and Australia*, 125.
62. Richardson, *British Immigrants and Australia*, 126.
63. Richardson, *British Immigrants and Australia*, 127.
64. Richardson, *British Immigrants and Australia*, 128.

Chapter 9

"STARTING FRESH, AGAIN AND AGAIN": FAMILY EXPERIENCES OF MULTIPLE MIGRATIONS TO AND FROM AUSTRALIA

Alexandra Dellios

"Becoming Australian" is a neat and linear narrative that features heavily in public and official histories of immigration. The historiography also stresses the difference between the post-World War II migration schemes of settler-colonial societies (Australia, Canada, New Zealand, and America) and the guest migration agreements of countries in Western Europe (especially Germany and France). Egon Kunz's characterization of the successful displaced persons (DPs) scheme typifies perceptions of the entire postwar immigration era: "Australia wanted loyal, enthusiastic life-long settlers first of all."[1] This rhetoric shaped the promotion of the immigration scheme to the mainstream Anglo-Australian population. It was matched with assurances that migrants would be assimilated into the "Australian way of life." The assumption of linear and permanent settlement can also be seen in the persistent official encouragement that migrants apply for Australian citizenship. But while this domestic assumption was apparent, the aspirations of migrants themselves are more complex than represented in popular and official depictions of the time. The permanence implied in the (still prevailing) "Becoming Australian" narrative does not always apply to their imaginations of their migration journeys.

European migrants arriving after World War II took advantage of the assisted passage offered by the Commonwealth government, without necessarily aspiring to total assimilation, Australian citizenship, or lifelong settlement. By the late 1960s, rates of return migration (especially to Italy and the Netherlands) began to exceed immigration, which some historians have attributed to poor work conditions and living standards for non-English-speaking migrants, and the lack of accessible support services.[2] Slow and incremental changes to settlement

---

1. Egon Kunz, *Displaced persons: Calwell's new Australians* (Canberra: Australian National University Press, 1988), 41.
2. James Jupp, *Arrivals and Departures* (Melbourne: Cheshire-Lansdowne, 1966), 49; Stephen Castles, "Italians in Australia: The Impact of a Recent Migration on the Culture and Society of a Postcolonial Nation," *Center for Migration Studies special issue* 11, no. 3 (1994): 346.

policies and rhetoric—the turn away from assimilation towards integration and eventually multiculturalism—were propelled by government anxieties over these high rates of return migration. They were also pushed along by the work of voluntary welfare agencies and ethnic community organizations trying to fill gaps in government-provided services and supports to new and longer-settled migrant communities. Reinforcing the dire needs of migrants on the ground, and with an ear to government, was the work of prominent sociologists and demographers—notably academics Jerzy Zubrzycki, Jean Martin, and David Cox (the latter, working within Christian welfare agencies).[3]

However, in order to fully understand the incidence of return migration and departure from Australia, further attention needs to be paid to the pre-existing desires, aspirations, and actions of migrant families. While familial stories and community memories can and do ascribe to an assimilatory settlement narrative, they can also offer emotional detail and complexity, as well as non-linear and anti-assimilatory perspectives that counter more nationalist, celebratory renderings of the migrant journey.[4]

In this chapter, I explore my family's circuitous migration/s—their departure, arrival, departure, and arrival. Like many Southern European migrants to Australia, my father, his brother, and their parents arrived with the intention of returning, and were able to do so after a period of time working and living in Melbourne. Australia was a distant but not permanent destination, not only for them but for most of the people with whom they traveled, including uncles, aunts, cousins, godparents, and close friends. It is telling that in the current Greek Australian Archives project, an oral history project hosted by the State Library of New South Wales, interviewers are required to ask of their Greek-born interviewees, "What was your plan? To stay for good or return in five years?" Nance Donkin's 1983 nonfiction blend of memoir and ethnography, *Stranger and Friend*, explores this topic of return and re-return, in an effort to underscore the deep connections between Greece and Australia.[5] Sociologist Gillian Bottomley's 1984 study of emigration and return migration to Greece, *The Export of People*, makes a similar point: "The assumption that people leave home as 'permanent' migrants has always been a dubious assumption."[6] Despite these early studies, there is little in the subsequent Australian historiography on the high incidence, and the familial context, of departure and return for postwar migrants.

3. Mark Lopez, *The Origins of Multiculturalism in Australian Politics 1945–1975* (Carlton, Victoria: Melbourne University Press, 2000), 130–40.

4. For more on assimilation, migrant adjustment, and emotional responses to assimilation's effective erasure of their pasts, see Joy Damousi, "'We are Human Beings, and have a Past': The 'Adjustment' of Migrants and the Australian Assimilation Policies of the 1950s," *Australian Journal of Politics & History* 59, no. 4 (2013): 501–16.

5. Nance Donkin, *Stranger and Friend: The Greek-Australian Experience* (Melbourne: HarperCollins Publishers Australia, 1983).

6. Gillian Bottomley, *The Export of People: Emigration From and Return Migration to Greece* (Wollongong: Centre for Multicultural Studies, University of Wollongong, 1984), 1.

This vision, of impermanence and return, shaped my family's orientations to migration, to the very idea of "settlement." From the perspective of departure—as a moment, as an event, and as an action—migration history extends, temporally and spatially, beyond single contained moments of arrival and settlement. The expectation of departure/s placed boundaries on the imagination of a family and a community. The story that follows is not one of economic or multicultural success, or even of integration—if anything, it is a story of anti-assimilation. The story is also framed by prior generations' experience of expulsion, dislocation, and internal mobility, and how those tragedies reverberate through family trees. I am also still making sense of this story, reconciling my desire for narrative meaning with a historian's sense of contingency, context, and the limits of agency.

I will provide a narrative account according to the oral history testimony I collected from my dad, Kyriakos, drawing out thematic and historical threads in his testimony, and matching it with primary and secondary research into modern Greek history and the Greek diaspora in the twentieth century. Ethically and emotionally, I regret not being able to match my dad's recollections with those of my grandmother, Dimitra—she's in the late stages of dementia.

In my mind, this is a family past shaped by the fickleness of one man (the family patriarch, my grandfather Anastasios), as well as the broader political realities shaping the push-and-pull factors of postwar European migration to and from Australia. I've attempted to tell this story with my dad, his voice indicated throughout using italics. My dad's story is also defined by complex patterns of place-making (imagined beyond the nation-state) that played out across a number of evolving urban and suburban contexts in Melbourne and in towns and cities in northern Greece. Emotionally, the story is shaped by strong sensory and affective memories of the various departures and goodbyes he experienced; and, overall, by a deep sense of nostalgia, loss and hope, of what *"could have been"* or should have been when embarking on (and thinking back to) dislocation and relocation. Accordingly, this account is an exploration of certain subjectivities. It attempts to complicate linear historical narratives about mass migration and settlement through personal and familial storytelling.

First Departure/Arrival (1969–74)

In early 1969, my paternal grandfather Anastasios decided that he, his wife Dimitra, and his two sons Kyriakos and Yianni needed a dramatic change. He made two applications for assisted migration, one to Germany and one to Australia. The Australian application was accepted first. In the eyes of my then eleven-year-old dad Kyriakos, the decision to leave their village of Therma in the Central Macedonian region of Greece seemed harried. The family *"jumped right into the decision to leave."* However, the rationalizations that Kyriakos provided will sound familiar to most historians of migration: *"life was hard."* His family were farmers, peasants. They worked the land: grew, picked, and sold tobacco and olives, tended to a flock of sheep, and made and sold cheese, like many others in that part of rural northern Greece.

Figure 9.1 Dellios family, 1965, Nigrita, Greece.

Well yeah, he was working the land. Well, mostly Yiayia [grandma, his mother], *he was at the kafenion* [coffee house]. *He would ah look after his sheep, and the sheep would be sleeping all day in the summer under the trees, and so would he. And Yiayia was busting her chops trying to collect the tobacco, which was horrible. We helped, the cousins used to help each other, we all helped each other because we all used to grow tobacco.*[7]

Those same cousins and other extended family were unsurprised when the papers for assisted passage to Australia came through and the Dellios family announced their departure—unsurprised, because many of them did the same. The papers for Germany came through weeks later, by which time the family had already committed to the idea of Australia, an Anglophone country on the other side of the world, the furthest any of them had ever traveled. That goodbye party, on the evening of their first departure, was a notable childhood memory for Kyriakos:

7. Gary Kyriakos Dellios, interview with the author, May 2, 2021.

Figure 9.2 Anastasios, Dimitra, and Kyriakos Dellios and other people from their village (Therma, near Nigrita)—sometime in the mid-1960s.

[W]e *were saying goodbye but it was always gunna be you know a trip for a few years, like they went to Germany for a few years and came back, that was always the plan. There was never, the plan was never to go there forever and "see you later" we never see you again. We had a very close bond—everybody, everybody in fact left, under the same circumstances.*[8]

Before continuing, I need to provide a longer historical context to the family's experience of migration and mobility. The modern founding of the village of Therma is linked to the exodus of refugees from Asia Minor in the 1920s.[9] The inhabitants of my father's village in the late 1960s were predominantly descendants of refugees from Anatolia and the region of Pontus on the coastline of the Turkish Black Sea. After the Greco-Turkish War of 1919–22, the Treaty of Lausanne in 1923 mandated a mass exchange of populations. This included approximately 1.5 million Greek-Orthodox Christians who lived in the Ottoman lands and 400,000 Muslims who resided in former Ottoman provinces annexed by Greece in the Balkan Wars of 1912–13 (notably, the region of Macedonia). The "dark days" of 1922, what became known to Greeks as the Asia Minor Catastrophe, and the

---

8. Gary Kyriakos Dellios, interview with the author, May 2, 2021.
9. However, excavations have revealed traces of the foundations of ancient buildings related to the use of thermal springs in the area.

Figure 9.3 Leaving Party, in the Dellios' home, Therma, July 1969.

violent ethnic cleansing of Christian Ottomans, has been the subject of much historical research in Greece since the late 1940s.[10] Understandably, much of the early historiography focused on the persecution of Christians before their exodus from Turkey, rather than the difficult and politically contentious process of incorporating the massive refugee population into the new Greek nation-state.[11]

Over 50 percent of refugees from the Catastrophe settled in the area of Greek Macedonia in the northern countryside.[12] The government also directed a large minority to Thessaly and Attica, and smaller numbers to Thrace.[13] New settlements were established in villages abandoned by departing Muslim populations. When it came to Macedonia, this directed settlement was also part of a wider government

---

10. Haris Exertzoglou, "Children of Memory: Narratives of the Asia Minor Catastrophe and the Making of Refugee Identity in Interwar Greece," *Journal of Modern Greek Studies* 34, no. 2 (2016): 345; Thomas Gallant, *Modern Greece: From the War of Independence to the Present* (London: Bloomsbury, 2016), 206.

11. For more on this historiography and its blind spots, see Georgios Kritikos, "Silencing inconvenient memories: refugees from Asia Minor in Greek historiography," *Journal of Ethnic and Migration Studies* 47, no. 18 (2020): 1–16.

12. Georgios Kritikos, "The Agricultural Settlement of Refugees: A Source of Productive Work and Stability in Greece, 1923–1930," *Agricultural History* 79, no. 3 (2005): 324.

13. Others too fled to Egypt, before having to flee again with the rise of Pan-Arab nationalism and the regime of Gamal Abdel Nasser in the 1950s. Many Pontic Greeks also

"Starting Fresh, Again and Again" 167

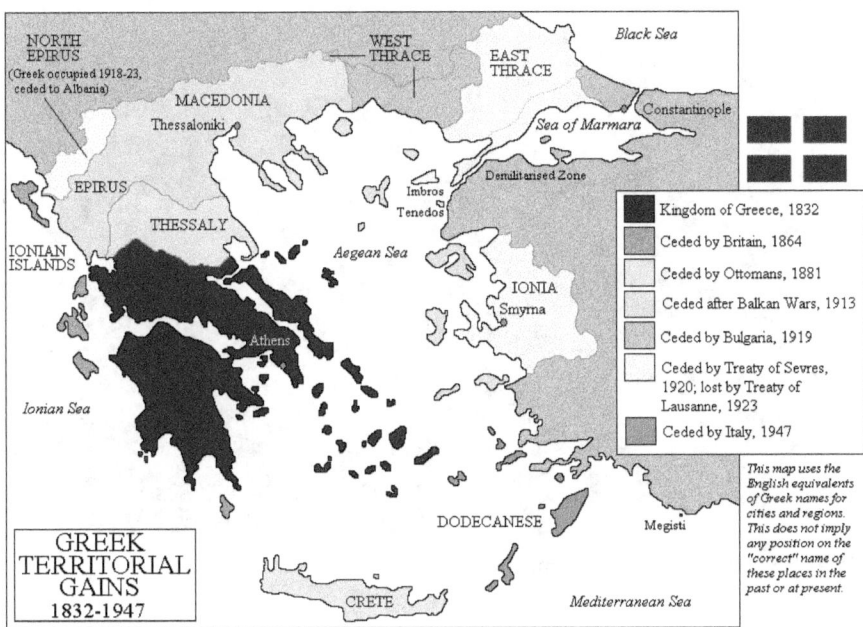

Figure 9.4 Map showing Greek territorial gains and losses, 1832–1947, Wiki Creative Commons License.

effort to "Hellenize" the Macedonian region of the new Greek nation-state. Some of these provinces were annexed by Greece after the Balkan Wars, including the area around the town of Florina in mountainous north-western Macedonia, which was home to many Slavic-speaking communities. This included my mother's parents, who spoke a Slavic dialect at home and Greek when official circumstances required it. Ironically, refugees from Asia Minor and especially from Pontus had distinct cultural and linguistic practices, which often marked them out from "so-called indigenous Greeks."[14] Their socio-economic integration, and the government's vision for national homogenization, faced many obstacles: linguistically, various waves of refugee groups differed, and as Greek historians writing since the late 1980s have argued, rural refugee settlements in Macedonia were culturally differentiated and held a sense of ethno-cultural belonging that did not always align with the Greek state. This served as a factor in their social stratification in the new Greece.

went to Russia, but were persecuted from the late 1930s under the Stalinist regime. Stalin deported most Pontic Greeks to Central Asia in the immediate postwar years, but, during the Greek Civil War, Greek Communist supporters became political refugees to the Soviet Union, where approximately 10,000 of them became permanent settlers; although, with the dissolution of the Soviet Union in 1990, many Greeks sought to emigrate to Greece. See Gallant, *Modern Greece*, 205.

14. Exertzoglou, "Children of Memory," 347.

Figure 9.5 Athanasios and Olympia Joseph, after they fled Smyrna in 1922.

Dimitra's mother, Marianthy Joseph, her parents Athanasios and Olympia, and her four teenage sisters were expelled from Smyrna on the Aegean coast of Anatolia (modern-day Izmir) in 1922, during the Great Fire of Smyrna, when the Turks retook the city at the effective conclusion of the Greco-Turkish War of 1919–22. An estimated 20,000 died in the Great Fire; some 200,000 Greek-speaking Christians were expelled; and approximately 30,000 "able-bodied" Greek and Armenian men were massacred by Ataturk's armies.[15] Athanasios was quite elderly by this point, and was spared. He was a middle-class merchant, and the family owned and operated fishing boats out of the port of Smyrna. They owned a house on the water. Like most Orthodox Christian refugees, they left everything behind—land, personal property, and wealth. Their lifestyles in their new homeland were a considerable downgrade from their life in Smyrna—not least because the government struggled to provide basic housing and sustenance to what amounted to a rapid 20 percent increase in the domestic population of Greece.[16] The government directed some 600,000 refugees to the agricultural labor market by providing plots of land (of varying sizes, and not all of it fertile). Given the numbers, this was an "achievement of incorporation," which also had the desired political effect of making many

---

15. Norman Naimark, *Fires of Hatred: Ethnic Cleansing in 20th Century Europe* (Cambridge, MA: Harvard University Press, 2002), 52.

16. *Statistical Annual of Greece: 1930–1931* (Athens: National Printing-Office).

dependent on the state, who promised to support their small farms and help pay off housing debts.[17]

After initially settling in government housing in Nea Artaki (in the region of Evia),[18] the family patriarch moved the family to the Halkidiki peninsula in northern Greece. Marianthy's sisters were *"married off"* to other Asia Minor refugees and settled throughout Macedonia. In this way, Marianthy was sent by her father to live further north with her sisters and their new families. She eventually married and settled in a village near the town of Serres, *"up near our way,"* as Kyriakos describes it. They were given land to farm in Therma and lived in a home vacated by Muslims in 1922, where my grandmother Dimitra was born in 1934. While the family had not been farmers in Asia Minor, this was the fate allocated to them as refugees in their own country. Before the exchange, Greek-speaking farmers in Asia Minor dominated tobacco farming, and unsurprisingly, given their settlement in the Macedonian region, tobacco quickly became the dominant cash crop there too—including in and around the mineral-rich soil of Therma.[19] As Kyriakos remembered, *"it was a horrible thing to grow."*

I've gone back to this period as a means of highlighting the mobility (both forced and voluntary) of successive generations—and because this familial history is not unique: it is a microcosm of modern Greek history and underscores the mobility of the Greek diaspora. They started fresh, again and again, notwithstanding the trauma of that initial and brutal expulsion from their homes in Asia Minor. I also return to this family story from my great grandmother's perspective because, like her daughter and grandchildren after her, her mobility after 1922 was largely dictated by the whims of the men in her life. Like her daughter, she also worked under physically demanding conditions and, wherever she moved to, was a key contributor to the family's economic, emotional, and social well-being.

Decades later, Greek Macedonia was devastated by the German occupation during World War II, and then again during the Greek Civil War from 1946 to 1949. Marianthy was murdered in 1946, as was her husband, each by opposing sides in this civil conflict. Complex family lore has made it now impossible to pinpoint their political alignments, which speaks to the wide-ranging and tragic effects of civil war on non-combative civilians. A narrative compromise seems to have shaped the narrative accordingly: Marianthy was sexually assaulted and murdered by Communist guerrillas for being in *"the wrong place at the wrong time."* Her husband was *"sold out"* to royalist forces by neighbors in his village; he was executed for smuggling food to Communist guerrillas hiding in the

---

17. Kritikos, "The Agricultural Settlement of Refugees."

18. This was a newly founded town of Greek refugees that replaced the former Muslim population. Nea (New) Artaki was a renaming of the Turkish town of Erdek.

19. Gallant, *Modern Greece*, 206.

Figure 9.6 Marianthy and Kyriakos Miltsos with baby Dimitra (my grandmother), 1934–5, eleven years before their deaths during the Civil War.

mountains. Horrific details have been shared with me, but I choose not to relay them here. Their deaths left my eleven-year-old grandmother and her younger sister Eleni orphaned. As we will see, her subsequent experiences of dislocation and relocation never failed to spark these dark memories. I grew up hearing a more censored version of this Civil War story from my dad (and with much of the politics expunged). He, too, stored it away as a defining aspect of his identity, an inherited memory. Joy Damousi has argued that for this generation, "who grew up listening to these stories about war being told over and over again," they became an integral part of their parents' and their Greek identity.[20]

After her parents were murdered, Dimitra and Eleni stayed in their childhood home in Therma, and one of their maternal aunts and her new husband came to care for them. This aunt soon had children of her own, and the girls became proxy caretakers to their two younger male cousins, in addition to taking on the bulk of household duties. Notably, during the remaining years of the Greek Civil War, the whole family would repeatedly flee this house when the situation in the village become unsafe, and return when they thought it was safe to do so—this was a period of uncertainty, and with each departure, they were unsure if they would return. Traditional customs continued, however. While their caretakers would have felt the burden of having to provide a dowry for the two girls, they were in a relatively good position: Dimitra and Eleni's parents had left them a lot of land and livestock. Kyriakos, rather cynically, cites this as the reason why Anastasios pursued Dimitra. She lived at home till she met Anastasios, who *"had a bad reputation in the village."*

The second youngest of twelve children, only five of whom survived, Anastasios Dellios had moved during the Civil War down to Therma from the tiny mountainous village of Lagadi near Serres with his two sisters, a brother, and his mother. His mother was also, like Dimitra's, a refugee from the Asia Minor Catastrophe. In the late 1940s, the family fled to Therma in order to escape the more violent fighting occurring in the mountainous regions of the country where Communist guerrillas were hiding. The northern countryside, bordering Communist Albania, Bulgaria, and Serbia, saw the heaviest fighting during the Civil War. For much of the war, this region, including the main town of Florina, was under Communist control.[21] This was also the area in which royalist government troops committed most of their atrocities.[22]

It is probable that Anastasios' paternal ancestors were from the region known today as Albania or North Macedonia, given the dialect of Greek they spoke. This too may have contributed to the ill reception they received in Therma, despite the fact that most people in Therma hailed from elsewhere (Smyrna or Pontus) and also spoke regional dialects. The cultural ambiguities and intermingling traditions

---

20. Joy Damousi, *Memory and Migration in the Shadow of War: Australia's Greek Immigrants After World War II and the Greek Civil War* (London: Cambridge University Press, 2015), 5–6; see also, 199–200 and Chapter 7. As she also explores, "others chose not to speak of traumatic pasts and … prefer silence as a means of dealing with family histories," which may account for the nature of some silences in the narrative Kyriakos tells. Dimitra was only eleven when her parents were murdered, and it has always been unclear whether she was a first-hand witness to the violence inflicted on her mother.

21. Damousi, *Memory and Migration in the Shadow of War*, 5, 15, 18.

22. Foreword in Allan Scarfe and Wendy Scarfe (eds.), *All that Grief: Migrant Recollections of Greek Resistance to Fascism, 1941–1949* (Sydney: Hale & Iremonger, 1994).

of this region was and is informed by the vast and bureaucratically complex reach of the Ottoman Empire—which shaped the cross-pollination and movement of music, ideas, language, and customs across the Balkans and Asia Minor from the fifteenth to the twentieth century.

Despite protestations from her family, Dimitra married Anastasios in 1957, when she was twenty-three and he was twenty-four. A year later, Kyriakos was born, followed in 1961 by another boy, Yianni. The region of Greece in which they grew up was socially and economically devastated by the Civil War. Accordingly, from the 1950s, the majority of Greeks applying for passage to Australia hailed from this region. By 1969, when my grandfather decided it was time to embark on another departure, the family had survived crippling poverty, bore their memories of loss, violence, and expulsion, and, from the advent of the 1967 military junta, withstood government sanctions and interventions in their private lives and commercial endeavors. The process towards departure may have seemed rushed to a young Kyriakos, but in many ways, it was several decades in the making.

Figure 9.7 Dimitra and Anastasios' wedding photo, 1957.

Figure 9.8 On board the ship *Patris*, 1969. The children putting on a play—dressed as pirates. Kyriakos is center-left, in the dark shirt.

Kyriakos has vivid memories of the first trip to Australia in July 1969, more so than subsequent departures. They flew from Athens to Djibouti in Africa, a necessary detour due to the closure of the Suez Canal in 1967. Kyriakos says it was the first time anyone on that flight had been on a plane—when turbulence struck, people screamed out in fear. Once in Djibouti, they boarded the immigrant ship *Patris*, along with over 1,000 other passengers. The *Patris* was the first liner in the Greek-owned Chandris fleet, purchased in 1959. It offered austere accommodation, although Kyriakos, a young boy, remembers the trip fondly—traveling with their family and friends, trying new foods (the first time they ate bananas), and seeing new places—punctuated by memories of his mother's sea sickness. They traveled through the Indian Ocean to Mauritius and from there continued on to Freemantle, where they docked for the day before departing for Melbourne. In all, the trip took four weeks.

After arriving in Melbourne, things progressed quickly. Housing was in short supply across the country, so the family lived in one-room in a house in Moreland, near the freeway. Kyriakos' godfather, who greeted them at the port when they arrived, rented the other room in this house, which was owned by a Greek family who had migrated years earlier. Kyriakos and Yianni went to school within days of arriving in Melbourne and their parents found work immediately. The industrial sector was still booming, despite short economic downtowns in 1952 and 1961, and employment was easy to find. They expected to find work immediately and begin to save. Temporally, their time in Melbourne had a clear beginning and end:

Look they made a decision to go. It was basically to work hard. She already bought shoes for work ... clothes. [Did she know what kind of work she'd be doing? Did Papou?] Yeah, she was going to work in a factory. He knew that too. They both organised themselves. They bought shoes and clothes for the factory. They were going to work. This was going to be their job for two or three years, four years, then go back. [What about the kids?] We were learning English on the ship ... we went to school pretty much straight away. They went to work, we went to school, within a day or two of arriving. They were already geared up in their minds. They were going to get jobs ... Manufacturing jobs, right. The idea was to work, pay off the debt to the government, which was, the agreement, for the period ... and get some money, and ah go back and do something with that money ... a lot of people did that. A lot of people went back after that period, 5, 10 years some of them, longer.[23]

Their settlement in Melbourne was therefore geared towards survival, rather than long-term social integration. Assimilation was never considered, nor was it necessary. All their friends and most of their colleagues and school friends were other Greeks, many of them from the same region of Greece. Their workplaces were filled with other migrants with a similar vision of their immediate future.

On the cusp of teenagerhood, and without a word of English, Kyriakos struggled academically at school, first at Moreland Primary School and then at Port Melbourne. Although there was a large Greek cohort in both schools, he has vivid memories of the racism he experienced from his Anglo-Australian peers—some of it physically violent: "*it was: 'shut-up wog', boof!*". The family moved away from the suburb of Moreland a few months after arriving in Melbourne "*because Papou was itching to go down to where all the other people from our village were, which was down in South Melbourne and Port Melbourne ... including relatives. People from our sort of area were all down there.*" Over 3,000 Greek-born immigrants lived in South Melbourne and Port Melbourne by the early 1970s, constituting 14 percent of the population in those two suburbs.[24] There were larger numbers again in the inner-city suburbs of Northcote, Prahran, Brunswick, Richmond, and Fitzroy, many of these concentrations predicated on chain migration and the proximity of factory work.[25] According to historian Michael Tsounis, this meant that there were "a lot of Spartans in Brunswick; Messenians in Prahran; Pontians in Yarraville."[26]

23. Gary Kyriakos Dellios, interview with the author, May 2, 2021.

24. A. M. Tamis, "The state of the modern Greek language in Australia," in Charles Price (ed.), *Greeks in Australia* (Canberra: Australian National University Press, 1975), 69; Ronald F. Henderson, Alison Harcourt, and R. J. A. Harper, *People in Poverty: A Melbourne Survey* (Melbourne: University of Melbourne Press, 1970), 121.

25. Victorian Ethnic Affairs Commission, "Greeks in Victoria: Policies, Directions, and Initiatives," in Price (ed.), *Greeks in Australia*, 181–203.

26. M. P. Tsounis, "Greek Communities in Australia," in Price (ed.), *Greeks in Australia*, 22–3.

Figure 9.9 Community event, South Melbourne, 1971–2.

Again, the Dellios family rented a house with another Greek family, but Anastasios had a disagreement with this family and decided to seek other accommodation. They were lucky enough to find a two-bedroom house at 210 Montague Street, South Melbourne (an address Kyriakos has never forgotten), which they bought from an elderly widow in fortnightly repayments amounting to $8,500. Sociological studies from the 1970s, conducted mostly by Anglo-Australian academics, spoke of the "single-minded determination" of Greek migrants to accumulate savings for investment in property.[27] This determination was also propelled by high rental costs and a competitive rental market.[28] From a contemporary perspective, it would be easy to view this as middle-class aspirationalism—and none have been lauded as much as the Greeks for adhering to the "model ethnic" stereotype—but that would ignore also the trials of those migrants, the high incidence of poverty, and overcrowded living situations among Southern Europeans in Melbourne, having to work multiple jobs at minimum pay, forced to take out second mortgages, and facing higher housing costs because of discrimination in the market.[29] The aim was not integration into existing social structures or establishing a foothold in Australian society, but rather, at least in my family's case and in the case of their close peers, to return to Greece with capital.

---

27. R. T Appleyard, "Issues of sociocultural adaptation and conflict," in P. R. De Lacey, Millicent E. Poole, and Bikkar S. Randhawa, *Australia in Transition: Culture and Life Possibilities* (Sydney: Harcourt Brace Jovanovich, 1985), 100.

28. Henderson, et al., *People in Poverty*, 136.

29. Henderson, et al., *People in Poverty*, 125, 131–3, 138.

Figure 9.10 Kyriakos posing outside their home in South Melbourne, 1974.

By this time, Kyriakos was attending South Melbourne Technical College. Although this was the dying days of assimilation, his name was anglicized to "Gary" (his brother Yianni became "John"). Migrants anglicizing their names is addressed in the literature, but in many cases, this was not a reliable sign of assimilation for Greeks—children in particular "adopted and practiced dual behaviour patterns" in an Anglophone country.[30] Both his parents worked late, and he became, in popular parlance, a "latchkey kid": arriving home after school with his brother to begin cooking the family meal before his mother returned from work. Dimitra was working in a printing shop, in a job she "*really loved, she was quite good at it.*"

---

30. Tsounis, "Greek Communities in Australia," 42–8.

Kyriakos' father was rarely home. Anastasios worked night shifts at the General Motors Holden factory in Port Melbourne (where he learnt *"every language but English, they spoke Greek, Italian, Yugoslav"*). The car manufacturing industry in the 1960s and 1970s had a higher number of migrant workers than any other industry in Australia—and those funneled into "low-skilled" or semi-skilled work were Southern or Eastern European migrants.[31] Anastasios also maintained an active social life in South Melbourne. *"The front of our house was like a kafenion sometimes, it was on a main thoroughfare. Yiayia was making coffees all day long when she was at home ... and Papou never did anything of course."* Although hospitality and being a good *nikokira* (loosely translated as "housewife") was a value Dimitra held dear, other aspects of her husband's social life in South Melbourne caused her anxiety, for it mainly revolved around alcohol (the men brewed their own tsipouro and ouzo, clear spirits *"strong enough to blind you"*) and other women. I was reluctant to include these memories, mostly because I am skeptical of the stereotype: the beleaguered Greek housewife, wringing her hands at home, while her husband indulges himself elsewhere. As stated, Dimitra loved her job during this time, and she was far from powerless in her social exchanges. She was a respected member of her tight-knit community, her *koinótita*. Her anxiety, I suspect, was linked to the importance of reputation within her "dominating kinship cluster," something Gillian Bottomley emphasizes in her study of the Greek community and networks in 1970s Sydney.[32]

But the social context of their relationship, the different freedoms afforded to her migrant husband, even though they both worked, warrants further reflection—especially because it has been used as a reason for return. For example, Dorothy Buckland-Fuller, a sociologist and social activist—and an Egyptian-born Greek who arrived in Sydney via England in 1961—observed in her work at the Redfern Baby Health Centre in the early 1970s a certain dynamic among the migrant women:

> that their husbands, and in fact all Greek men, are better off in Australia than they were in Greece for they have more money, more Greek cafes, gambling places and nightclubs to spend it on. Women, on the other hand, are worse off because they stay at home most of the time, and they have no family nearby to visit as they did in Greece. They tend to feel lonely, isolated and friendless and wish they were back home.[33]

---

31. Constance Lever Tracy and Michael Quinlan, *A Divided Working Class: Ethnic Segmentation and Industrial Conflict in Australia* (London: Routledge & Kegan Paul, 1988).

32. However, she is careful to state that this "defining field of action" was not uniform across all Greek community settlements in Australia. Gillian Bottomley, "Community and Network in a City," in Price (ed.), *Greeks in Australia*, 112–42.

33. Dorothy Buckland-Fuller, "Immigrant Women in Australia," *SAANZ* [*Sociological Association of Australia and New Zealand Conference*] *Conference*, University of Waikato, Hamilton NZ, August 23–26, 1975, 14–15.

Some of Buckland-Fuller's comments here, and in her other generalized references to Greek migrant women, are condescending, sometimes erring on derisive. Unlike the majority of her Greek-speaking contemporaries, in her life Buckland-Fuller had benefitted from access to better educational opportunities, and spoke English fluently when she arrived in Australia. Despite, and perhaps because of, their class differences, Buckland-Fuller advocated on behalf of immigrant women, publicizing their poor treatment in the workforce and in the home.[34] While certain stereotypes about Southern European migrant women are overblown, stereotypes arise out of a base reality. Admittedly, Anastasios more accurately reflects the stereotype Buckland-Fuller cites above. Dimitra was not "isolated and friendless" in Melbourne—and perhaps it is worth stressing, in reference to Buckland-Fuller's research, that Sydney is not Melbourne. Higher numbers and chain migration in the postwar era meant the demographic was different in Melbourne, and by the 1960s, Greeks there had established over 200 brotherhoods, regional fraternities, and community organizations.[35] The sheer strength of the community in 1970s Melbourne—the availability of all-night Greek clubs, espresso bars, Greek cinemas, Greek dances "at least every weekend," Greek soccer games, political clubs, and Greek gambling dens—gave Anastasios plenty of options, as a Greek-speaking man.[36]

However, far from feeling stuck at home, Dimitra considered her job in the printing press better than picking tobacco in Greece. Although, like most married Greek women of her generation, most of her activities beyond work were conducted as part of the family unit. In this, she prided herself and her family on their regular attendance at the Greek Orthodox Church in South Melbourne. They attended weekly services, and every baptism, name day celebration, engagement, and wedding within the community. Religion—or her reputation as a devout woman adhering to Greek Orthodox (and therefore "ethnic") customs—was a consistent and grounding feature of her life, both in Australia and in Greece. Isolation was a non-issue in their inevitable aim to return (undeniably, Dimitra missed her sister Eleni back in Greece).

The diasporic community in which they lived was not only a geographical entity (inner-city Melbourne) defined by ethnicity ("Greekness"—a concept I hope I've complicated in the discussion above), or even only by regional identity (descendants of war and expulsion, first from Asia Minor, then from Greek Macedonia). For the Dellios family and their contemporaries in South and Port Melbourne, it was also a moral community: bound by codes of "honour and shame," premised on family and reputation, and linked to conservative rural

---

34. Buckland-Fuller established the Australian-Migrant Women's Association in 1974 and was a commissioner on the Ethnic Affairs Commission of New South Wales.

35. Dominique Francois De Stoop, *The Greeks of Melbourne* (Melbourne: Transnational Publishing Company, 1996), 50.

36. David Cox, "Greek Boys in Melbourne," in Price (ed.), *Greeks in Australia*, 145.

worldviews and a rural social structure.³⁷ Ultimately, women policed, maintained, and were judged according to these codes. Undeniably, Anastasios' freedom in Melbourne was not matched in Dimitra's life; but this reality applied in Melbourne as much as it did in their village of Therma. Recognizing these continuities (as well as the differences) is an important part of understanding the nature of their (multiple) returns and departures.

Less than five years later, in early 1974, the family prepared to return, as they'd always planned. The South Melbourne house was sold for a small profit. Dimitra and Anastasios left their jobs—both with pains in their hands and backs from the strain sustained during their repetitive factory work (more on this later). Kyriakos and Yianni left school (as it would turn out, for good). Their long-awaited return was an exciting time for fifteen-year-old Kyriakos:

We all flew back. We all flew back, like I said, Harry's dad [his godfather], *Harry, my uncle already had* [were you excited?] *Very! Yes, oh my god, it was the most exciting time, darling, we thought, ah good, I'm going to see my cousins again, go back to the village. But it wasn't the same. It really wasn't. A lot of people had already left.*³⁸

The issue of assimilation, the pressure to be, as Damousi explores, "grateful" migrants—to deny the past (and with it, the baggage of traumatic war memories)—must have been present, to some degree, for my grandparents.³⁹ But perhaps as later arrivals (arriving at the tail-end of the immigration boom, and just before the introduction of multiculturalism), their horizons were expanded; they had endured and survived the Civil War, its aftermath, and the deprivations and political uncertainties in Greece, had even lived for a few years through the junta's rule—as had their contemporaries, their neighbors and friends in South Melbourne. Outwardly, Anastasios would wryly comment on being "*New Australians now,*" but within their circles and the social spheres that dominated most of their day-to-day lives, there was no question of needing to repress or juggle their "Greekness" in Australia. Kyriakos and Yianni—or Gary and John—did not agonize over their role as cultural brokers (notwithstanding the pressure they faced as occasional translators); they were not, as the literature proposes, migrant children "torn" between two worlds. Return was a given. Kyriakos' sense of regret and loss, of being unable to belong in either place, came much later. It emerges later in his life, as he looks back and narrates his second (or was it third?) return to Australia, and now these feelings manifest each and every time he departs to and from Greece.

In one evocative sensory memory, Kyriakos describes being a young teenager, thrilled to be back in his village of Therma—reflecting on how he brought little parts of Australia back with him:

---

37. *Greek Families in Hawthorn and Clifton Hill* (Melbourne: General Studies Dept., Swinburne College of Technology, 1974), 6–16.

38. Gary Kyriakos Dellios, interview with the author, May 2, 2021.

39. Damousi, *Memory and Migration in the Shadow of War*, 203.

We got these two big tin boxes, tin. You know the Arnott's biscuits? The Assorted Creams, and a box of Teddy Bear biscuits. These two boxes, tin boxes, quite large tins. They went into the suitcases and went into the ship, and in the horio [village], *after* [laughs] *after we returned, I'd fill up my pockets, I'd go volta* [walking/out] *in the horio, eating biscuits from Australia, it was funny.*[40]

Second Departure/Arrival (1974–5)

They arrived back in Greece months before the junta's rule ended on July 24, 1974. Kyriakos states that the political situation in Greece had little impact on their decision to return: "*We missed our relatives and the lifestyle.*" But it quickly became apparent that life would be no easier after their stint in Australia. In the months before July 24, Anastasios attempted to renovate an old deli in Therma into a kafenio. He spent most of the profits gained in Melbourne on this endeavor, but the military police "*wouldn't give him a license to serve alcohol, because they didn't like him. I think it was a political thing, in those days.*" It's unclear whether Anastasios had any clear political allegiances, or whether he simply found himself too often on the wrong side of the law in Greece. He has never been a member of any

Figure 9.11 Therma, taken in 2005.

40. Gary Kyriakos Dellios, interview with the author, May 2, 2021.

political organization or party, although Australian historians have commented on the left-leaning tendencies and politicization of postwar Greeks in Melbourne.[41] Anastasios proceeded without a license, but after being fined a few times, he abandoned the endeavor. But as Kyriakos describes it, *"the old man was not able to settle, again."* They packed up and moved to Chalkida, where some of Dimitra's family still lived. However, *"he would not settle again. He got a job, he didn't like it. I liked it. I would've loved to have stayed there. After two months of renting this old house down there, he decided nah, we're going to go to Thessaloniki now. Kept moving, he just couldn't settle."*

After their next move, they rented an apartment in the heart of Thessaloniki, where Kyriakos thrived: *"it was the place to be."* Both he and his brother worked in hospitality, and gained a freedom that had not been possible in their rural village—a reality underscored by the exodus of Greek youth from villages to cities that had begun in the 1950s. Ironically, Anastasios found himself once again working with tobacco, albeit not in harvesting, but in production—he packaged cigarettes in a factory.

Figure 9.12 Anastasios working in a tobacco factory in Thessaloniki, 1974.

---

41. Michael Tsounis, "The Greek Left in Australia," *Australian Left Review* 1, no. 29 (1971): 53–60. Con Allimonos in his history of Greek Communist activity in Melbourne argued that the support for Communist guerrillas created a reliable support base in Australia, where Melbourne Greek Communists, in the form of the Democritus League, were able to cement their base among Greek migrant workers. Con K. Allimonos, "Greek Communist Activity in Melbourne: A Brief History," *Labour History* 86 (2004): 137–8.

And then, "*The Turks attacked Cyprus.*" Kyriakos recalls the chaos, and the urge to flee—but also how this atmosphere, the perceived imminent danger, triggered other traumatic memories of departure for his mother:

> *The whole of Greece mobilised. The men were called to arms . . . People were leaving the cities. Because they thought Turkey was going to bomb the cities. It was a horrible, horrible time. Everybody left. I got on the back of a ute, because Yiayia and Uncle John* [Yianni] *went with a bus, I couldn't fit . . . we were going back to the village. Supermarkets were stripped bare, everyone left the cities, all the boys went to report to their units, even Papou went, but he was forty-odd by then, and they rejected him . . . We just ran . . . Yiayia was telling me that night, because she remembers she was a child with the second world war the army was gathering near her house, and she could hear the horses when she was a child and all that brought back memories for her . . . She was pretty traumatised I guess.*[42]

After this, the family's trajectory changed once again: "*Papou thought, ah f*ck this.*" Somehow, Anastasios had ensured that the family's passports allowed them to return to Australia: he "*kept the door open to Australia . . . He did have just enough money to buy 4 Qantas tickets. And he did.*" They spent Christmas in Thessaloniki, and then once again "*said our goodbyes.*" By this point, emigration from Greece to Australia had slowed down, although the Australian immigration figures aren't able to account for those who departed and returned.

Kyriakos was sixteen. At this point in the oral history interview, I asked why he didn't refuse to leave Thessaloniki, a city he loved. I failed to comprehend the familial and societal codes that applied to sons and daughters, children of the Civil War and dislocation, and the reputational obligation to family unity that ultimately meant Kyriakos consented to leave for Australia with his parents and brother:

> [Anastasios] *did ask—and I said no, I'm not going back, I don't want to go back, I love it here. I was not happy, I wanted to leave* [him] *you know, go and hide. Of course, I didn't . . . In hindsight, who knows where we would've been. But we did come back. I was pretty depressed. I was not looking forward to—to coming back here. We arrived back in Melbourne around New Year's 1975 . . . We left everybody behind, we had to start fresh, again, again.*[43]

Starting again, a continuous theme in this story, was difficult for Kyriakos. But they had not left everyone behind. His godfather went back to Australia within six months of returning to Greece in late 1973, and his cousins had settled in Clayton in south-east Melbourne. After they arrived back in Australia in 1975, life fell into a familiar pattern. They rented in Brunswick then Fawkner (Dimitra refused to go back to South Melbourne, where she feared Anastasios might adopt the same habits in that social scene—importantly, her decision prevailed). Anastasios

---

42. Gary Kyriakos Dellios, interview with the author, May 2, 2021.
43. Gary Kyriakos Dellios, interview with the author, May 2, 2021.

worked the night shift in a factory making toilet bowls, where he *"did his back,"* becoming one of the many non-English-speaking migrants vulnerable to industrial injury.[44] The mainstream media and politicians maligned them as exploiting the compensation system. They were derisively dismissed as suffering from "Mediterranean Back," as malingering or psychosomatically inflating their industrial injuries.[45] Dimitra worked in a confectionary factory, where her old RSI re-emerged. They both retired early, in their fifties, due to their injuries. Kyriakos got a job through a friend from his village—pumping petrol *"from 5am to 10pm"* at a station in Broadmeadows in Melbourne's outer west, which did nothing for the depression he felt at being back in Australia.

Eventually, the family followed other Northern Greeks to the new suburbs in Melbourne's outer north, in Epping and Lalor (again, there was a regional aspect to this internal chain migration). They were part of another exodus, this time internal, of postwar migrants "upgrading" from the cramped, run-down housing of the industrial inner-suburbs to the more spacious (and sparse) blocks of the outer suburbs. It wasn't always a matter of upgrading, however; manufacturing was declining in Australia. Also, Henderson's inquiry into poverty in Melbourne in the 1970s argued that Southern European migrants had positively "transformed" the inner-city areas of Melbourne, turning the "dingy and depressing" old terrace houses into homes that then became attractive to Anglo-Australians—which in turn raised prices, and made it difficult for migrants to find accommodation, even by the 1970s.[46]

The Dellios family did not take up citizenship, despite the Department of Immigration's concerted advertising in the Greek language press throughout the 1970s.[47] According to the census and voting figure estimates in 1973, over one million migrants had not sought Australian citizenship, yet a large proportion had been in Australia well over the five years needed in order to apply. The intention was always to depart, again—at least, in Kyriakos' mind. This too was the reason underpinning many migrants' decisions—including stateless peoples fleeing the

---

44. Community groups like the Australian-Greek Welfare Society found that non-English-speaking migrants had higher rates of workplace accidents and serious injuries, but were unaware of their rights under the Compensation Act. They stressed that workplaces needed "to make extensive use of the migrants' own language, on the job, in union offices and publications." Australian Greek Welfare Society, *Ethnics in Industry: A Submission by the Australian Greek Welfare Society* (Melbourne: AGWS, 1976), n.p.

45. Annette Rubinstein, "Mediterranean Back and Other Stereotypes: A Review of the Australian Literature Dealing with Industrial Back Injuries," *Australian Journal of Social Issues* 17, no. 4 (1982): 295–303.

46. Henderson et al., *People in Poverty*, 139.

47. These efforts to encourage the take-up of citizenship included posting regular advertisements in ethnic-community newspapers and in community languages throughout the late 1970s, especially in *Neos Kosmos*, but also in mainstream papers like the *Herald Sun*: "This is my invitation to you, to belong to Australia as a citizen." "Message from A.J Grassby," *Herald Sun*, January 18, 1974.

Figure 9.13 Kyriakos, family, and friends (his godparents) seeing a "friend from the village" perform at a pub in Brunswick, 1976.

Soviet Union—to delay the adoption of Australian citizenship. It was only when he met and married his Greek-born wife Irini Rossidis (while working as a storeman at a Coles supermarket in Lalor) that he was compelled to apply for citizenship. He had found that a Greek passport did not allow him enough freedom of movement during his honeymoon in 1979, while traveling from Noumea to the New Hebrides. In 1980, at twenty-two, he applied for Australian citizenship so he could get a "*proper passport.*" His parents applied at the same time, eleven years after they had first migrated. In another act of anti-assimilation, they never learnt to speak English, nor did most of their friends. They still intended to return to Greece.

A Third Departure/Arrival? (1985–6)

In 1985, Kyriakos, with his one-year-old son Tasso (Anastasios) and Irini, attempted another return. A flight took them to Athens on an "*open ticket.*" I'm counting this as a third departure:

> I've always wanted to go back. In fact, when I married your Mum the plan was to move to Greece . . . we did. We went with a ticket that didn't have a return date on it. Because we thought, we don't know when we'd come back, or if we come back.[48]

---

48. Gary Kyriakos Dellios, interview with the author, May 2, 2021.

Figure 9.14 Back in Greece, 1984, visiting the village, Therma.

And yet, their comically low expectations of Greece were present even during that departing flight: Irini and Kyriakos joke to this day about the volume of nappies they packed in their suitcases, dubious about Greece's ability to provide basic commodities. And so, after nearly six months, they departed Greece again for many of the same reasons that compelled the Dellios family's previous departures, and for which people leave today:

> After two or three months, we could see that things were still tough in Greece ... there was still political issues, the infrastructure wasn't there like we have here. Here life was simpler, easier ... In Greece they bust their arses, they work hard, but they don't get paid, and you know there's a lot of corruption.[49]

A sense of *"what could have been"* is strong throughout Kyriakos' testimony; what could have been if not for the *"old man's inability to settle"*, but also if not for the civil conflict, forced relocations, and economic deprivations. The fact that *"it could just as easily have been Germany"* does not change the fundamental intention and situation of the family, and of similar Greek families in the postwar era: to return after a few years of work, hopefully with money saved. In fact, my maternal grandfather completed this journey on his own, as a guest worker in Germany in the 1950s, leaving his family behind in Greece for a few years. And today, Kyriakos can point to the spread of his extended family working across many countries:

49. Gary Kyriakos Dellios, interview with the author, May 2, 2021.

Figure 9.15 Back in Greece, 1984, Athens trip.

second cousins spent their childhoods between Greece and Germany, and now live and work in Germany and return to Greece during the holidays; others are more recent guest workers in the United Kingdom, and then there's more recent temporary residents in Australia, who continue to go back and forth. Furthermore, due to their many internal relocations within Greece, there was never just one place to return to—granted, "the village" holds a nostalgic allure in the memories of many postwar migrants.

There are many points at which the linear historical narrative of "Becoming Australian" can be disrupted, most notably in the multiple moments of departure whose effects extend beyond the current generation. The characteristic of any diaspora (whether the Greek, Irish, or Chinese diaspora) is that the "migrant journey" is not one-way, nor does it always have a clear end-point. Multiple (both forced and voluntary) departures (and sometimes, the delay of departure) punctuate this history and spread across continents. I've said nothing of the Greek families who found it more difficult to return, including the political exiles who were effectively barred from returning (however temporarily) to Greece during the rule of the military junta. For their part, Dimitra and Anastasios returned to their village and their home multiple times throughout their lives, for months and sometimes years at a time, as many of their generation did. This too reinforced their resistance to assimilating into Australian society. The situation was different for Kyriakos (a member of the 1.5 generation), and it is not without some regret that he comments that *"starting fresh again and again"* was draining, socially, emotionally, and financially, but that is *"what everyone did."* He still wants to go back.

Chapter 10

STAYING OR DEPARTING: DISPLACED YOUTH IN AUSTRALIA

Karen Agutter

Introduction

At the end of World War II, over 8 million people in the western zones of Europe were officially labeled as Displaced Persons (DPs).[1] By July 1947, when the International Refugee Organization (IRO) assumed the care of these refugees, approximately 1.2 million DPs remained, the majority of whom were stateless or had refused to repatriate.[2] Thereafter, under the IRO, the focus shifted from repatriation to one of resettlement in a third/receiving nation.

Among these remaining DPs were over 4,000 so-called unaccompanied children.[3] Many of these children, officially defined as being under the age of seventeen and separated from relatives and homelands, had been brought to Germany, from as young as nine or ten years of age, as forced laborers. Numbers continued to swell as more youths crossed into Western Europe, claiming fear of persecution from Communism, and sought the protection the IRO.[4]

---

1. G. D. Cohen, "The 'Human Rights Revolution' at Work," in S.-L. Hoffmann (ed.), *Human Rights in the Twentieth Century* (New York: Cambridge University Press, 2011), 45.

2. The IRO was tasked with the care of DPs at the end of the United Nations Relief and Rehabilitation Administration (UNRRA) mandate. T. Judt, *Postwar: A History of Europe Since 1945* (London: Vintage Books, 2006).

3. This total included 1,417 Polish, 400 classified as stateless, 123 of undetermined nationality, and 2,550 from over thirty nationalities. See L.W. Holborn, *The International Refugee Organization: A Specialized Agency of the United Nations, Its History and Work, 1946–1952* (London: Oxford University Press, 1956), 315. These figures do not include children who were considered "enemy nationals" and therefore outside the IRO mandate. See T. Zahra, *The Lost Children: Reconstructing Europe's Families after World War II* (Cambridge, MA: Harvard University Press, 2015), 8.

4. For more on the situation in Europe, see, for example, Zahra, *The Lost Children*; R. Balint, "Alexander and Anastayzia: The separation and search for family among Europe's displaced," *History of the Family* 22, no. 4 (2017); L. Taylor, *In the Children's Best Interests: Unaccompanied Children in American-Occupied Germany, 1945–1952* (Toronto: University of Toronto Press, 2017).

Increasingly aware of the need to find a solution for the children who could or would not be repatriated, the IRO determined that, like their adult counterparts, resettlement would be the preferred option.[5] Accordingly, in May 1948 the Director of Resettlement for the IRO, wrote to George Vincent Greenhalgh, the Chief Migration Officer of the Australian Military Mission in Europe that "It appears to us that Australia, a country anxious to obtain single and strong young people, might be willing to consider the allocation of a quota of its immigration requirements to this age group."[6] This letter was followed, some two months later by one from Aleta Brownlee, Chief of the Child Welfare Branch of the IRO, to the Australian Minister for Immigration, Arthur Calwell. Brownlee's request was more specific as she outlined the plight of the large number of children in Austria who she felt should or could not return to their country of origin, but, rather, needed to be resettled. These children, she explained, included "young people from 14 to 21 years ... mostly boys, brought here as slave labour by the Germans and placed on farms where they have remained in practically the same position, without education, without the privileges of Austrians; and often without pay."[7] She finished by saying, "We think these children, with some investment on the part of a country which is interested in them, could become very fine citizens."[8]

Perhaps in response to this emphasis on strength, youth, and future citizenship, all factors highly valued by Australia, in October 1948 the Department of Immigration sought advice from the Department of Labour and National Service regarding the ability to absorb 4,000 DP youths aged sixteen to eighteen into the work force. It was determined that there was in fact a very great shortage of juvenile labor and therefore there would be no difficulty in finding employment for these displaced youths.[9]

In January 1949, a meeting was held between Tasman Heyes (Secretary of the Department of Immigration), Major General Lloyd (Chief of the IRO for Australia and New Zealand), and IRO child welfare officer Dorothy Marshall. During this meeting Marshall asked a number of questions which were indicative of the IRO's beliefs that the ongoing welfare of these children needed to revolve around their physical and emotional care and their educational and legal security.[10] And, on paper at least, Australia appeared to adhere to these ideals when it agreed to accept

---

5. Although the global publicity surrounding the plight of these unaccompanied children had prompted a number of governments to agree to accept them, very few of these schemes actually materialized, or at best were very small in scale and highly selective, largely for fear of the potential burden the children might pose to the state in the immediate and long-term future. See Taylor, *In the Children's Best Interests*, 244–7.

6. National Archives Australia: A434, 1950/3/1145; Unaccompanied Youths and Children.

7. July 2, 1948, National Archives Australia; A434, 1950/3/1145.

8. July 2, 1948, National Archives Australia; A434, 1950/3/1145.

9. National Archives Australia; A434, 1950/3/1145.

10. Taylor, *In the Children's Best Interests*, 234.

unlimited numbers of unaccompanied youth aged sixteen to eighteen under a specific set of assurances:

- That the Minister for Immigration would act as each youth's guardian until the age of 21.
- That trained Welfare Officers would supervise their adjustment to his or her new surroundings.
- That family groups would not be separated.
- That they would be able to apply for naturalization when eligible.
- That all educational facilities available to Australian children would be available to these youths and, if circumstances required, the government would meet the cost of the maintenance, education and medical care during their minority.
- That the youths would be encouraged into apprenticeships and the continuance of technical education with consideration given to choice of occupation, and opportunities made for "the development of outstanding talents." AND
- That the Government would arrange individual sponsorship for the foster placement of the youth.[11]

Given the situation in Europe, the reluctance of other nations to accept these unaccompanied youth, the promises made by the Australian authorities, and the rapidly approaching end of the IRO's mandate,[12] it is hardly surprising that, according to historian Lynne Taylor, this plan "generated considerable excitement, both because of what it offered ... and because it addressed an otherwise very difficult group to place—older youth."[13]

The Unaccompanied Youth in Australia

The first group, a small cohort of twelve—nine boys and three girls—arrived in April 1949 and Calwell was quick to claim that Australia would "give these fine young Baltic people an opportunity to establish themselves in a new country ... [and added that] Australians will be given the opportunity of taking them into their families as foster children."[14]

In line with this objective, government-initiated positive publicity of the early youth arrivals was regularly featured in official press releases and follow-up articles. This publicity highlighted the young people's happiness, for example, at being sent

---

11. National Archives Australia; A434, 1950/3/1145.
12. This was scheduled for June 30, 1950 although they were seeking an extension and did extend until January 1, 1952.
13. Taylor, *In the Children's Best Interests*, 250.
14. National Archives Australia; A434, 1950/3/1145.

to work as domestics for professional families, or how a £5 cheque from an Adelaide woman had allowed one young man to buy the tools he so desperately desired.[15] However, very quickly these young DPs became part of the general intake and remained outside the public gaze unless they were the victims of accidents or as a result of criminal activity. How then can one identify and track the lives of these people?

In order to establish exactly who migrated under this particular scheme, I have consulted the nominal rolls of the ships which arrived after the first cohort in April 1949. These rolls list the names of passengers under categories of migration: single men; single women; family groups, and so on; and in this case, "Unaccompanied Youth." This information includes the migrant's full name, birthdate, and nationality. Entered into a database, this information provides the basis for my longitudinal study of these youths. To reconstruct their lives in Australia, and in some cases, after departure, I have consulted a variety of other archival sources, including those available online through the Arolsen Archives; immigration, alien registrations, naturalization and other files held by the National Archives of Australia; naturalizations gazetted by the Commonwealth; and newspapers.[16] I have also called on various genealogical tracing tools including those relating to births, deaths, and marriages, and electoral rolls.

To date I have identified over 300 unaccompanied children, the vast majority of whom arrived in the first months of the scheme, and it is the cohort of 269 individuals who arrived between April and December 1949 which I will consider here. The youngest of these youths was fourteen and the oldest twenty: 88 percent were aged between sixteen and eighteen years.[17] There were 240 boys and twenty-nine girls; their nationalities, as given in the nominal rolls, are provided in the table below. Given when this scheme operated, it is not surprising that the number of youths who gave their reason for protection as "escaping communism" outnumber those who had been bought to Germany as slave labor during the war.

---

15. See, for example, *The Argus* (Melbourne), January 13, 1950: "They had the thrill of a new job," 3; *The News* (Adelaide), August 12, 1949, "YOUNG MIGRANT IS HAPPY NOW," 3.

16. During and in the years following World War I (1916–26) and World War II (1939–72), Australia required all "aliens"—that is, those inhabitants over the age of sixteen who were not Australian/British citizens—to register their details with the authorities. Once registered, migrants had to notify of any change of address, name, job, or marital status.

17. Because of the time between assessment, departure, and arrival, some of those youths, who were almost nineteen when selected, had reached the age of twenty on arrival. The age of majority at this time in Australia was twenty-one. It must be noted that age was also particularly difficult to determine accurately and was sometimes manipulated. See A. Burgard, "Contested Childhood: Assessing the Age of Young Refugees in the Aftermath of the Second World War," *History Workshop Journal* 92 (Autumn 2021): 174–93.

Table 10.1 Data sourced from ships nominal rolls held by the National Archives of Australia

Identified Nationality	Number
Czech/CSR	103
Polish	49
Hungarian	29
Yugoslavian	24
Lithuanian	15
Latvian	10
Slovenian	10
Romanian	8
Ukrainian	7
Russian	6
Estonian	3
Romanian	2
Bulgarian	1
German	1
Undetermined	1
Grand Total	269

After Arrival—Promises Made and Never Kept

Despite their differences of nationality, reasons for seeking IRO protection, and subsequent resettlement in Australia, it would seem that hardly any of these young DPs were beneficiaries of the promises that had been made to them by the Australian authorities in Europe. Contrary to the agreement made with the IRO, there is little evidence of the promised education, apprenticeships, choice of occupation, or opportunities for "the development of outstanding talents."[18] The Department of Immigration responded quickly to questions about the promised education and claimed that the youths had been warned before selection that they would be "directed to mainly rural and domestic employment for a period of two years after arrival." However, they excused this by arguing that "efforts will be made to assist them later to take up occupations for which they appear more suited"— that is, after the two-year work contract was completed.[19] There is very little evidence of assistance either immediate or delayed. In reality, on arrival the youths were sent to the migrant Reception and Training Centres, including Bonegilla and

18. National Archives Australia; A434, 1950/3/1145.

19. August 8, 1949, Tasman Heyes to Director Bonegilla Centre in National Archives Australia: PP6/1, 1949/H/3021; Displaced persons—International Refugee Organisation Youths—14 to 18 yrs unaccompanied.

Bathurst.[20] From these centers they were allocated jobs, generally in menial positions: the boys as general laborers on farms, in public utilities, and industry, especially the railways; and the girls as domestics in both private homes and in public settings such as hospitals. Like their adult counterparts, these youths were also subject to a compulsory two-year work contract, at the end of which they were left to their own resources.[21] Later, social workers noted that it was not surprising that these youths "became either rebellious and have run away, or [are] confused and depressed about their future prospects."[22]

Although the Minister for Immigration acted as their guardian until the age of twenty-one, so that, for example, when Vera K. wished to marry at aged nineteen she had to get the permission of Minister Calwell,[23] most of the supervision of these children was delegated to the respective Child Welfare departments in each state.[24] Individual sponsorship and foster placement did not occur and unfortunately many of these teenagers fell through the cracks. Individual stories provide examples of youths such as Zigfrid K. who habitually absconded from work contracts, and of criminal activity from petty offences, such as Zofia C.'s habitual shoplifting, Antonin R.'s appearances in the children's court for breaking and entering, and numerous young lads' court appearances for petty theft and for speeding and motorbike offences, through to more serious crimes including allegations of rape and murder.[25] Again, social workers noted that many of these criminal activities might have been avoided if "personal guardianship had been available from the beginning" to direct the young people in their activities and choices.[26]

20. Post-World War II, Australia established a system of accommodation facilities which consisted of Reception and Training Centres for processing newly arrived DPs and other European migrants, Holding Centres for the dependent wives and children of migrant workers, workers hostels, and other general hostels which were open to all assisted migrants to Australia. See K. Agutter, "More than Just a Roof over Their Heads: Migrant Accommodation Centres and the Assimilation of 'New Australians' 1947–1960," Ph.D. thesis, School of Humanities: History, University of Adelaide, 2017.

21. For more on the DP work contracts, see K. Agutter, "Displaced Persons and the 'Continuum of Mobility' in the South Australian Hostel System," in M. A. Kleinig and E. Richards (eds.), *On the Wing: Mobility Before and After Emigration to Australia*, Visible Immigrants, Vol. 7 (Spit Junction, NSW: Anchor Books Australia, 2013); A. Dellios, "Displaced Persons, Family Separation and the Work Contract in Postwar Australia," *Journal of Australian Studies* 40, no. 4 (2016): 418–32.

22. National Archives Australia: A445, 276/2/12; Social Welfare—Special Problems—young people—unaccompanied youth etc.

23. National Archives Australia: A441, 1951/13/505; Kremnewa, V.

24. National Archives Australia; PP6/1, 1949/H/3021.

25. During my investigation into these youths, I have noted that some are still living and out of respect to them and in the interest of their, and their descendants' privacy, I have chosen to use first names and surname initial only throughout this chapter.

26. National Archives Australia; A445, 276/2/12.

There are few examples of the separation of family groups, but those that do exist indicate that although work contracts might have initially separated them, as was the case with brothers Hans and Allan G., they were, within months, working in the same city; or Ruth W., who, when found to have family in Australia, was at least placed in work nearby. Finally, and fortunately for this study, naturalization was encouraged and, in the case of these youths, could be obtained after much shorter periods of residence than for other migrants and DPs.

Given that the promises made by the Australian authorities were not upheld, and that the opportunities available to these youths in the first two years of residence were far from what they may have hoped for, it might be expected that there would have been a general desire to move on from Australia, either to attempt to return to Europe or perhaps migrate to other destinations. This longitudinal study seeks to test this hypothesis.

Staying or Departing?

Of the 269 youths under consideration, only six definitively departed while 210 were still resident in Australia ten years after arrival and can be found as adults on electoral rolls after 1960 and through death registrations. The remaining fifty-three are mystery cases who seemingly disappear from the public record soon after arrival.

The Departures

All of the six departure cases outlined below have been crossed-checked using confirmatory information including date and place of birth and parents' names. The first, Henryk S., was born in 1932 in Poland. Henryk's mother died when he was young, and his father followed in 1941. After their deaths, he was living with his sister when they were taken by the Germans as slave labor; Henryk was aged eleven. After the war he attached himself to the US army until he was placed in the Bad Aibling Children's Camp, where he expressed a desire to go to Australia. Soon after his arrival, Henryk faced charges of theft and larceny for a series of offences and in January 1951 he was reported as having left the Commonwealth. In 1958, Henryk, and his wife Herta, traveled from Southampton (UK) to New York, giving his permanent address as Florida. Henryk died in France in 2005. Given his departure from Australia just fourteen months after his arrival, and the fact that there is no record of his naturalization, we must question if his criminal activities resulted in deportation. As Jayne Persian notes (see Chapter 3 of this collection), the names of migrants who faced deportation are not efficiently recorded and, consequently, to date I have found no proof that this was the case with Henryk. However, one of the reasons for obtaining Australian citizenship was to secure a passport to replace non-existent or temporary identity and travel documents, so it is difficult to imagine how, outside of deportation, he would have been able to travel so soon after arrival and with no evidence of naturalization.

Very little is known of my second individual, Alfred S., who was born in Czechoslovakia in 1932. Alfred's father was deceased, and he left the country with his mother's consent, seeking IRO protection and claiming fear of the Communist regime. There is no record of Alfred naturalizing in Australia, and I can find nothing about him until the registration of his death in Marseille, France, in 1996.

By contrast, Erna O. is among those DPs whom the Department of Immigration chose to feature in the Australian newspapers and in the *New Australian*.[27] Born in 1932 in Lithuania, Erna's mother had died in 1934. Her father remarried and he, Erna, and her stepmother fled when the Russians approached in 1944. In Germany they worked on a farm and her father subsequently died in a factory accident. After the war, Erna, reunited with her brother and sister, tried to emigrate together to Australia, but they were refused and Erna was recommended for the Unaccompanied Youth scheme by the Children's center. On arrival in Australia, Erna was sent to work as a domestic. She naturalized in 1951 and was granted her citizenship during a ceremony at the Jubilee Citizenship Convention, bringing her further publicity. She is next noted as departing Sydney for London in May 1956, where she listed her address as care of her sister who had settled there. Five months later, Erna was a passenger on the French SS *Liberte* traveling from Le Havre to Detroit, her travel documents identifying her as a twenty-four-year-old Australian. In February 1957, Erna married Clarence W. in Los Angeles, California. In the 1960s, she was reunited with her sister and brother who joined her in America. Family reunion was likely a strong motivator for her departure.

In a similar migratory trajectory, three male youths departed Australia for Canada and the United States. Ferdinand H., born in 1931 in Slovenia, was reported as having departed the Commonwealth on December 12, 1952, having become naturalized in 1951. Ferdinand married and went on to become a naturalized American citizen, going on to serve in the US army in Vietnam. He died in 2013.

Jozsef K., who was born in 1930 in Hungary, left his parents and came to Australia, also claiming a fear of the Communist regime. In 1955 he was working as a laborer for the Victorian Railways when he applied for Australian citizenship; in 1957 he traveled from Sydney to Hawaii. In 1958 he married a German-born migrant in Toronto, Canada, and in 1965 he applied for US citizenship, claiming that he had lived continuously in the US since 1959.

Finally, Eugen M. was born in Hungary in 1933. A Jew, Eugen had survived the concentration camps but sadly his family did not. In coming to Australia, he noted on his immigration papers that he had an aunt in New York. He became naturalized in 1953 and then traveled to the US in 1957, dying in New Jersey in 1990.

Erna, Ferdinand, Jozsef, and Eugen might be described as what Kunz calls "transit naturalizations"; that is, those who obtained documents in order to leave

---

27. The *New Australian* was a monthly publication produced by the Immigration Department specifically for European migrants. Its aim was to inform and educate new arrivals in the Australian way of life, highlight DP success stories, encourage naturalization, and remind DPs of their obligations, especially with regard to the two-year work contract.

Australia for other destinations of settlement relatively soon after arrival.[28] It is impossible to know if this was always their intention, if they were influenced by finding family or pursing opportunities as they arose, or even if their departure was prompted by the fact that they found life in Australia not what they had hoped for or been led to expect.

The Stayers

Of the 210 unaccompanied youth that can be traced, the vast majority (169) became Australian citizens. Because they naturalized, these individuals are easier to trace as they usually appear on electoral rolls and hence mobility, changing occupation, and the growth of families can be monitored. Those that did not naturalize may be found through other sources such as marriage or death records or, in some cases, through articles in newspapers.

Although death may seem an unlikely criterion to measure evidence of a lack of departure, the registration of death, and subsequent burial records and monumental inscriptions, provide vital information in the reconstruction of the lives of this DP cohort.

Sadly, the mortality rate among DPs, especially at a younger age, was significant. Leading causes of death included accidental drowning, motorcycle fatalities, and industrial accidents largely as a result of the types of labor in which they were employed.[29] Tragically early deaths are evident within this cohort and include Yugoslavian-born Giorgie Z. who died just two years after arrival aged nineteen when he dived into shallow water, and Hungarian Gyula M. who died aged twenty-five after a fatal motor vehicle accident. For twenty-five-year-old Czech Milan E., a long history of petty crimes resulted in a series of prison sentences, and he took his own life aged twenty-five whilst incarcerated. However, for the vast majority of the 210, death records indicate long lives, with many living into their eighties and nineties and more than half marrying and having children.

Obviously, not all of the stayers adjusted to, or were happy with, life in Australia. The Department of Immigration used the threat of deportation as a method to control behavior, especially regarding fulfillment of the work contract, although this tactic often backfired. Czech youths Jindrick C. and Miroslav H. certainly tested the threat of deportation, claiming that they intentionally committed crimes in order to be returned to Europe. Appearing in court less than eighteen months after their arrival, they outlined their unhappiness through an interpreter, claiming that promises made to them by consular officials before they left Europe had not been fulfilled. The youths said they were brought to Australia from a children's camp in Germany, having been told that on arrival in Australia they would be

---

28. E. F. Kunz, *Displaced Persons: Calwell's New Australians* (Sydney: ANU Press, 1988), 221.

29. Kunz, *Displaced Persons*, 222–3.

allowed to choose their own trade or profession, would be taught local customs and the English language, and looked after in a camp or adopted into private homes. Instead, they had been sent to work on the railways where they stated the pay was so inadequate that they could not afford to buy clothes or shoes. Jindrick told the court that they had heard they would be deported and returned to Europe if they committed a crime.[30] Although they were not deported, they did receive some acknowledgment of their complaint when the judge agreed that they had been the victims of the system, although he put this down to a "lack of co-ordination somewhere" rather than misrepresentation. Nevertheless, in saying that, the judge went on to state that if the Department of Immigration had taken greater interest in their welfare, they might not have engaged in criminal behavior. His compassion did not extend to a dismissal of the charges, as he sentenced Miroslaw to two years' imprisonment and released Jindrick on a good behavior bond.[31] Jindrich, later known as Henry, stayed in Australia and was naturalized in 1957. Miroslaw extended his criminal record after his release but remained in Australia and died in New South Wales aged sixty-five.

For those migrants who were seen to exhibit repeated disobedience, especially in regard to not fulfilling their work contracts, or who committed more serious crimes, the Australian authorities did actually seek their deportation. When Lithuanian-born Pranas A. absconded from his work contract, in response to the request for deportation, the IRO/Combined Travel Board recommended counseling rather than removal.[32] Heyes, using this case as an example, noted that such refusals were often made without the IRO having full knowledge of the mitigating circumstances, in this case a previous charge of assault and attempted rape.[33] Pranas was naturalized in 1957 and is on the electoral rolls as a driver in the 1960s. Similarly, in April 1951, the Australian authorities approached the IRO to arrange the return to Germany of Sandor M. and Johann N. who were convicted of the murder of a Greek seaman in 1950.[34] The request for deportation was refused. Sandor served a seven-year sentence and on release committed other crimes, the last of which saw him receive a life sentence. Johann was sentenced to five years which he served at HM Prison Pentridge, Melbourne. I have been unable to find

30. "Lied To By Official," *Newcastle Morning Herald and Miners' Advocate* (New South Wales), February 24, 1951, 3.

31. "Lied To By Official," *Newcastle Morning Herald and Miners' Advocate*.

32. National Archives Australia: A6980, S250240; Deportation of displaced persons—Policy.

33. Heyes to Head of Australian Military Mission Berlin, July 1951, in National Archives Australia; A6980, S250240. This case had been dismissed when a judge determined that although a prima facie case had been made, no jury would convict. See "Jury Would Not Convict, Says Magistrate," *Newcastle Morning Herald and Miners' Advocate* (New South Wales), July 19, 1950.

34. National Archives Australia; A6980, S250240.

any subsequent records for this young man. So, although deportation was a constant threat, I am yet to find hard evidence that it was a method of departure for these young DPs.

The Missing

The missing youths represent 20 percent of the total cohort studied, a percentage that far exceeds Egon Kunz's missing 7 percent which, in his groundbreaking study, contributed to his overall estimate of a 10 percent departure rate.[35] Do we assume, as he did, that half of these missing individuals should be counted as having departed from Australia?

Unlike Kunz's sample, which consisted only of male DPs, the cohort studied here includes female youths who actually represent eight (15 percent) of the missing fifty-three individuals. Female migrants are particularly difficult to trace as, in this period, they generally marry and adopt their husbands' names, making it harder to reconstruct their lives. This might seem incongruous given the compulsory recording of so-called life milestones such as marriage, however these certificates are not always available as digital records through genealogical and other platforms. For example, while the online search engines for New South Wales and Victorian registrations are excellent and cover extended time periods, Western Australian marriages are only available between 1841 and 1936, well prior to this study.

Therefore, even if we restrict the missing to male youths, this still leaves forty-five individuals unaccounted for and the question remains—do we assume all or, as Kunz indicates, half of these departed the Commonwealth?

Of the forty-five missing male subjects, thirteen naturalized but do not subsequently appear on any available public record beyond their initial arrival and very early alien registration documents. These are particularly interesting cases. Australian citizenship would have enabled access to a passport and therefore the natural assumption might be that they departed, but there are other possibilities which must be considered. Although some changes or anglicizations of names are established from alien registrations, the gazetting of naturalizations and the publication of changes by deed poll, I am sure that some were never official. While Edvard to Edward or Smolertschuk to Smoler are obvious changes, if others changed from Pokorny to Benson, Boskovics to Charles, and Popilko to Wilson, as happened, then tracking is difficult, if not impossible. As Kunz notes, some of these men may also have been constantly on the move, living hand to mouth and outside official records or, given the traumas they had previously suffered and the incidence of mental health issues, may have been in institutions.[36]

To do a like for like comparison with Kunz (i.e., considering only the male unaccompanied youth), then there were five departures and forty-five missing from a total male cohort of 239. Kunz calculated his overall 10 percent departure

---

35. Kunz, *Displaced Persons*, 224.
36. Kunz, *Displaced Persons*, 269.

rate based upon the total number of departures (7 percent) and 50 percent of the missing to arrive at a 10 percent overall departure rate. Using this formula, the corresponding figures here give a total departure rate of 11.5 percent, which is comparable to the general DP male population.

Conclusion

At the outset of this chapter, I postulated that these unaccompanied youth might have had good reason to depart from Australia, as they had been misled about the educational opportunities and familial and/or emotional support that would be available to them. While there is evidence of unhappiness and dissatisfaction, exhibited directly and possibly indirectly through the significant incidence of petty criminal behavior amongst this cohort, there were other factors that made their departure particularly difficult. Many of these youths had experienced uncountable horrors during the war. As UNRRA worker Francesca Wilson explained, "hangings, shootings, murder, robbery, crimes of the basest kind. Nothing had been kept from them."[37] Traumatic associations that it might be argued were best left behind, at least geographically, if never physically or psychologically? Additionally, for the majority of these youths, their homelands no longer existed or were under Soviet control, and while some left family behind, others had no known family to return to.

On arrival in Australia the application of the two-year work contract generally meant low-paid menial jobs with little or no opportunity to save money or to train and gain any sort of qualification to improve future prospects, although there are rare exceptions. For example, Hungarian-born Jeno B. had completed eleven years of schooling in Europe before he left and in 1952 he was successful in applying for a Commonwealth university scholarship, going on to study law and became a solicitor. However, for those who were taken as slave labor, who lost parents, or who were directly affected by war in other ways, any form of prior education was absent or severely lacking, making occupational and economic advancement difficult. Although Kunz argues that "Australia turn[ed] out to be close to paradise for the least educated" and therefore they rarely left, I would argue that their economic circumstances, especially in the first decade after arrival, were a significant restraint.[38] Furthermore, as noted above, a significant percentage of the unaccompanied youth married, establishing new lives and families, forming ties with Australia and, at the same time, potentially further restricting their desire and/or financial ability to leave.

37. Quoted in K. Rossy, "The (Bio)Politics of Relief: UN Food Policy Towards Displaced Children in Post-War Germany (1945–49)," in B. Scutaru and S. Paoli (eds.), *Child Migration and Biopolitics: Old and New Experiences in Europe* (Oxon: Routledge 2020), n.p. (e-book).

38. Kunz, *Displaced Persons*, 225.

In his twenty-year longitudinal study, Egon Kunz was limited to the records available to him. However, as he admits, he was significantly helped by being able to engage with members of his cohort. Kunz utilized ethnic organizations, chaplains, and fellow passengers to trace DPs directly and indirectly through important information about name changes, last known addresses, and occupations and workplaces.[39] In trying to reconstruct the lives of these unaccompanied youths seventy years after their arrival, while there have been great advances in the accessibility of records (through indexing and digitization), challenges remain in terms of those who left few or no public records. Therefore, although the longitudinal study of this migrant cohort can provide some statistical information about who and how many stayed or departed, the actual motivations for staying or departing remains informed conjecture.

---

39. Kunz, *Displaced Persons*, 268.

Chapter 11

DEPARTURE BY DIPLOMACY: A HISTORY OF REFUGEE RESETTLEMENT OFFERS BETWEEN AUSTRALIA AND THE UNITED STATES

Claire Higgins

On several occasions since the 1960s, Australia and the United States have offered to resettle refugees whose original journey to one or the other country was politically contentious. While a 2016 agreement between the two states is the most recent and prominent example of what some Australian politicians have called refugee "swaps," earning international headlines and the ire of former US president Donald Trump, in fact this practice of "departure by diplomacy" has a longer history, involving generations of refugees from Cuba as well as many Vietnamese, Haitians, and others who sought asylum by boat.[1]

These resettlement offers have been upheld by both governments as a sign of bilateral goodwill and framed as a linear migration process. But for the individuals concerned, the prospect of being redirected halfway around the world was a new detour in their search for protection, one greeted with mixed emotions and results. For some, hopes to reunite with loved ones or join diaspora communities were diverted. For those held in detention, accepting a transfer was understood—or framed by the state—as the *only* way they could physically leave a liminal space between country of origin and country of refuge.

This chapter will chart the history of these departures by diplomacy and consider the individual impact of bilateral refugee policymaking between Australia and the United States. With a primary focus on the Australian context, this chapter draws on newspaper reports, congressional and parliamentary hearings, and archival records from presidential libraries and United States and Australian government repositories. The agreements themselves are not usually formalized or, if they are, the text is not publicly available. A 2007

---

1. Azadeh Dastyari, "Swapping Refugees: the implications of the 'Atlantic Solution,'" *UTS Law Review* 9 (2007): 93.

Memorandum of Understanding remained confidential, according to legal scholar Azadeh Dastyari, as is the 2016 agreement.² Simon Henshaw, then Acting Assistant Secretary of State, told a congressional hearing in 2017 that "we have an agreement with the Australians that, if they classify a report, it is classified under our system."³

Legal scholar Eve Lester has observed that in the popular understanding of Australia's refugee policy "the refugee appears to be a secondary consideration, regarded as merely incidental or instrumental in fulfilling geopolitical interests and priorities," an observation that others have made in the broader global context, and which historians have urged forced migration scholars to overcome.⁴ Historically, in terms of the various resettlement offers issued between Australia and the United States, the needs and hopes of individuals themselves have been largely absent from media coverage. Recently, in the Australian context the advent of modern telecommunications has helped, to some degree, those refugees and asylum seekers who are detained offshore to tell their own stories and communicate directly with advocates and journalists (in spite of the severe restrictions placed upon detainees' access to mobile phones and the internet), which represents a small victory against what legal scholar Michael Grewcock has called a "deliberate strategy of institutional obfuscation and silence" and the "everyday, structural violence of Australia's border policing operations."⁵ The experiences of those refugees subject to earlier diplomatic negotiations, however, are much harder to unearth. Thus, where the accounts of individual refugees are not available, in this chapter I will attempt to think creatively about the people whose lives were disrupted or diverted by the departures discussed in the above-mentioned government archival documents and other sources, to reconstruct the context in which these refugees were displaced, and to reflect on the way that their intentions and trajectories may have been impacted by the political and diplomatic maneuverings of their preferred destination state.

---

2. Dastyari, "Swapping Refugees," 95.

3. United States, 115th Congress, House of Representatives Committee on the Judiciary, Hearing before the Subcommittee on Immigration and Border Security, "Oversight of the United States Refugee Admissions Program," 26 October 2017, Hon. R. Labrador to S. Henshaw.

4. Eve Lester, "Australian Responses to Refugee Journeys: matters of perspective and context," in Jordana Silverstein and Rachel Stevens (eds.), *Refugee Journeys: Histories of Resettlement, Representation and Resistance* (Canberra: ANU Press, 2021), 24; Lauren Banko, Katarzyna Nowak, and Peter Gatrell, "What is Refugee History, Now?" *Journal of Global History* 17, no. 1 (August 2021): 4.

5. Michael Grewcock, "Our Lives is in Danger: Manus Island and the end of asylum," *Race & Class* 59, no. 2 (2017): 72.

The Role of Resettlement Arrangements in Australian Asylum Policy

In an interview with the *Guardian* newspaper in late 2017, Iranian refugee Arash Shirmohamadi was distraught. Having been detained on Nauru some four years earlier under Australia's hardline asylum policy, Arash was blocked from entering Australia and therefore reuniting with his wife and young daughter. Australian officials were now encouraging him to apply for admission to the United States, under a refugee resettlement deal signed between Canberra and Washington in 2016. It was America or a life in the impoverished island nation of Nauru. But to qualify for departure to the United States, Arash would have to be a single man, separated from his wife and without custody of his daughter. Australia had presented him with no choice at all.[6]

Arash's story is an example of the Australian government's increasing preference for negotiating resettlement arrangements with other countries as a way of removing particular cohorts of refugees—those who have been held in onshore or offshore detention because they attempted to reach Australian territory by boat without a valid visa and who have been banned from ever making a life in Australia, under a policy introduced by the then Labor government in mid-2013 and upheld by the incoming Liberal government under a policy of "border protection." Australia has sought to make deals with several developing countries, such as the Philippines and (reportedly) Kazakhstan and Kyrgyzstan.[7] A vaunted 2014 deal with Cambodia cost Australia A$55m in aid and yielded poor results, with only a handful of refugees ever choosing to leave Nauru to resettle in that country and— due to inadequate human rights protections—very few ultimately staying permanently.[8] In comparison, while the 2016 arrangement with the United States has taken a long time to come to fruition—with stop-start processing and long delays—it has offered one of the only avenues through which refugees who arrived

---

6. Ben Doherty, "Border Force tells Nauru refugees to separate from family if they want to settle in US," *Guardian*, December 6, 2017, https://www.theguardian.com/world/2017/dec/06/border-force-tells-nauru-refugees-to-separate-from-family-if-they-want-to-settle-in-us. See also Refugee Council of Australia, *Australia's Man-made Crisis on Nauru*, October 4, 2020, https://www.refugeecouncil.org.au/nauru-report/.

7. See Lisa Martin, "Philippines refugee deal on the cards," *News.com.au*, October 9, 2015, https://www.news.com.au/national/breaking-news/deal-with-philippines-to-settle-refugees/news-story/e6031e0a085ad14c3cf1c90a1dc76080; Lindsay Murdoch, "Remaining two refugees in Cambodia rue leaving Nauru," *Sydney Morning Herald*, March 13, 2016, https://www.smh.com.au/world/remaining-two-refugees-in-cambodia-rue-leaving-nauru-20160312-gnh7mo.html.

8. Refugee Council of Australia, *Australia's Man-made Crisis on Nauru*.

by boat since mid-2013 can access a safe, sustainable, and long-term solution to their displacement and detention.[9]

According to Australia's most senior immigration policymaker, the US–Australia agreement is underpinned by a "collaborative spirit" between the two countries, which in this context means a shared interest in the deterrence of people seeking asylum and in the selective resettlement of refugees through a controlled annual program.[10] The two countries have a "longstanding history" of working together in this area of policy.[11] That collaboration involves not only the transfer of refugees, but a range of knowledge-sharing arrangements in policy and intelligence on immigration matters, through both bilateral exchanges and multilateral forums such as the Five Eyes intelligence partnership.[12] Legal scholars such as Daniel Ghezelbash have described how the Australian government has copied the United States' past use of policies such as remote offshore detention and the "interdiction and deflection" of asylum seekers at sea through these forums for "legal and policy transfer" between the two countries.[13] According to geographer Allison Mountz, while such deterrence policies may be ill conceived and have poor consequences for those individuals who are interdicted or detained, states of the global North "do not operate in a vacuum," but rather "look to peers for 'best practices.'"[14]

Australia and the United States also liaise with many other countries in their efforts to control entry to their territories. For example, through what Amy Nethery and Carly Gordyn have identified as "incentivised policy transfer," Australia has secured, using "substantial financial and diplomatic incentives," Indonesian

---

9. For information on the US–Australia resettlement deal, see further Claire Higgins, "The US–Australia resettlement deal: the diplomacy and uncertainty of a 'very big deal,'" *Australian Journal of Politics and History* 68, no. 2 (June 2022): 197–217. The UN refugee agency, civil society groups, and private individuals have helped to organize the resettlement of a relatively small number of refugees to Canada and some European countries. See "Canada 'like a dream' for refugee who spent 6 years in Australia's Manus Island camp," *CBC News*, November 8, 2019, https://www.cbc.ca/radio/asithappens/as-it-happens-friday-edition-1.5353214/canada-like-a-dream-for-refugee-who-spent-6-years-in-australia-s-manus-island-camp-1.5353217.

10. Australia. Senate Legal and Constitutional Affairs Committee, Estimates: Immigration and Border Protection Portfolio, October 23, 2017, Mike Pezzullo to Senator Jane Hume, 21.

11. Australia. Senate Legal and Constitutional Affairs Committee, Estimates: Immigration and Border Protection Portfolio, October 23, 2017, Mike Pezzullo to Senator Jane Hume, 21.

12. See Daniel Ghezelbash, *Refuge Lost: Asylum Law in an Interdependent World* (Cambridge: Cambridge University Press, 2019), 25–6; Penelope Mathew, "Australian Refugee Protection in the Wake of the Tampa," *American Journal of International Law* 96, no. 3 (2002): 670.

13. Ghezelbash, *Refuge Lost*, 4.

14. Allison Mountz, *Seeking Asylum: Human Smuggling and Bureaucracy at the Border* (Minneapolis: University of Minnesota Press, 2010), xvi.

assistance in combating people-smuggling operations and detaining asylum seekers.[15] Furthermore, the regional ministerial initiative known as the Bali Process, led by Australia and Indonesia, is another forum through which states in the region seek to prevent people smuggling. According to legal scholar Asher Hirsch, unlike visa requirements or other unilateral forms of immigration management, bilateral or multilateral arrangements between Australia and its Southeast Asian neighbors are forms of "cooperative deterrence," through which the Australian government seeks to emphasize the responsibilities of source and transit countries in the management of migration.[16] For its part, the United States works closely with Canada and Central and South American governments to access information about would-be arrivals, in an intelligence gathering effort that is "primarily motivated by security concerns" (anti-drug smuggling, anti-terrorism, for example), but which also serves to block access to asylum.[17]

Although beyond the scope of this chapter, that bi- and multilateral collaboration must be seen in a global context in which states have sought ways to avoid their responsibilities for refugee protection.[18] As Goodwin-Gill, McAdam and Dunlop have noted, policies such as interdiction at sea or the offshoring of detention facilities in third countries, both utilized by the United States since the 1980s and Australia since the 2000s, are an attempt to deny asylum seekers access to their territories and to somehow therefore avoid obligations under international law.[19]

Cuban Refugees in the 1960s and 1980s

From late 1962, following the Cuban Missile Crisis, Cubans looking to flee their country for the United States were forced to either risk a journey by boat to Florida or Mexico, or risk the ire of authorities in seeking a plane ticket from Havana to Madrid.[20]

---

15. Amy Nethery and Carly Gordyn, "Australia–Indonesia cooperation on asylum seekers: a case of incentivised policy transfer," *Australian Journal of International Affairs* 68, no. 2 (2014): 186.

16. Asher Hirsch, "The Borders Beyond the Border: Australia's extraterritorial migration controls," *Refugee Survey Quarterly* 36, no. 3 (2017): 70.

17. David Fitzgerald, *Refuge Beyond Reach: How Rich Democracies Repel Asylum Seekers* (Oxford: Oxford University Press, 2019), 66.

18. See Christian Joppke, "Asylum and State Sovereignty: A Comparison of the United States, Germany and Britain," *Comparative Political Studies* 30, no. 3 (June 1997): 263–4.

19. Guy S. Goodwin-Gill and Jane McAdam with Emma Dunlop, *The Refugee in International Law*, 4th edn. (Oxford: Oxford University Press, 2021), 416.

20. Between 1963 and 1965 the United States admitted almost 7,000 Cubans who fled to Florida by boat, and almost 60,000 who fled via Mexico and Spain—see Jorge Duany, "Cuban Migration: A Postrevolution Exodus Ebbs and Flows," Migration Policy Institute, July 6, 2017, https://www.migrationpolicy.org/article/cuban-migration-postrevolution-exodus-ebbs-and-flows.

For the next three years there was no longer any opportunity for Cubans to take a commercial flight directly into the United States to access protection.[21] Instead, Cubans looking to board a plane to the United States had to fly via Europe. The Spanish national airline Iberia remained one of the few carriers that continued to operate direct flights out of Havana to Madrid, while the Havana office of Dutch airline KLM continued to issue connecting tickets to Madrid via South American capitals.[22] It was because of this transatlantic route that the Australian government first came to offer resettlement places for Cubans as a form of diplomatic goodwill to the United States.

Under the Communist regime led by Fidel Castro, Cubans wishing to leave on one of these flights had to apply for a passport—braving "Communist-oriented hoodlums" who beat and harassed those queued outside the relevant government ministry—and then present themselves for scrutiny by the Cuban intelligence agency, whose approval hinged on the individual not being named on a list compiled by local "neighbourhood vigilance committees."[23] For those Cubans who did receive exit visas, they then needed a visa to another country (a difficult document to obtain) and were forced to wait several weeks, if not months, for a reservation on an outbound flight. Once at the airport in Havana, intelligence officials would again scrutinize their identity and permission to depart, calling individuals aside for questioning and, in some cases, strip searching.[24] When a person had finally secured a reservation and boarded a flight to depart Havana, they may have faced multiple stopovers—in Curacao, Paramaribo, and Lisbon—before reaching Madrid, if they flew with KLM.[25] With their assets confiscated by the Cuban state following their departure, these refugees arrived with only what they had with them. In Spain, they may have connected with distant relatives, or joined other exiles in boarding houses or crowded accommodation and been reliant on the provision of food and other services from Catholic or Jewish relief agencies.

By 1964 the United States government was beginning to view the travel of Cubans to Madrid—and prospectively onward to the United States—as a problem.

---

21. In 1965 the US government negotiated with the Cuban government, via the Swiss, for an orderly departure program to fly Cubans directly to the United States. This program, the "Cuban airlift," ceased in 1973, and required prospective departees to be approved by both the Cuban and US governments. See John F. Thomas, "Cuban Refugees in the United States," *International Migration Review* 1, no. 2 (1967): 47, 52–4.

22. Maryellen Fullerton, "Cuban Exceptionalism: Migration and Asylum in Spain and the United States," *University of Miami Inter-American Law Review* 35, no. 3 (Summer, 2004): 556; United States Embassy Madrid to Department of State, October 30, 1964, in "Cuba—Refugees, 10/63–7/65," Country Files, NSF, Box 30, LBJ Presidential Library.

23. "Cuban Refugees Face Red-Tape Nightmare," *Canberra Times*, July 26, 1961, 2.

24. "Cuban Refugees Face Red-Tape Nightmare," *Canberra Times*, July 26, 1961, 2

25. United States Embassy Madrid to Department of State, October 30, 1964, in "Cuba—Refugees, 10/63–7/65," Country Files, NSF, Box 30, LBJ Presidential Library.

There were two concerns. The first stemmed from "congressional pressure" on the US government to prevent Cubans arriving via Madrid to access "the very generous relief programme" and becoming "a permanent charge on the United States Treasury."[26] The second was security. According to a cable from the Department of State to the US Embassy in the Hague, of June 30, 1964, the "principal consideration" for "all free world airlines" in isolating Cuba from global travel networks was that "Cuba uses air links to free world countries to move subversive trainees and couriers to and from Cuba."[27] The Department of State indicated a concern that if non-diplomats, in the form of refugees, were allowed onto these flights to Europe, then others may be as well. The United States government thus sought and received assurances from the Dutch airline KLM and the government of the Netherlands "that KLM would limit its services to Cuba to those required for foreign embassies" and "would take out of Cuba only minimum numbers [of] refugees at request of foreign embassies" and "would notify [government] in advance of all such flights."[28]

In late 1963 the Intergovernmental Committee for European Migration (ICEM), known today as the International Organization for Migration (IOM), which was led by the US, approached the Australian government about the possibility of resettling some of the refugees.[29] As far as Canberra understood it, efforts had been made "without any particular success at this stage to find alternative outlets for these Cuban refugees."[30] With a "bank up" of between 7,000 and 10,000 Cubans in Spain, Australia's departments of External Affairs and Immigration saw the possibility of selecting from their numbers "some good types of migrants"—blue-collar workers in particular—and excluding any "radical" anti-communist "elements" that would attract a negative public reaction in Australia.[31] The exercise was driven, therefore, by economic rather than humanitarian interests. An additional—and highly appealing—consideration was whether Australia could acquire "political credit" with Washington for making this resettlement

26. Letter from the Permanent Mission of Australia to the European Office of the United Nations, to the Secretary of the Department of External Affairs, Canberra, April 13, 1964, subject: "Cuban refugees in Spain," in A9737 1991/1765 Part 1, Cuba Refugees Australia Relations: Feb 7, 1964 to June 17, 1991, National Archives of Australia.

27. Department of State to United States Embassy The Hague, June 30, 1964, in "Cuba—Refugees, 10/63–7/65," Country Files, NSF, Box 30, LBJ Presidential Library.

28. United States Embassy Caracas to Department of State, October 30, 1964, in "Cuba—Refugees, 10/63–7/65," Country Files, NSF, Box 30, LBJ Presidential Library.

29. Secretary of the Department of Immigration to Secretary of the Department of External Affairs, February 18, 1964, in A9737 1991/1765 Part 1, Cuba Refugees Australia Relations: Feb 7, 1964 to June 17, 1991, National Archives of Australia.

30. Permanent Mission of Australia to the European Office of the United Nations, to the Secretary of the Department of External Affairs, Canberra, April 13, 1964.

31. Secretary of the Department of Immigration to Secretary of the Department of External Affairs, February 18, 1964.

contribution.³² After all, these Cubans were stuck in Spain because the United States had shut them out, and Washington was a driving force behind the ongoing calls by ICEM and the UN refugee agency for other countries to step in.

The preferences of the Cubans themselves were considered in Canberra's thinking as a measure of the likelihood of these potential newcomers settling successfully into Australian society. It is worth trying to explore these preferences further to illuminate individual decision-making amid, as Lester phrased it, "geopolitical interests and priorities." Among the thousands "banked up" in Madrid, ICEM claimed that up to eighty Cubans "had displayed interest in coming to Australia," but after Australian consulate staff in Madrid made their own inquiries, the number proved to be less than five.³³ For the majority of those waiting in Spain, a lack of knowledge about Australia, combined with its limited Cuban diaspora, were no doubt among the factors weighing on their minds (in the post-1945 era fewer than fifty Cubans obtained Australian citizenship).³⁴ In comparison, both Madrid and the hoped-for destination of Miami were linguistically and culturally familiar environments, where Cuban exiles could share their experiences and visions for the future. Perhaps also of significance was the vast distance from Australia to Cuba, a distance that was not quickly (or affordably) traversed. The Department of State advised the Australians that the refugees in Madrid viewed Florida as "the best jumping off point for a re-entry into Cuba" when (they believed) conditions in their country would soon improve, and thus "if Cubans seemed uninterested in Australia it would be for this reason."³⁵

Regardless of this lack of interest, the Australian government maintained the offer of resettlement places through the late 1960s and into the early 1970s.³⁶ The reason, it appears, was entirely political, an attempt to earn goodwill with other governments as both the ICEM and the UN refugee agency continued to call on member states to admit Cubans from Spain. Prominent US Senator Ted Kennedy helped to publicize this call.³⁷ A 1971 report in the *New York Times*, titled "Cuban Refugees in Spain Prefer the U.S.," noted that "just a handful" of the more than 14,000 Cubans waiting in Spain, around 131 people in the previous two years,

---

32. Permanent Mission of Australia to the European Office of the United Nations, to the Secretary of the Department of External Affairs, Canberra, April 13, 1964.

33. Secretary of the Department of Immigration to Secretary of the Department of External Affairs, February 18, 1964.

34. Australian Consulate General Geneva to Department of External Affairs, November 28, 1968, in A9737 1991/1765 Part 1, Cuba Refugees Australia Relations: Feb 7, 1964 to June 17, 1991, National Archives of Australia; Australia. *Official Yearbook of Australia: no. 61, 1975 and 1976* (Canberra, 1976), 167.

35. Australian Embassy Washington DC to Department of External Affairs, April 1, 1964, memorandum 413/64, in A9737 1991/1765 Part 1, Cuba Refugees Australia Relations: Feb 7, 1964 to June 17, 1991, National Archives of Australia.

36. Editorial, "Still More Refugees," *Canberra Times*, June 15, 1967, 2.

37. "Cuban Aid Plea," *Canberra Times*, May 12, 1966, 6.

could be "induced" to resettle elsewhere—a "meager result."[38] Australia was named alongside Latin American countries as one of the states that had offered resettlement places, indicating that a very small number of Cuban refugees decided to set aside their hopes of reaching the United States and begin life in Australia instead.[39] Ghassan Hage has argued that individuals "engage in the physical form of mobility that we call migration because they are after existential mobility ... where they feel they are going somewhere as opposed to nowhere."[40] With thousands more Cubans flying into Madrid each year only to be left in limbo, and no sign that conditions in Cuba would improve as hoped, it is possible that those who chose to come to Australia in the late 1960s and early 1970s felt that moving on was their best option.

Less than a decade later, Australia would again offer to resettle a small number of Cuban refugees. This time it was under very different circumstances. In the northern spring and summer of 1980, more than 125,000 Cubans made landfall in Florida. The "Mariel boatlift," as it became known, began when President Castro opened prisons and encouraged Cubans to depart for the United States, strategically causing trouble for the Carter administration through what political scientist Kelly Greenhill has called "coercive engineered migration."[41] President Carter was advised by a senior administration official that "other countries have left us isolated" and "we need an aggressive international campaign."[42] By early May 1980, Australia's then Fraser government had responded to "formal approaches" by the governments of the United States and of Peru (which was sheltering Cubans in its embassy in Havana) and offered to resettle up to 200 Cubans.[43] Evidence indicates that only around fifty refugees ultimately came to Australia.[44] Scholars of US

38. "Cuban Refugees in Spain Prefer the US," *New York Times*, February 7, 1971, 12.

39. Data from the Australian Bureau of Statistics shows that for the year to June 1975, some fourteen Cubans joined the small diaspora community in obtaining Australian citizenship, an act that required residence of at least three years. See Australia. *Official Yearbook of Australia: no. 61, 1975 and 1976* (Canberra, 1976), 167.

40. Ghassan Hage, "Waiting Out the Crisis: On Stuckedness and Governmentality," in Ghassan Hage (ed.), *Waiting* (Carlton: Melbourne University Press, 2009), 98.

41. Kelly M. Greenhill, *Weapons of Mass Migration: Forced Displacement, Coercion and Foreign Policy* (Ithaca, NY: Cornell University Press, 2010) 2.

42. James T Mcintyre to President Jimmy Carter, Memorandum, April 30, 1980, Stephen Page's subject files 1977–1981; Records of the Cabinet Secretary, Cuban, Haitian and Indochinese Refugees 5/1980, Box no. 126, 654742, in Jimmy Carter Presidential Library and Archives.

43. See Eugene Eidenberg to Charles Renfrew, Sept 5, 1980, folder "Cuban–Haitian Memos," Cabinet Secretary & Intergovernmental Affairs: Eidenberg, box 43, Jimmy Carter Presidential Library and Archives; Briefing paper titled "Cuban asylees," April 22, 1980, folder "Cuba: refugees, 4/13–25/80," NSA: Staff Material—North/South, Pastor—Country File, box 17, collection 24, JCL; "200 Cubans accepted," *Canberra Times*, May 8, 1980, 1.

44. Department of Foreign Affairs to Mexico City, "Deportation of Cuban Nationals," January 8, 1991, A9737 1991 / 1765 Part 1, Cuba—refugees—Australia relations, NAA.

immigration have pointed to the racialized contrast between the US government's relative welcome of Cuban refugees before Mariel, and the attempts to exclude, both legally and physically, the often "Afro-Cuban and working-class people" who arrived amid the "boatlift."[45] In 1980 those without family connections were "in limbo in tent cities in southern Florida" or detained on military bases around the country.[46] According to Klaus Neumann and Savitri Taylor, the small number of Cubans who were resettled in Australia that year were mostly young male "semi-skilled workers" interviewed at military bases in Pennsylvania and Florida, and for some their settlement in Sydney was fraught with difficulty.[47] One wonders what future these young people saw for themselves when they made a decision to give up on their plans for a life in America and instead depart for a migrant hostel in Cabramatta. According to Cuban-American academic Dr. Sonia Chao, among the new arrivals living in tents in Florida "the fear was palpable and the mental and physical exhaustion apparent," because "they weren't guaranteed they would actually get to stay" in the United States.[48] Given that the Carter administration was now labeling the Cubans "entrants" rather than refugees, which according to historian Jana Lipman "made it easier for the government to begin exclusion proceedings"—and, the archival record shows, administration officials even briefly canvassed the idea of dropping the arrivals back into Cuba by helicopter in the dead of night, fifty people at a time—perhaps the Cubans who chose to fly to Sydney were led to believe, by US or Australian officials, that a secure future in the United States was not possible.[49]

Vietnamese Refugees in the 1970s

Within historical scholarship on Australia's response to Vietnamese refugees, the role of Australia–United States diplomacy has attracted brief attention, and archives of the United States government have been largely overlooked until now.

---

45. Jenna M. Lloyd and Alison Mountz, *Boats, Borders and Bases: Race, the Cold War, and the Rise of Migration Detention in the United States* (Berkeley: University of California Press, 2018), 57.

46. Jana Lipman, "A Refugee Camp in America: Fort Chaffee and Vietnamese and Cuban refugees, 1975–1982," *Journal of American Ethnic History* 33, no. 2 (2014): 71.

47. Klaus Neumann and Savitri Taylor, "He has to take his chances: the resettlement of a refugee in Australia and his deportation to the country he had fled, 1980–1992," *History Australia* 16, no. 3 (2019): 462.

48. Amanda M. Perez, *40 Years Later: Cuban Americans Reflect on the Mariel Boatlift* (Miami: University of Miami, 2020), https://news.miami.edu/stories/2020/04/40-years-later-cuban-americans-reflect-on-the-mariel-boatlift.html.

49. Lipman, "A Refugee Camp in America," 60; Staff Material—Defense/Security Files NSA 31, Refugees (SCC Meeting), 8/1–27/80, Box no. 81, in Jimmy Carter Presidential Library and Archives.

Records of the Department of State reveal that a "close" liaison developed between the two governments from late 1977 onward, when the number of Vietnamese fleeing to Australian shores by boat began to increase and Canberra became a more active participant in international efforts to address the significant displacement of Vietnamese into the Southeast Asian region.[50] And based on this close liaison, in April 1978, a delegation from the Australian government met with their Department of State counterparts to seek Washington's support for its efforts to discourage Vietnamese from sailing south.[51] Relatively benign in comparison to contemporary deterrence measures, these efforts included the attempts of Australian immigration officials working in regional refugee camps to identify and select for resettlement those Vietnamese who were otherwise inclined to sail to Darwin.

At this meeting the United States also agreed that where a Vietnamese person in a refugee camp had been approved for resettlement in the United States by US Immigration officials (INS) but then—put off by a long wait—decided to sail to Australia instead, the individual would be transferred from Australia to the United States. In a cable to US missions across Southeast Asia and in Canberra, Secretary of State Cyrus Vance wrote that "in order to encourage [Australia] to continue its generous policy of admitting at least 4,000 Indochinese refugees in the first six months of this year, we will accept all boat refugees arriving on their own in Australia from countries of temporary asylum who had previously been approved by INS." The agreement went even further, as Vance wrote:

> If pressed by [Australia] ... [the US] would also be prepared to consider on case-by-case basis any post recommendations for parole for other boat refugees arriving in Australia who are closely associated with the US.[52]

This is an early and obscure example of refugee departures arranged through diplomacy between the two states. Archival evidence suggests that ultimately very few Vietnamese were transported from Australia to the United States under this agreement—a mere twenty-one people by April 19, 1979, after which it appears the US government wanted to cease the practice.[53] But records of the Department of

---

50. Department of State to all East Asian and Pacific Diplomatic Posts, Jan 28, 1978, folder "Australia 1978 #3," series "subject files," box 13, P 483, RG 59, National Archives and Records Administration, College Park, MD.

51. Claire Higgins, *Asylum by Boat: Origins of Australia's Refugee Policy* (Sydney: NewSouth, 2017), 97–8.

52. Secretary of State Washington DC to United States Embassy Canberra, April 10, 1978, in RG 59 P483, Box 13, File no. 3, National Archives and Records Administration, College Park, MD.

53. Office of Humanitarian Affairs, Department of State, to Immigration and Naturalization Service, April 19, 1979, in RG 0059 P483, Box 34, File: "Refugees in Australia," National Archives and Records Administration, College Park, MD.

State do point at the upheaval experienced by those who were subject to the agreement—and their lack of choice in their destination.

In the early months of 1978, Truong Van Dau and Nguyen Van Sau fled Vietnam and reached a crowded island refugee camp off the coast of Malaysia. In their very early twenties, the two men were fisherman by trade, with experience crewing small vessels. While they had no known relatives in the United States, both young men were interviewed by officials from the United States' Immigration and Naturalization Service (INS) and approved for admission. With poor English skills, each man was assigned a sponsor in the United States who would support their resettlement. But for reasons that are not explained in the archival file, both men then chose to instead depart Malaysia in a small vessel and, after sailing through the Indonesian archipelago and across the Timor Sea, they arrived on Australian shores on May 30.

While Australian authorities soon discovered that the two young men had previously been approved for resettlement by the INS, the United States consulate in Sydney did not begin processing their cases until February 1979, by which time both men were living in Adelaide.[54] They would have spent time in a migrant hostel, perhaps taken classes to improve their English skills, and gained employment. Even by April 1979 the consulate was still trying to assemble the relevant paperwork for the young men, and staff expressed hope that "some arrangements can be made to take them to the US in spite of the backlog" in processing resettlement cases.[55] It is unclear when the men ultimately departed for the United States.

Archival records indicate that Mr. Truong and Mr. Nguyen's decision to forgo resettlement in the United States and embark on a sea voyage to Australia was not uncommon among Vietnamese refugees in Southeast Asian camps during late 1977 to mid-1978. It is possible that the young men had been located at the refugee camp on Pulau Tengah, an island 16 km off the east coast of Malaysia, because this was reportedly a popular starting point for organized departures to Australia at that time.[56] Perhaps they chose to change course and jump on a departing boat because of the rudimentary living conditions in the growing camp, where several thousand refugees slept under wooden structures without walls and with roofs made of coconut leaves, facilities hastily constructed on the island by UNHCR and

---

54. United States Consul Sydney to Secretary of State Washington DC, March 7, 1979, in RG 0059 P483, Box 34, File: "Refugees in Australia," National Archives and Records Administration, College Park, MD.

55. United States Consul Sydney to Secretary of State Washington DC, April 12, 1979, in RG 0059 P483, Box 34, File: "Refugees in Australia," National Archives and Records Administration, College Park, MD.

56. United States Embassy Bangkok to United States Embassy Canberra, April 27, 1978, in RG 0059 P483, Box 13, File no. 3, National Archives and Records Administration, College Park, MD.

local authorities.⁵⁷ Perhaps they—and others like them—tired at the prospect of waiting several months for US authorities to transfer them to Kuala Lumpur and on to a flight to the United States.

Similarly, in around early 1978, six members of one family were interviewed by INS officials in a Malaysian refugee camp and, though approved for resettlement in the United States, chose to forgo the wait for departure and make their own way to Australia by boat. The family, consisting of Tran Met and Tran Thi Nuoi, along with four children between the ages of seven and eighteen, were settled in Perth. Sometime later, in June 1978, Australian authorities realized that Mr. and Mrs. Tran's three other children, a nephew, and several grandchildren were already in the country, having arrived by boat early that year. They too had received prior approval for resettlement in the United States during their temporary stay in a refugee camp.

Notably, the Australian government (referred to as "GOA" in the US cables) took its time deciding whether to "enforce their departure."⁵⁸ As the US embassy in Canberra explained in a cable back to Washington, "working levels" in the Australian government—meaning civil servants—"were reluctant to ship out a family which had decided it wanted to stay in Australia."⁵⁹ Those higher up, such as the Minister for Immigration and Ethnic Affairs, thought differently: "Political levels have overruled them, apparently electing to use this family as an example of the GOA's insistence that it alone shall set the criteria for immigration into Australia."⁶⁰

The deterrent value of this measure is questionable, particularly because evidence suggests that less than two dozen Vietnamese were ever transferred to the United States and the case does not seem to have attracted media attention. Decision-makers in the Australian government, however, were keenly aware that the exodus from Vietnam was reaching record highs in mid-1979, and feared that many thousands of Vietnamese could still sail south to Darwin. Thus, the value in the Tran family's transfer was politically symbolic, for even this small number of refugees constituted proof that the United States would continue to support Australia's efforts to prevent boat arrivals: "No less than Immigration Minister MacKellar himself has told us that the GOA regards this as a test case of US willingness to honor its commitment to accept (this handful of) refugees it had previously agreed to take in Malaysia."⁶¹

---

57. Danny Dang, as told to Linda Ching, *Running on the Edge of the Knife: A True Story*, ed. Pamela Hitchcock (n.p.p.: Lulu.com, 2012), 139–42.

58. United States Embassy Canberra to Secretary of State Washington DC, February 26, 1979, in RG 0059 P483, Box 13, File no. 3, National Archives and Records Administration, College Park, MD.

59. United States Embassy Canberra to Secretary of State Washington DC, February 26, 1979.

60. United States Embassy Canberra to Secretary of State Washington DC, February 26, 1979.

61. United States Embassy Canberra to Secretary of State Washington DC, February 26, 1979.

Staff at the US embassy in Canberra had delayed processing the paperwork required for the family's transfer to the United States until a firm decision was made in Canberra, and it appears that the authorities organized for the fifteen family members to travel to the United States together in late 1979.[62] This was well over a year after these refugees had landed on Australian shores aboard various boats and begun the task of rebuilding their lives in cities across the country. The children would have enrolled in primary and high school, tried to make friends, and learn English. The adults—ranging in age from their twenties to their early sixties—would have navigated the job market and secured rental accommodation. As the US embassy reported, the family "had decided [they] wanted to stay in Australia." But the decision was not theirs. Instead, they—like Mr. Truong and Mr. Nguyen—were left in limbo for months, waiting with an administrative cloud hanging over their fate. To borrow from anthropologist Maree Pardy's 2009 essay on waiting, once they reached Darwin the Tran family "had already waited, sometimes patiently sometimes not, to learn English and to engage with the world and the local spaces they moved through. They had waited to blend in, so to speak; to become part of the landscape of multicultural Australia."[63] On Minister MacKellar's insistence—for purely political reasons—these refugees now had to *re*settle in a foreign country and begin that same process all over again.

Refugees Held Offshore

On several occasions since the admission of fifty Cubans in 1980, the Australian government and the United States have offered to resettle refugees who had been refused entry to one or the other country and detained in third countries. A little-known example occurred after Castro's government encouraged a renewed exodus to Florida in 1994, when thousands of Cubans were intercepted at sea by US authorities and detained at the US naval base in Guantanamo Bay, Cuba. The following year the US government put out a call through its overseas missions for offers of resettlement for Cubans held at Guantanamo Bay. Out of the few states that replied to the United States' request, the Australian government was noted as expressing "considerable interest" in the prospect of resettling Cubans from Guantanamo.[64] Similarly, according

---

62. United States Consulate Perth to Secretary of State Washington DC, July 17, 1979, in RG 0059 P483, Box 13, File no. 3, National Archives and Records Administration, College Park, MD.

63. Maree Pardy, "The Shame of Waiting," in *Waiting*, 202.

64. Memorandum, from Rick Sherman to Brunson McKinley, Terry Rusch [...], March 28, 1995, National Security Council, Democracy, Human Rights and Humanitarian Affairs Office, and Jonathan Noetzel, "Guantanamo (GTMO) Updates [4]," Clinton Digital Library, https://clinton.presidentiallibraries.us/items/show/53991. The nature of Australia's offer is a subject of my ongoing archival research.

to Dastyari, the Australian government agreed to resettle a Haitian couple from Guantanamo Bay in mid-2002.[65]

Later resettlement offers have attracted media attention. In 2007 the United States and Australia signed a Memorandum of Understanding (MoU) under which the US committed to resettling 200 refugees held by Australia in remote offshore detention on Nauru and Manus Island, Papua New Guinea.[66] In exchange, Australia agreed to consider admitting refugees held at Guantanamo Bay, which initially involved the resettlement of 150 Cuban refugees.[67] Dastyari writes that at the time, the United States had also been approaching other countries to resettle refugees from the naval base, such as Canada and the Czech Republic.[68]

The 2007 MoU with Australia prompted a warning in the *Sydney Morning Herald* in May 2007 that Haitians may risk their lives attempting to reach the United States as a way of settling in Australia. The headline read: "US–Australia refugee swap deal tempts Haitians." As the newspaper reported, in that country few ordinary Haitians "even know where Australia is," but one local woman said she had heard "Australia is a rich country" where "life will be better."[69] In this telling, prospective departees desired economic security, in a simplified image that overlooked the myriad reasons why people may choose to leave their life behind, board a small vessel, and risk their lives on a dangerous clandestine sea journey. As eminent legal scholar Harold Koh remarked when representing asylum seekers in the 1990s, the so-called "magnet effect" did not take account of the civil disorder, collapse of democratic institutions, and resulting lack of hope that prompted Haitians to flee their country.[70]

More recently, in 2017, Australian newspapers reported Canberra's decision to resettle seventeen Cubans who had attempted to sail to Florida (and were reportedly found clinging to a lighthouse) before being denied entry to the United States and detained for a year at Guantanamo Bay.[71] One member of the group, Vergara Lopez, told media on arrival in Brisbane that "it's a dream—we are very happy." Yet Vergara and the others were pinning their hopes on an appeal currently before the US courts. "Maybe if we win the case we can leave Australia and go to the States," he said. The appeal of accepting resettlement in Australia, it seems, was

65. Dastyari, "Swapping Refugees," 97.
66. Dastyari, "Swapping Refugees," 94.
67. Dastyari, "Swapping Refugees," 97.
68. Dastyari, "Swapping Refugees," 97.
69. "US–Australia refugee swap deal tempts Haitians," *Sydney Morning Herald*, May 7, 2007.
70. Brandt Goldstein, *Storming the Court: How a Band of Law Students Fought the President and Won* (New York: Scribner Publishing, 2005), 114, 194.
71. See Helen Davidson, "Australia resettles Cuban refugees found clinging to a lighthouse off Florida Keys," *Guardian*, August 22, 2017, https://www.theguardian.com/australia-news/2017/aug/22/australia-resettles-cuban-refugees-found-clinging-to-lighthouse-off-florida-keys.

to leave the harsh and liminal space of Guantanamo Bay—to go *somewhere*, as Hage phrased it, rather than nowhere. As the Cubans' lawyer in Florida put it, the group were "happy to finally attain full freedom."[72] Thus, the point of this diplomatically-organized departure was about one state—Australia—supporting another in blocking unwanted asylum seekers from its shores.

The 2016 agreement signed between Australia and the United States, involving refugees held on Nauru and Manus Island, is based on the same imperative. The agreement has brought great relief to those who have finally departed the tarmac of Port Moresby or Nauru International Airport and landed in America. Rohingya man Faisal Parvez, who was detained on Nauru for years, was "crying with happiness" when he reached Chicago.[73] Young Rohingya writer Imran Mohammad has said the day he landed in Chicago was "the day I consider myself reborn."[74] But with long delays in processing (some claims are still in train years later), there are some refugees who are still waiting, fearing being coerced to return to their countries of origin or the insecurity of life on Nauru or in Papua New Guinea, and in distress at not knowing whether they can ever leave the legal limbo in which Australia has put them.[75]

For those senior members of the US Department of State who were first approached by Australian officials about the idea of negotiating this resettlement deal, the awfulness of long-term detention on Nauru and Manus Island was forefront in their minds. By then, the UN refugee agency, UNHCR, as well as UN and national human rights observers had issued well-publicized reports of the hot, humid, and rudimentary living conditions—and the attendant impact on detainees' mental health—and the unsuitability of Nauru and Papua New Guinea for permanent settlement.[76] "When the Australians first came to us," former US Assistant Secretary of State Anne Richard has said, "my motivation was let's do

---

72. Davidson, "Australia resettles Cuban refugees found clinging to a lighthouse off Florida Keys."

73. Tasha Wibawa, "Australia's unwanted refugees are living with 'nightmares' while building new lives in the US," *ABC News*, December 30, 2018, https://www.abc.net.au/news/2018-12-30/meet-the-people-who-australia-did-not-want/10666244.

74. Imran Mohammad, "Pain, Refuge and Freedom: Imran's story," Amnesty International, March 22, 2019, https://www.amnesty.org.au/pain-refuge-and-freedom-imrans-story/.

75. Ben Doherty, "Three countries, eight years: one refugee's nightmare odyssey through Australia's detention system," *Guardian*, July 17, 2021, https://www.theguardian.com/australia-news/2021/jul/17/three-countries-eight-years-one-refugees-nightmare-odyssey-through-australias-detention-system.

76. UNHCR, *UNHCR Mission to the Republic of Nauru, 14 December 2012* (2012), 7–9, https://www.refworld.org/docid/50cb24912.html; UNHCR, *UNHCR Mission to the Manus Island, Papua New Guinea, 15–17 January 2013* (2013), 63, https://www.refworld.org/pdfid/5139ab872.pdf; UNHCR, *UNHCR monitoring visit to the Republic of Nauru, 7 to 9 October 2013* (2013), 2, https://www.unhcr.org/en-au/58117b931.pdf; UNHCR, *UNHCR*

this, let's make this happen, we have got to get these individuals to a better place."⁷⁷ In an opinion piece for Australian media in 2019, Richard wrote that the US signed on to the deal because it wanted to get the refugees out of "hellacious" conditions and "off those islands" as quickly as possible.⁷⁸ Former Deputy Secretary of State Heather Higginbottom backed up this account, writing in an opinion piece for US media that the administration signed the deal because it sought to "immediately relieve the suffering of these refugees."⁷⁹ At this point in time, the Obama administration was planning a substantial increase to the USRAP for financial year 2017–18, perhaps making it easier for policymakers to incorporate some 1,250 places for refugees detained by Australia. The Trump administration, however, slashed the USRAP to record lows, and while it grudgingly maintained the agreement with Australia for diplomatic reasons, long delays in processing meant that refugees subject to this arrangement were left waiting an unnecessarily long time, compounding the harm already inflicted by Australia's system of offshore detention.⁸⁰

Conclusion

The nature of individual choice in the international protection regime is gaining greater attention in forced migration scholarship, as part of a greater emphasis on

---

monitoring visit to Manus Island, Papua New Guinea, 23 to 25 October 2013 (2013), 1, https://www.refworld.org/docid/5294aa8b0.html; United Nations Committee against Torture and Other Cruel, Inhuman or Degrading Treatment or Punishment, "Concluding Observations on the Combined Fourth and Fifth Periodic Reports of Australia" (CAT/C/AUS/CO/4-5, 2014), 17; Australian Human Rights Commission, *The Forgotten Children: National Inquiry into Children in Immigration Detention*, (Sydney: Australian Human Rights Commission, 2014), 58–9.

77. Zoe Daniel and Stephanie March,"US refugee deal: architect of deal says arrangement loosely based on Australia 'doing more'," *ABC News*, March 22, 2017, https://www.abc.net.au/news/2017-03-22/us-refugee-deal-architect-says-based-on-australia-doing-more/8375250.

78. Helen Davidson, "US believed Australia would take more refugees in exchange for Nauru and Manus deal," *Guardian*, November 18, 2018, https://www.theguardian.com/australia-news/2018/nov/18/us-believed-australia-would-take-more-refugees-in-exchange-for-nauru-and-manus-deal; Anne Richard, "Australia's loss is America's gain': the Nauru and Manus refugees starting anew in the US," *Guardian*, January 29, 2019, https://www.theguardian.com/commentisfree/2019/jan/29/what-happened-to-the-deal-and-the-refugees-surviving-australian-and-us-politics.

79. Heather Higginbottom, "You probably missed the big story buried in the latest Trump leaks," *Time*, August 9, 2017, https://time.com/4894058/donald-trump-malcolm-turnbull-refugees-famine/.

80. See Higgins, "The US–Australia resettlement deal."

the participation of refugees in decision-making.[81] As legal scholar Tristan Harley and others have noted, in the ordinary resettlement process administered by the UN refugee agency (UNHCR), refugees have little ability to choose where to be resettled.[82] Instead, UNHCR identifies those refugees who are most in need of resettlement in a third country, and the states then choosing to accept them.[83] Harley and co-author Harry Hobbs have argued, however, that even if refugees had a choice in the durable solutions process, "it will mean little if there are no solutions on the table" or if only one solution is available.[84] While the departures by diplomacy discussed in this chapter sit outside the UNHCR resettlement process, Harley and Hobbs' argument here is highly relevant, because many of the individuals whose fates are discussed in the second and third sections of this chapter were ostensibly given a choice to apply for resettlement in Australia or the United States, but—as Arash Shirmohamadi's story so clearly demonstrates—that choice was presented within a context in which, as Grewcock has put it, these refugees had few meaningful rights and were instead reduced to being simply a tool through which the Australian or United States governments could publicly demonstrate a tough approach to "border control."[85]

Far from a linear narrative of mobility involving movement from one state to another, Critical Refugee Studies scholar Yen Le Espiritu has noted that for refugees themselves, a journey may be filled with "confusion, ambivalence, and even misgivings," "full of detours and snags."[86] Attempting to think through these perspectives, in and around the available historical sources, is an important step in understanding the impact of bilateral resettlement offers beyond the goodwill generated between two countries. The departures by diplomacy explored in this chapter indicate that for refugees subject to these kind of resettlement offers, an ability to meaningfully exercise a choice in their destination may be limited;

---

81. Resettlement "involves the selection and transfer of refugees from a State in which they have sought protection to a third State which has agreed to admit them—as refugees—with permanent residence status"—see UNHCR, *Resettlement Handbook*, revised edition (Geneva: Division of International Protection, 2011), 3.

82. Tristan Harley, "Refugee Participation Revisited: the Contributions of Refugees to Early International Refugee Law and Policy," *Refugee Survey Quarterly* 40, no. 1 (2021): n. 89.

83. Annelisa Lindsay, "Surge and selection: power in the refugee resettlement regime," *Forced Migration Review* 54 (February 2017): 11.

84. Tristan Harley and Harry Hobbs, "The Meaningful Participation of Refugees in Decision-Making Processes," *International Journal of Refugee Law* 32, no. 2 (2020): 222.

85. Grewcock, "Our Lives is in Danger," 84–5.

86. Yen Le Espiritu, *Body Counts: The Vietnam War and Militarised Refuge(es)* (Berkeley: University of California Press, 2014), 2.

instead, the challenge of their displacement is exacerbated by the exclusionary policies of their preferred destination state.

Acknowledgments: I would like to thank Dr. Tristan Harley, Dr. Jordana Silverstein, and the authors represented in this collection for scholarly conversations that expanded my thinking on departures, mobility, and individual choice in refugee resettlement.

Chapter 12

MOVING ON: WHEN MIGRANTS DEPART, AND WHY IT MATTERS

Tara Zahra

The migration histories that we are most familiar with are success stories: individuals or families leave one home, fleeing persecution or seeking a better life, and settle permanently in another. They may struggle along the way, but their children and grandchildren prosper—and pass their stories on as part of family and national history. Yet, as this volume has shown, this is hardly the universal experience of migration in the past or the present.

A recent *New York Times* article tracked the phenomenon of so-called "failed" migration. Up to 25 percent of today's immigrants around the world, the article reported, return to the place they came from. In some cases, the returnees never make it to their destination, their journeys cut short by border guards, corrupt smugglers, scorching deserts, turbulent waters, or a lack of cash to continue onward. Other migrants return home in defeat. Yaya Guindo left his home in a fishing village in Senegal at the age of nineteen. Eight years later, which he spent living and working itinerantly in construction and restaurants, he returned broke and demoralized from a Libyan detention center. He had wanted to come home sooner but was ashamed to do so. "I didn't have anything. I was embarrassed."[1]

These experiences of return or "failure" are not new, but they have rarely been explored in depth by historians of migration. This book has focused on the invisible flip-side of global migration: migrants who move on, who "depart" from the places to which they had migrated. In the essays assembled here, the original destination was Australia in the second half of the twentieth century. Some departed to return home (to Greece, Germany, the USSR, Great Britain, and elsewhere), while others engaged in what Susan Ossman calls "serial migration," moving from one place to another.[2]

---

1. Anemona Hartecolis, "A Hard Lesson for Migrants who Give up: There May be No Welcome Mat Back Home," *New York Times*, September 15, 2019, https://www.nytimes.com/2019/09/15/world/africa/africa-migrants-return-home.html.

2. Susan Ossman, *Moving Matters: Paths of Serial Migration* (Stanford, CA: Stanford University Press, 2007).

Sometimes these departures were voluntary, sometimes they were forced, and sometimes they took place in the large gray zone between forced and voluntary migration.

Not every departure was a failure, however. In some cases, returning home or moving on was always the plan. Ruth Balint highlights the extent to which Australia was a second or even third choice for many postwar displaced persons who were settled there by international organizations. They went to Australia in the first place because they had no other options.[3] For these migrants, moving on to another destination was a "success," seen from their own perspective, even if it was considered a "failure" by international organizations or the Australian government. For others, such as members of the Dellios family in this volume, Australia was always intended to be a temporary home.[4]

In this chapter, intended as a final reflection, I focus on why departures matter, and what they can tell us about the history of migration more broadly. I've chosen to use examples from my own research, many of which come from Europe and the United States in the first half of the twentieth century.[5] Although the focus of this book is on Australia after World War II, I hope this only reinforces a central point of the volume: departures are an important facet of migration history regardless of the time or place. Of course, departing from the United States in 1890 had a different political significance from departing from Palestine in 1930 or from Australia in 1950. As the chapter in this volume by Justine Greenwood suggests, departures from Australia were considered particularly alarming to state authorities, given the state's desire to recruit rather than deter (white) immigrant labor. Australia is therefore an especially fruitful starting point for an in-depth exploration of departure. Hopefully, however, this book will inspire historians of migration to explore the experiences and significance of departure in other contexts.

The essays gathered here demonstrate that departures matter, first of all because they challenge national myths founded on the narrative of migration as a one-way journey. In Australia, Ruth Balint argues, the history of departures tests a narrative about the triumph of a "multicultural" Australia after World War II. In the United States as well, the successful integration of immigrants has been central to a progressive vision of American identity and history for over a century. This mythology was not only a product of politics—it has also been sustained by biases in sources and in individual and collective memory. The history of migration to the United States is often written based on oral histories and testimonies from immigrants who *stayed* rather than those who left. For example, the Ellis Island Oral History Project is a treasure trove of oral histories taken from people who arrived in the United States from Europe, mostly during the late nineteenth and early twentieth century. These were all migrants who came and stayed in the USA.

3. Balint, in this volume.
4. Dellios, in this volume.
5. Tara Zahra, *The Great Departure: Mass Migration from Eastern Europe and the Making of the Free World* (New York: W.W. Norton, 2016).

Reflecting on their experiences many decades later, there is an overwhelming tendency to see whatever hardships they experienced as worthwhile because they have made their lives in the USA, and their children and grandchildren see themselves as Americans.

But in focusing on arrivals, and not on departures or returns, we miss out on the stories of the 30–40% of migrants who arrived in the United States during the period of the Great Migration from Europe who either returned home or moved on. In any context, the fate of departees is harder to track down. When Karen Agutter attempted to trace a cohort of young displaced persons who arrived in Australia after World War II, for example, it required sleuthing in archives in several countries and languages.[6] Some migrants changed their names or simply disappeared from official records entirely. The history of those who stay is simply easier to write than the history of those who leave.

In the United States in the early twentieth century, many migrants only wanted to stay long enough to achieve their goals: work hard and earn enough money to buy some more land or build a house back home. But others returned to Europe bitter and disappointed with America, and warned friends and family members not to make the same mistake they had. For example, the writer Louis Adamic, who emigrated to the United States from the Austrian Empire, was enticed to emigrate by dazzling stories of America as a "Golden country." But as he planned his own journey overseas, he heard other stories about the fate of emigrants, whispered among neighbors:

> Mother knew of . . . men in villages not remote from our own who had returned from the United States without an arm or minus a leg, or in bad health. There was an *Amerikanec* in Gatina, the village near Blato, who had come home with a strange, sinful, and unmentionable disease, which he later communicated to his wife, who, in turn, gave birth to a blind child.[7]

In Australia, essays in this volume show, some displaced persons who arrived after World War II were also disillusioned by the reality of the working and living conditions. As Karen Agutter shows, young displaced persons who had been promised education and opportunity in Australia found themselves indentured in low-wage jobs in poor conditions. Some migrants, lacking the documents or resources necessary to leave Australia, even resorted to committing a crime in order to try to get themselves deported. Former Soviet citizens complained of intolerable poverty and miserable work conditions in their appeals to return to the USSR, in Sheila Fitzpatrick's account. And young British emigrants to Australia may have been disappointed or frustrated by the lack of leisure opportunities, the harsh climate, and other aspects of social life in Australia, as Rachel Stevens'

---

6. Agutter, in this volume.
7. Louis Adamic, *Laughing in the Jungle: The Autobiography of an Immigrant in America* (New York: Harpers & Brothers, 1932), 3–4, 8.

chapter suggests. In each case, the experience of migrants challenged the ways in which Australian authorities wanted their country to be seen by the outside world—as a land of opportunity, modernity, and the good life.[8]

Departures were deeply disruptive to national narratives and mythologies in many contexts beyond Australia and the United States. As Ori Yehudai's work demonstrates, many Jews who moved to Palestine or to Israel did not see the state as their permanent homeland, but rather as a waystation to more desirable destinations. After World War II, some displaced persons made their way to Palestine and then immediately returned to displaced persons camps in Germany, having found that they couldn't adapt to the climate or conditions of life in Palestine. These departures were deeply disturbing to the Israeli state, as they disrupted the claim that Jews could only be at home in Israel.[9]

In Eastern Europe in the aftermath of World War II, meanwhile, many newly Socialist states were desperate to recruit labor in order to rebuild their countries. The return of citizens from abroad came to be seen as a referendum on entire societies and political systems, and a serious state security concern. The chapters by Sheila Fitzpatrick and Ebony Nilsson in this book illustrate the political importance placed on the return of Soviet citizens from Australia to the Soviet Union during the Cold War, in both Australia and the USSR. Even if the numbers were few, the stakes were very high.

Throughout Eastern Europe, Socialist states attempted to entice emigrants in the West to come home—sometimes with offers of big apartments, choice jobs, and other benefits. They encouraged such departures in part because they needed labor, but also because returns could be celebrated as a great ideological victory. Returnees were heralded as symbols of national and social liberation. "For more than 100 years, our compatriots have departed for every corner of the earth, in search of a living to support themselves and their families, because they could not subsist at home," explained Bedřich Steiner of the Czechoslovak Foreign Institute. "After the liberation in 1945, the first priority of the government was to enable this diaspora to return home."[10] In later decades, so called "repatriation" or "amnesty" campaigns, which encouraged citizens to "depart" from the West, were rarely very successful in numerical terms, but return stories provided valuable material for state propaganda efforts.[11]

It would be a mistake, however, to reduce the meaning of departures to the political significance that they acquired for states. Indeed, one advantage of studying departure through individual or family biographies is that these personal stories offer a more nuanced perspective on movements that are often explained

---

8. Agutter, Fitzpatrick, Stevens, in this volume.

9. Ori Yehudai, *Leaving Zion: Jewish Emigration from Palestine and Israel after World War II* (New York: Cambridge University Press, 2020).

10. Poslanec Dr. Bedřich Steiner, Carton 85, Československý ústav zahraniční–II (ČÚZ-II), Národní archiv, Prague (NA).

11. See Zahra, *The Great Departure*, chapter 6, for more on these campaigns.

mechanically. The chapters by Alexandra Dellios and Kay Dreyfus in this volume offer rich portraits of individual round-trip journeys. They highlight the emotional factors that played a role in individual decisions to move on or return home, alongside the political forces and economic opportunities. In spite of the tendency of states to think about departure as a referendum on a society, a way of voting with one's feet, departures were frequently motivated by highly personal or emotional factors—homesickness, the desire to grow old and die in one's land of origin, to join family members or get away from one's family, to connect with one's past or ancestors, or to have an adventure and see the world.[12]

Departures also matter because they profoundly shaped both individuals' life trajectories and the societies to which the departees returned. What do migrants bring back with them, if they return home or move on? Money if they are lucky, illness and disillusionment if not. In Eastern Europe, many officials worried that returnees also brought home new ideas about things like democracy, gender, and the family. American officials certainly believed that time in the USA would serve to "civilize" and "democratize" Europe. The report of the 1911 Dillingham Commission asserted the allegedly transformative effects of emigration on European peasants:

> He leaves his village, a simple peasant in his peasant dress, usually not only unable to read and write, but not even desiring to. Ingrained in him are the traditions of his obligations to the church and to his superiors ... When he goes back to his old home he is a different man. He is more aggressive and self-assertive. His unaccustomed money gives him confidence and he is no longer willing to pay deference to his former superiors. Frequently too, the church has lost the influence it had had with him. Moreover, if he has not learned to read and write himself, he has at least seen the value of that ability and is more anxious than before to send his children to school.[13]

While this is clearly a self-congratulatory narrative, it was sometimes shared by migrants. John Szabó of Chicago, writing in 1909, reflected, "Although in the beginning I had to do without, and even now I am not bathing in milk and honey, I feel that now I am that man who at home I only had a presentiment that I had a right to be, that is: an independent, free man."[14]

At a more material level, return migrants brought new forms of technological and managerial expertise. Thomas Bat'a, the founder of the Bat'a shoe company, visited the United States for six months in 1905; when he returned he built a new three-floor factory modeled on the one he had seen there. He came to be known as the Henry Ford of Europe, as well as the "King of Shoes."

---

12. See Dellios and Dreyfus in this volume.

13. William Paul Dillingham, *Reports of the Immigration Commission: Emigration Conditions in Europe* (n.p.p.: Franklin Classics 2018), 388.

14. Cited in Julianna Puskás, *Ties that Bind, Ties that Divide: 100 Years of Hungarian Experience in the United States* (Boulder, CO: Lynne Rienner, 2000), 56-7.

It wasn't only factories that were transformed—it was also the material culture and landscape of the Old World, as return migrants built what were often called "American" homes with the money they had saved. The fact that these migrants were often called "the Americans" suggests that they adopted distinctive ways of living that made them identifiable. This trend continues to this day among migrants from Mexico and Central America.[15]

Of course, these transformations were not always seen positively. After World War I, while Polish nationalist associations and societies in the United States encouraged migrants in the USA to return home as a patriotic duty, many Polish officials in Warsaw worried about the ability of remigrants to adapt to life in war-devastated Poland. As an official from the Ministry of Labor explained, "Polish-Americans are accustomed to better conditions. They are going to demand goods, machines, livestock and equipment, means of communication. We don't have any of that here."[16]

Some Poles, such as Polish economist Sigismund Garga, believed that remigrants from America would be

> a welcome gift to the newly established fatherland. They are bringing great experience of the most modern state system, they will doubtlessly be equipped with a great deal of technical knowledge ... they should generally possess substantial capital ... They will also bring home a true understanding of the meaning of national sovereignty.[17]

In reality, many of the returnees did have a hard time adjusting. Some observers blamed returnees themselves for their problems adapting. They had allegedly become too "Americanized." A guide for returning Poles denounced remigrants who "returned home with dollars and all started to act like lords, and to waste money on servants and luxuries." But Polish nationalist propaganda continued to insist that Poland had much to offer returning migrants, even if it was not in the form of modern conveniences. Returnees "admittedly recalled American amenities and big city life" with nostalgia, the guide continued. "But all of them decidedly agreed about one thing, namely, that America had sucked away their health, nerves,

---

15. Sarah Lopez, *The Remittance Landscape: Spaces of Migration in Rural Mexico and Urban USA* (Chicago: University of Chicago Press, 2015).

16. Protokol z dnia 3 marca 1920 z posiedzenia w sprawie reemigracji Polaków z Ameryki, Sig. 9943, B26353, Ministerstwo Spraw Zagranicznych, Archiwum Akt Nowych (AAN), Warsaw; Mieczysław Szawleski, *Kwestja emigracji w Polsce* (Warsaw, 1927), 81; Adam Walaszek, *Reemigracja ze Stanów Zjednoczonych do Polski po I wojnie światowej (1919–1924)* (Krakow, 1983), 58–64.

17. Sigismund Gargas, Das polnische Auswanderungsproblem, Berlin 1919, sig. 3, Panstowy Urząd Emigracyny, AAN.

and strength for work." Only upon return to Poland could an individual "enjoy a truly humane life."[18]

Departures matter, in addition, because they were not always voluntary. Particularly in the twentieth century, they became a tool of state policy, a lever pulled to manipulate labor markets or demographics. Adam Goodman's work on the history of deportation from the United States reveals that at least 57 million immigrants have been expelled from the US in the last 140 years, but that 75 percent of them have been what are euphemistically called "voluntary departures," the result of what Goodman calls "self deportation." Especially in the second half of the twentieth century, unwanted migrants in the United States have been systematically coerced, encouraged, or tricked into signing waivers promising that they will not contest deportation proceedings and will voluntarily leave the country (90 percent of these have been Mexicans).[19]

While the numbers may not have been as high, it is clear that a similar process was at work during the Great Depression in the US and other countries of mass immigration like France. Writing in 1937, the International Labor Organization observed that the Great Depression had produced "a virtual reversal of migratory currents. Countries that have traditionally been lands of immigration have been transformed into lands of emigration, and the typical countries of emigration have taken on the form of countries of immigration."[20] In 1931 the US Immigration Commission even offered to pay for the repatriation of migrants who had arrived within the last three years and were receiving public assistance.[21] These "journeys of despair" alarmed social workers on both sides of Europe and the Atlantic. Suzanne Ferrière of the International Migration Service in France lamented:

> The process followed in the U.S. is being copied all over Europe and it becomes worse every month. Be it expulsion, or repatriation, every country in Europe now tries to get rid of its unemployed foreigners. The situation is appalling.[22]

George Warren, director of the American Branch of the International Migration Service, observed in 1931:

---

18. No author, Informator dla Reemigrantów, Poradnik dla tych, którzy myśla o powrocie do Polski (Warsaw, 1933), 18, 49–50.

19. Adam Goodman, *The Deportation Machine: America's Long History of Expelling Immigrants* (Princeton, NJ: Princeton University Press, 2020).

20. Societé des Nations, Le problème des migrations, Report of the ILO to the Assembly of the SDN, September 9, 1937, 4, Carton 517, V. Sekce-6. bežná spisovna, Ministerstvo zahraničních věcí (MZV), NA.

21. Raport emigracyny Konsulatu Generalnego R.P. w Nowym Yorku za lata 1930 i 1931, sig. 128, Konsulat Generalny RP w Nowym Yorku, Archiwum Akt Nowych, Warsaw.

22. To U.S. from H.Q. (Suzanne Ferrière), April 19, 1932, Folder 28, SW109, Social Welfare Archive, University of Minnesota.

This flow of individuals and families back to Europe ... is perhaps satisfying to the economist, to the politician, and to the man in the street who visualizes more elbow room here, more jobs for citizens, lighter relief burdens for our communities and a reduction in those elements of our population supposedly contributing to our more recent forms of criminal activity. But to the social worker sensitive to the social considerations surrounding this migration, to the shattered hopes and the atmosphere of defeat and despair in which these returns are made, questions immediately arise as to the intangible and immeasurable losses created by this disruption in family life.[23]

East European authorities deplored the moral, political, and social impact of destitute returnees: Czech officials lamented that "People who emigrated full of hope that they would improve their social situation are returning as beggars loaded with debts ... Men who were once independent will now be dependent [on charity] until they die."[24] French officials estimated that between 1932 and 1934, 20 percent of Polish workers left France, close to 64,000 people.[25] Officials in the French Labor Ministry denied rumors of systematic deportations, insisting that the government was merely trying to "facilitate" the return of migrants to Poland.[26] To workers themselves, however, the distinction between "facilitating repatriation" and "deportation" was less obvious.[27]

Departure didn't even have to happen to have real consequences. The threat of departure was and continues to be a way of regulating and disciplining migrant labor. Chapters by Jayne Persian and Ruth Balint in this volume highlight the ways in which the threat of deportation was used as a disciplinary tool in postwar Australia.[28] This was not a new phenomenon, nor was it limited to Australia and the United States. For example, a large number of the East European agricultural workers employed in interwar France were single women, and their sexual and "moral" comportment was closely monitored. Julie Šalmiková, aged eighteen, arrived in France in January 1938. That summer, she received a letter of reprimand:

> The consulate of the Czechoslovak Republic in Strasbourg has been informed that you go out every evening and return late in the night. On July 14, 1938, you

---

23. George Warren, "The Widening Horizon in our Service to Foreign-Born Families," National Conference of Social Work, June 15, 1931, Folder 28, SW109, Social Welfare Archive, University of Minnesota.

24. Navrh na úpravu evidence vystěhovalecké, June 20, 1924, Carton 4048, MSP, NA.

25. Émigration polonaise en France, August 24, 1934, sig. 433, Pologne, Z-Europe, Archives Diplomatiques, Paris (ADP).

26. Le Ministre du Travail à Monsieur le Ministre des Affaires Étrangers, April 28, 1934, sig. 433, Pologne, Z-Europe, ADP.

27. Sdružení čsl. krajanských spolků v severní Francii, October 6, 1935, Carton 456, Sekce–6. běžná spisovna, MZV, NA.

28. See Persian and Balint in this volume.

were out until 5 AM. You are consorting with three young men in Jussey, and your behavior is inciting scandal in the community. If you are deported from France for your bad behavior, you should not expect this office to provide you with any assistance.[29]

The presumption of eventual departure has also been used as a pretext to limit the rights and opportunities of migrants in the postwar era. Guest worker programs—such as the Bracero program in the United States, which employed Mexicans on a temporary or seasonal basis, and the Guest Worker program in postwar Germany—relied on the presumption of departure to deny migrants citizenship rights as well as social and labor rights. In reality, many so-called "guest workers" stayed in Germany, as did their children, who could not become citizens until the age of fifteen. Germany even tried paying these so-called "guest" workers to return home. But interestingly, the myth of eventual departure was also upheld by Turkish authorities, because mass emigration was considered an embarrassment, and the Turkish state wanted to retain financial and cultural ties to its emigrants.[30]

An important insight that comes from studying the history of departures is that departures increase when borders are more open than closed. Before 1914, 30–40% of migrants to the United States returned home. But after the Johnson-Reed Act of 1924 shut down mass migration from Southern and Eastern Europe, that number decreased dramatically. That was because migrants knew that if they left the US they might not ever be able to return again. They focused on bringing their family members over to join them, a process that often took years. A similar dynamic emerged in Europe after major restrictions on migration were passed in the wake of the oil crisis in the early 1970s. Migrants stopped going home and focused on getting their families to join them permanently in Europe.[31]

Opening borders, by contrast, increases return and circular migration. This was one result of the expansion of the European Union. Young East European migrants to the UK became highly sensitive to changing economic conditions at home and abroad, and they came and went based on where the best opportunities could be found. Thanks to relatively few barriers to mobility, return migration is more common among East Europeans who migrate within the EU than those who come

---

29. Julie Šalmiková, 1938, Carton 4054, MSP, NA.

30. See, for example, Michelle Kahn, "The Long Road Home: Vacations and the Making of the 'Germanized Turk' Across Cold War Europe," *Journal of Modern History* 93, no. 1 (March 2021): 109–49.

31. See Lauren Stokes, *Fear of the Family: Guest Workers and Family Migration in the Federal Republic of Germany* (Oxford: Oxford University Press, 2022).

to the United States, where the difficulties of obtaining a visa make back-and-forth trips problematic.[32]

Finally, departures matter because not everyone is able to depart. One problem with the "nation of migrants" paradigm in US history is that it doesn't apply to Native Americans who didn't migrate here, or slaves, who didn't come voluntarily— and couldn't choose to leave and go home. Slaves and, to a lesser degree, other forms of contract labor or penal migrants did not have the option of "moving on."[33] There are also many historical examples of migrants who could not depart because they didn't have the resources or documents they needed, or because of the shame they would experience back home. This "shame" was sometimes gendered: for example, it applied to men who failed to make a living, to single women who became pregnant, or women whose marriages didn't work out as hoped.

Departure from Australia was contingent on the possession of a passport. Ironically, as authors in this volume indicate, that meant that some stateless refugees who wanted to permanently leave Australia had first to become Australian citizens. Red tape could be as effective as barbed wire in preventing departures. Joseph Roth aptly described what he called the "metaphysical affliction" of refugeedom in 1937: "You're a transient and you're stuck; a refugee and a detainee; condemned to rootlessness and unable to budge."[34]

In the case of migrants who couldn't depart, departure draws our attention to the power of states and the importance of citizenship. But departure also matters because it highlights the limits of state power. One surprise in writing about the history of migrant colonialism in the nineteenth and twentieth century—whether the colonists were Zionists in Palestine, Russians and Poles in South America, Italian fascists in Libya or Ethiopia, or Germans in Eastern Europe—is the sheer amount of failure and return. This goes for both internal and overseas colonization. For example, beginning in the late 1920s, Italy's fascist authorities promoted internal and external colonization as politically preferable alternatives to emigration. The idea was to prevent the state from "losing" its migrants to American cities and instead use them as a resource to expand the Italian Empire and to become more self-sufficient in food production, by colonizing unproductive land.

32. Kathy Burrell (ed.), *Polish Migration to the UK in the "New" European Union after 2004* (Farnham: Ashgate, 2009), 9; Marta Anacka and Marek Okólski, "Direct Demographic Consequences of post-Accession Migration for Poland," in Richard Black et al., (eds.), *A Continent Moving West? EU Enlargement and Labour Migration from Central and Eastern Europe* (Amsterdam: Amsterdam University Press, 2010), 143–5; Bozena Leven and Michal Schwabe, "The Impact of Changing Entry Barriers on Polish Migration," *Journal of Global Economics, Management, and Business Research* 2, no. 1 (2015): 25–34.

33. Adam Goodman, "Nation of Migrants, Historians of Migration," *Journal of American Ethnic History* 34, no. 4 (Summer 2015): 7–16.

34. Joseph Roth, *The Wandering Jews*, trans. Michael Hofmann (New York, W. W. Norton, 2001), 127.

"Today, the real America for all Italians is Libya," preached one fascist slogan.[35] Or in the Agro Pontino, a short hop from Rome.

The new settlements at home and in Africa even included reserved spots for migrants who had returned home from places like America or France.[36] The results were far from successful, however. In the Agro Pontino in 1939, 477 individuals arrived in Mussolini's so-called new towns. But in the same year, 488 individuals left—whether because they requested repatriation or were expelled for bad conduct. Many got sick with malaria or other illnesses, which the regime covered up.[37]

Historians can learn a lot from these failures. Efforts to use migrants as tools for demographic or social engineering failed when it turned out that the Italian farmers from the Veneto had no idea how to farm land in the Agro Pontino or Africa. They failed when supposed "Germans" from the Baltics turned out to have more in common with local Poles or Ukrainians than with Germans from the Third Reich. They failed when migrants had different priorities to the state, and they failed when the organizers of these projects imagined that they were sending people into "empty space" and ignored the presence and claims of native populations. Australia's history of departures offers similar insights into the history of migration, showcasing the extent that the individual choices, preferences, and strategies of migrants mattered. They often interfered with the state's economic or ideological goals.

Shifting our focus away from the migrants who stayed and towards those who left has the potential to tell us a great deal about individual migrants, state efforts to govern migration, and the interaction and conflict between the two. These stories of departure challenge national myths about the "success" of migration and help us to better understand migration at the level of individual experience rather than mass movements. The departed are not always easy to find, but tracking them down offers rich rewards.

35. Cited in Donna Gabaccia, *Italy's Many Diasporas* (New York: Routledge, 2000),144.

36. Pamela Ballinger, "Colonial Twilight: Italian Settlers and the Long Decolonization of Italy," *Journal of Contemporary History* 51, no. 4 (2016): 813–38.

37. Relazione sull'attività della Delegazione di Littoria in Agro Pontino, nell'Anno 1939, Busta 35g, Commissariato Generale per Le Migrazioni e la colonizzazione Interna, Archivio Centrale dello Stato, Rome (ACS).

INDEX

Page numbers in italics refer to figures and tables.

activism 9
adventurers 93–4
Africa 13, 231
Aliens Act 1947 21–3
Aliens Deportation Act 1949 56, 56 n.33
America, *see* United States
Anpassen 134–5, 135 n.41, 144
Appleyard, Reginald T. 5, 33, 105–6, 157–8
ASIO, *see* Australian Security Intelligence Organization (ASIO)
assimilation 161
    and migration registration 23
    and migration studies 5
    and Soviet DPs 72–3, 83
Athens *186*
Australia
    Border Force 22, 34
    "border protection" 8, 202–3
    citizenship oath 31
    and culture 131
    DP attitudes to 35, 38–9
    and migration history 37
    migration studies in 3
    see also Australia–United States resettlement agreement
Australian Security Intelligence Organization (ASIO)
    and Soviet repatriation 67–70, 70 n.11
    DP assimilation 72–3, 83
    espionage 70–1, 97–100
    re-entry 78–83
    repatriation workers 74–8
    "Return to the Homeland" Committee 74–6
    and war criminals 64
    see also Spry, Charles
Australia–United States resettlement agreement 201–5
    and "border protection" 202–3
    and Cuban refugees 205–10, 214–15
    and Guantanamo Bay 214–16
    and Manus Island 215–17
    and Nauru 203, 215–17
    and Vietnamese refugees 210–13

Bad Hersfeld 132, 132 n.30
Balint, Ruth 8, 16
Berlin 127
Border Force 22, 34
"border protection" 8, 202–3
Borrie, W. D. 5
Bosworth, Richard 37–8
Bottomley, Gillian 149–51, 162
Britain
    British arrivals 104, *104*
    British return 36–7, 37 n.9, 103–6, *106–8*, 146, 157–60
    "£10 Poms" 2
    and anti-British attitudes 109
    "boomerang poms" 49 n.74
    and class 107
    and climate 109
    homesickness 108–9
    and migration studies 3–4, 8
    British youth 103–4, 120–3
    see also essay contest
    emigration by sea 105, *105*
Brownlee, Aleta 188
Buckland-Fuller, Dorothy 177–8

Calwell, Arthur 21, 40, 53–4, 56, 63
Canada 2, 158–9
Casanova 140
Castro, Fidel 206, 214
children, *see* youth
"China" Russians 86–7, 94–6
citizenship
    and Dellios family 183–4
    oath 31
    Soviet 88

class 107, 118
climate 109, 117–18
Cohen, Robin 14–15
Cold War 52, 68, 85, 224
Communism
   Fidel Castro 206, 214
   and deportation 59–60, 60 n.58
   and DPs 85–6
   Greek 181 n.41
   and migrant selection 54
convicts 1, 3
crime
   and deportation 49, 57–8, 195–6
   youth 192, 195–6, 198
   see also war criminals
Cuban Missile Crisis 205
Cuban refugees 205–10, 214–15
culture
   and Australia 131
   British youth 120–3
   German musical 131, 136

Damousi, Joy 16
Dellios family
   and Asia Minor refugees 165–7
   in Athens *186*
   and citizenship 183–4
   Dimitra *170*, *172*
   factory work 174, 177, 181, *181*, 183, 183 n.44
   farming 163–4, 169
   and gender 177–9
   and Greek Civil War 169–72
   "Greekness" 179
   Kyriakos *173*, *176*, 184–5
   Marianthy *170*
   in Melbourne 173–5, *175*, 176, *176*, 177–8, 182–3, *184*
   in Nigrita *164*
   on *Patris* 173, *173*
   and Smyrna 168, *168*
   in Therma 165–6, 169, 171, 180, *180*, *185*
   in Thessaloniki 181, *181*, 182
Dell'Oro, Alfredo 20–3, 33
democracy 225
departure 17, 19, 69, 160, 221–3
deportation 18, 48–9
   Aliens Deportation Act 1949 56, 56 n.33

   and Arthur Calwell 56
   and Communism 59–60, 60 n.58
   and Eastern Europe 57
   and Hungary 61
   and IRO 47–8, 59
   and Italy 47
   and labor 228
   and misrepresentation 61–2
   numbers 57
   of refugees 11
   refusal to work 46, 57–8
   and United States 227
   war criminals 51, 58, 63
   and youth 195–7
   see also extradition
diaspora 14–16, 186
Diner, Hasia 15
displaced persons (DPs)
   adventurers 93–4
   attitudes to Australia 35, 38–9
   and Communism 85–6
   deportation, *see* deportation
   and Eastern Europe 11, 38
   extradition, *see* extradition
   Jewish 42 n.37, 63, 224
   and labor 36, 41, 72, 90–1, 223
      refusal to work 46, 48, 57–8
      skilled migrants 43, 91–2
      unskilled migrants 29
   and Roy Maslyn 39–40
   and mental illness 92–3
   migrant selection 40, 53–4
   and Orthodox Church 99
   and United States 41–3
   war criminals, *see* war criminals
   and World War II 1, 11, 187, 223
   youth 187–91, *191*, 192–8
   see also International Refugee Organization (IRO); refugees
DPs, *see* displaced persons (DPs)
Dreyfus, Alfred 126, 126 n.2, 127–30
Dreyfus, George 17, 125, 128, 131
   and *Anpassen* 134–5, 135 n.41, 144
   in Bad Hersfeld 132, 132 n.30
   Casanova 140
   and departure 143
   and Volker Elis Pilgrim 141
   and film composing 134–5
   George Dreyfus—Live! 136

and German musical culture 131, 136
The Gilt-Edged Kid 141
and the Holocaust 130, 137–9
and musical style 133
and opera 134, 139–42
Rathenau 142
and Karlheinz Stockhausen 133–4
Surviving 136–7
and trauma 142
in Vienna 133
Dreyfus, Hilde 127–9
Dreyfus, Wilhelm 127 n.5

Eastern Europe 2, 11, 13, 18, 38, 57, 224
ECAJ, *see* Executive Council of Australian Jewry (ECAJ)
education 189, 191, 198
Ellinis 145–6, 151–2, 154
emotion 147, 163, 225
espionage 70–1, 97–100
    and re-entry 78–83
essay contest
    and Australia tour 115–16, *116, 119*
        class 118
        climate 117–18
        culture 121–2
    and publicity 110–14
    and social attitudes 111
Europe 31, 37, 229
    and United States 225–6
    see also Eastern Europe
European Union 229
Executive Council of Australian Jewry (ECAJ) 62, 64
extradition 51, 65–6, 66 n.99
    see also deportation

factory work 174, 177, 181, *181*, 183, 183 n.44
failure 221–2, 230–1
family 91, 162–3
    see also Dellios family
farming 163–4, 169
Fitzpatrick, Sheila 17
Florida 208–10, 214–16

Gatrell, Peter 11
gender 14, 31 n.54, 177–9, 230
George Dreyfus—Live! 136

Germany
    and George Dreyfus 125–6, 130
    Holocaust 130–1, 137–9
    and Jewish students 127–8
    Kristallnacht 128
    musical culture 131, 136
    and war criminals 51–2
Gilt Edged Kid, The 141
Gordeev, Anatoly 72 n.30, 86–91, 93, 99
government
    departure statistics 24
    Menzies 24–5
    and migration registration 20–4
    passenger cards 25–6
    and politics of emigration 19–20
    and settler loss 27–8, 30, 32, 32 n.58, 33
Grassby, Al 23, 32–3
Great Depression 227
Greece 17
    Gillian Bottomley on 149–51
    Civil War 169–72
    Ellinis, see Ellinis
    Greek Communism 181 n.41
    Greek return 149–51, 162–3
    Greek social life 150
    Greek stowaways 146, 149, 151–2, 155
    map of territories *167*
    military junta 153–5
    Patris 145–6, 151–5, 173, *173*
    refugees from Asia Minor 165–7
    Smyrna 168
    see also Dellios family
"Greekness" 179
Green, Nancy 19
Grewcock, Michael 202, 218
Guantanamo Bay 214–16
guest workers 229
Gulag 88, 88 n.8

Haiti 215
Handbook on Return Migration 13
Heyes, Tasman 22
history, *see* migration history
Holborn, Louise 47, 52
Holocaust 130–1, 137–9
Holt, Harold 59, 63–4
homeland
    and diaspora 16

and George Dreyfus 125
"Return to the Homeland" Committee 74–6
homesickness 31, 31 n.54, 108–9
housing 175
Hulme, Kathryn 41
humanitarianism 9
Hungary 61, 66

immigration program
   cost 26 n.30, 29 n.43
   and departure 24–5
   and permanent settlement 20, 24
   Soviet sabotage of 74, 76, 78–9, 83
   see also essay contest
International Refugee Organization (IRO)
   and deportation 47–8, 59
   and DPs 35, 187
   and Soviet Union 85
   and war criminals 53, 58
   and youth 188–9, 191
   see also displaced persons (DPs); refugees
IRO, see International Refugee Organization (IRO)
Israel 18
Italy 31, 47, 230–1

Jews 4
   and diaspora 14–16
   Executive Council of Australian Jewry (ECAJ) 62, 64
   Holocaust 130, 137–9
   and Israel 18
   Jewish DPs 38 n.12, 42 n.37, 224
   Jewish students 127–8
   Kristallnacht 128
   and migrant selection 54
   and war criminals 63–4
   see also Dreyfus, George
Johnson-Reed Act 1924 229
Jupp, James 8

Kalman, Julie 8
King, Russell 14
Kovacs, Michael 44
Kristallnacht 128
Kunz, Egon 43, 161, 197, 199

labor 6
   convict 3
   and deportation 228
   and DPs 36, 41, 72, 90–1, 223
   factory work 174, 177, 181, *181*, 183, 183 n.44
   farming 163–4, 169
   guest workers 229
   refusal to work 46, 48, 57–8
   skilled migrants 28–9, 43, 91–2
   unskilled migrants 29
   and youth 187–8, 191–2, 198
laws
   Aliens Act 1947 21–3
   Aliens Deportation Act 1949 56, 56 n.33
   Johnson-Reed Act 1924 229
   National Security (Aliens Control) Regulations 1939 21
Lynch, Phillip 29

Macedonia 166–7
Manus Island 215–17
Martin, Jean 5, 38–44
Melbourne 173–5, *175*, 176, *176*, 177–8, 182–3, *184*
memory 147–9
mental illness 92–3
Menzies government 24–5
migrant selection 30, 40, 53–5
migration history
   and Australia 37
   and departure 19, 69, 160, 163, 221–3
   and emotion 147, 163, 225
   and James Jupp 8
   and life history 108
   and memory 147–9
   and ships 146
   and youth 120
migration registration 20–4
migration studies
   and activism 9
   and Africa 13
   and assimilation 5
   in Australia 3
   and Britain 3–4, 8
   and diaspora 14–16
   and gender 14
   and labor 6

migration history, *see* migration history
and non-British migrants 6
and refugees 8
and Eric Richards 16
and social science 5
and war criminals 7
and "whiteness" 4
and Mark Wyman 12
Mischka's War 17
mobility 16–17, 209
   and diaspora 15–16
   and refugees 218
   and skilled migrants 28–9
   transilients 28
multiculturalism 3, 8, 33, 222
music
   culture in Germany 131, 136
   musical style 133
   opera 134, 139–42
   see also Dreyfus, George

National Security (Aliens Control) Regulations 1939 21
naturalization 2, 18, 45–6
Nauru 203, 215–17
Nazis 7, 63–4
Nigrita *164*

Obama administration 217
opera 134, 139–42
Orthodox Church 99, 178

Palestine 128, 224
passenger cards 25–6
passports 2, 18, 45, 158, 230
Pavlov, Dmitry 86–7, 99
permanent settlement 20, 24, 44, 158–9, 161
Petiss, Susan 35
Petrov, Vladimir 71, 77, 77 n.58, 87–8, 90, 98–9
Pilgrim, Volker Elis 141
Poland 226–7
Price, Charles 5, 25, 27–8, 33
Proudfoot, Malcolm 36
publicity
   and deportation 57
   and displaced youth 188–9

and essay contest 110–14
and Roy Maslyn Williams 39
and Queensland 116

Queensland 116, 118, *119*

racism 174
   White Australia Policy 4, 31 n.49
Rathenau 142
refugees
   from Asia Minor 165–7
   and Australia–United States resettlement agreement 201–5
   Cuban refugees 205–10, 214–15
   Manus Island 215–17
   Nauru 203, 215–17
   Vietnamese refugees 210–13
   and "border protection" 8, 202–3
   deportation of 11
   and humanitarianism 9
   Jewish 38 n.12
   and mobility 218
   Soviet 52
   United Nations High Commissioner for Refugees (UNHCR) 216, 218
   and World War II 11–12
   see also displaced persons (DPs); International Refugee Organization (IRO)
Refugee Settlers 38
registration, *see* migration registration
repatriation workers 74–8
return
   Africa 13
   British 36–7, 37 n.9, 103–6, *106–8*, 146, 157–60
   "£10 Poms" 2
   and anti-British attitudes 109
   "boomerang poms" 49 n.74
   and class 107
   and climate 109
   homesickness 108–9
   and migration studies 3–4, 8
   and diaspora 14–16, 186
   and Eastern Europe 11, 13, 224
   and failure 221–2, 230–1
   gendered 14
   Greek 149–51, 162–3
   homesickness 31, 31 n.54

non-British 156–7
rates 8, 37 n.9, 106, *106*, 161
transatlantic migration 10
"Return to the Homeland" Committee 74–6
Richards, Eric 16–17
Richardson, Alan 157–60
Richmond, Anthony 28, 158
Round-trip America 12
Russia, *see* Soviet Union
Russian Social Club 86, 88, 90, 96

sea travel 105, *105*
   see also ships, migrant
security, national
   and Communism 60
   and deportation 59–60
   and espionage 70–1, 97–100
   migrant selection 53–5
   National Security (Aliens Control) Regulations 1939 21
   and re-entry 78–83
   and repatriation workers 74–8
   and "Return to the Homeland" Committee 74–6
   and Soviet Union 67–8
   and war criminals 52–3, 64
   see also Australian Security Intelligence Organization (ASIO)
selection, *see* migrant selection
serial migration, *see* third-country migration
settler loss 27–8, 30, 32, 32 n.58, 33
ships, migrant 10, 18, 44–5, 147
   Ellinis 145–6, 151–2, 154
   and Greek military junta 153–5
   and memory 147–9
   and migration history 146
   Patris 145–6, 151–5, 173, *173*
   and stowaways 146, 149, 151–2, 155
skilled migrants 43, 91–2
   and mobility 28–9
slaves 230
Slezkine, Yuri 15
Smyrna 168, *168*
social science 5, 30, 37
social services, *see* welfare
Soviet Union 17
   and ASIO surveillance 67–70, 70 n.11

DP assimilation 72–3, 83
espionage 70–1, 97–100
re-entry 78–83
repatriation workers 74–8
"Return to Homeland" Committee 74–6
"China" Russians 86–7, 94–6
citizenship 88
forced repatriation 85, 94
Gulag 88, 88 n.8
and IRO 85
and Orthodox Church 99
refugees 52
repatriates
   adventurers 93–4
   and family 91
   and labor 90–2
   marital status 89
   and mental illness 92–3
   nationality 89
repatriation agents 86–7
   Anatoly Gordeev 72 n.30, 86–91, 93, 99
   Dmitry Pavlov 86–7, 99
   Vladimir Petrov 71, 77, 77 n.58, 87–8, 90, 98–9
Russian Social Club 86, 88, 90, 96
"White Russians" 68, 86
spies, *see* espionage
Spry, Charles
   and DP assimilation 73, 83
   and Soviet re-entry 79–82
   and Soviet Union 67
   and war criminals 64
statistics, departure 24–8
Stockhausen, Karlheinz 133–4
stowaways 146, 149, 151–2, 155
Suez Canal 147
Surviving 136–7

Tasmania 118
temporary settlement 34, 44, 49
Theme from Rush 135
Therma 165–6, 169, 171, 180, *180*, 185
Thessaloniki 181, *181*, 182
third-country migration 16, 18, 37 n.9, 221
transatlantic migration 10
transilients 28
trauma 142, 171 n.20, 182

travel
    sea travel 105, *105*
    see also ships, migrant
Trump administration 217

UNHCR, *see* United Nations High
    Commissioner for Refugees
    (UNHCR)
United Kingdom, *see* Britain
United Nations High Commissioner
    for Refugees (UNHCR)
    216, 218
United Nations Relief and Rehabilitation
    Agency (UNRRA) 52, 85
United States 2
    and deportation 227
    and DPs 41–3
    and Europe 225–6
    and migration history 222–3
    see also Australia–United
        States resettlement
        agreement
UNRRA, *see* United Nations Relief and
    Rehabilitation Agency
    (UNRRA)
unskilled migrants 29

Vienna 133
Vietnamese refugees 210–13

war criminals 51–3, 58
    and extradition 51, 65–6, 66 n.99
    and migration studies 7
    Nazis 7, 63–4

welfare
    child 188–9
    and settler loss 32, 32 n.58
White Australia Policy 4, 31 n.49
"White Russians" 68, 86
Wiesenthal, Simon 64
Williams, Roy Maslyn 39–40
Wilton, Janis 37–8
women 177–9, 228, 230
work, *see* labor
World War II
    and DPs 1, 11, 187, 223
    and Eastern Europe 11
    prewar migration 3
    postwar migration 5–10
    and refugees 11–12
Wyman, Mark 10, 12–13

youth 193–5
    British 103–4, 120–3
        see also essay contest
    child welfare 188–9
    crime 192, 195–6, 198
    death 195
    deportation 195–7
    education 189, 191, 198
    and IRO 188–9, 191
    labor 187–8, 191–2, 198
    missing 197
    ship rolls 190, *191*
Yugoslavia 65–6

Zahra, Tara 10–11, 41
Zubrzycki, Jerry 5

www.ingramcontent.com/pod-product-compliance
Lightning Source LLC
Chambersburg PA
CBHW071828300426
44116CB00009B/1472